Gothic Fantasy

THE FILMS OF TIM BURTON

First published in Great Britain and the United States in 2007 by
MARION BOYARS PUBLISHERS LTD
24 Lacy Road
London SW15 1NL

www.marionboyars.co.uk

Distributed in Australia and New Zealand by
Peribo Pty Ltd, 58 Beaumont Road, Kuring-gai, NSW 2080

Printed in 2007
10 9 8 7 6 5 4 3 2 1

#Z0699019

A CIP catalogue record for this book is available from the British Library.
A CIP catalog record for this book is available from the Library of Congress.

ISBN 0-7145-3132-4
13 digit ISBN 978-0-7145-3132-8

Set in Baskerville 11/14pt
Printed in England by Cox & Wyman

Gothic Fantasy
THE FILMS OF TIM BURTON

by Edwin Page

MARION BOYARS
LONDON • NEW YORK

Dedicated to Charlotte & Ellen

'Thanks for all your support'

&

With a special mention for Hannah Lucy Ross

Contents

Introduction

After being immersed in the work of Tim Burton for a while things can get a little strange. You see movement in the shadows and when you turn to look there's nothing there. Life feels slightly unreal. There's a sense of the mysterious hanging in the air like the fog in his film *Sleepy Hollow*. You see things in a different light.

When watching the stylised movies that have made Tim Burton a household name, it is easy to see why they can have such a profound effect. They are like fairy tales, communicating to us on a symbolic level, speaking of things far deeper within our conscious and subconscious minds than most films would dare to delve.

Issues of alienation, insanity and a wish for acceptance are among those raised in expressionistic and gothic surroundings. The films explore life and death, tackling fundamental moral questions that stem from the balance of dark and light within each of us. Most importantly, they have the power to connect with us on a personal level, a power gained from the fact that Burton invests so much of himself into each movie that he works on. There is a humanity present that can reach out from the screen and touch us in a way that isn't possible with the run-of-the-mill Hollywood movies, which are so often devoid of such a personal touch, communicating only on a level of pure entertainment.

This is not to say that Tim Burton's work isn't entertaining, it is – and often very much so – but his work transcends this basic function of film. Burton is one of the few filmmakers who retains both integrity and passion, he won't agree to do a film unless he feels a personal connection with it – which is fortunate for his audience who can reap the benefits of this absolute commitment.

Burton's films aren't so much about the plot as they are about creating a mood, conveying emotion and communicating through the use of symbolism. This is why they resonate so strongly with such a wide audience. They talk to us individually about what it is to be human. They take us on an emotional journey: from the laughter of *Beetlejuice* to the tears of *Big Fish*, from the bittersweet fairy tale of *Edward Scissorhands* to the heart warming story of *Charlie and the Chocolate Factory*, from the horror of *Sleepy Hollow* to the vibrant playfulness of *Mars Attacks!*, and from the brooding darkness of *Batman* to the hopeful naivety of *The Nightmare Before Christmas*.

During the course of this book each of his major feature films will be examined and the trademarks evident within them will be identified. The extent of his personal involvement will become clear, as well as other characteristic Burton traits such as his recurring collaborations with various actors and crew members.

I started writing the book as a fan and have ended it as a devotee who marvels at the depth of imagery created by one of modern cinema's truly great directors. So, let the journey begin. Read on and explore the unique cinematic experience of the films of Tim Burton.

1. Tim Burton:
The Man Behind the Movies

Tim Burton is a tall man usually dressed in black. His dark hair is often wild and unruly, Johnny Depp stating that 'a comb with legs would have outrun Jesse Owens given one look at this guy's locks.'[1] All his films have been affected by his childhood experiences, experiences which still have a strong resonance with Tim Burton the man. This personal touch has meant that his movies communicate a deep sense of humanity to those that see beyond the stunning visuals and often playful plotlines.

Born on 25th August 1958, Timothy William Burton spent the first ten years of his life living with his parents and younger brother in Burbank, California. Burbank is the location of a number of film and television studios, including Disney, NBC and Warner Brothers, so even as a boy he was close to the industry he would eventually become part of.

He couldn't understand why his parents sent him to Sunday school when they weren't really religious or why they had a certain picture hanging on their lounge wall despite the fact they didn't seem to have any real feelings for it. He also couldn't understand why they blocked up the windows of his bedroom, leaving only high slits for the light to shine through. So, distanced from his parents and younger brother due to his perceived 'difference', Burton moved in with his grandmother at the age of ten and remained with her until leaving high school.

He saw the suburban life as lacking in passion, as a kind of colourless, flat landscape in which no one really knew anyone else beneath the façade of normality. He has said of his experience of living in suburbia that there was 'no passion for anything, just a quiet, kind of floaty kind of semi-oppressive blank palette that you're living in.'[2]

In order to escape these oppressive feelings Burton would indulge in creative and quite ingenious pranks. At one time, with the help of some other children, he distributed debris and stamped footprints around a local park, and then persuaded other kids that aliens had crash-landed there. He also faked fights in the neighbourhood and once convinced another child that a killer had died after falling into a swimming pool, their body having dissolved due to the fact that the pool had recently been cleaned with chloride (the tall tale was supported by some clothes he'd thrown into the water).[3]

Due to his suburban upbringing, Burton developed the belief that society tries to suppress any creativity and passion an individual may feel, while at the same time a particular culture is enforced upon us, almost suffocating any creative urges we may possess. Because of this he says that individuals need a 'certain kind of strength and simplicity' in order to break through the enforced, cultural framework.[4] This 'strength and simplicity' is exactly what Burton employed in his passion for drawing, a passion that continues to this day. It is also evident in his films on a visual level, making his movies highly identifiable.

The symbolism Burton uses in his films provides clear evidence of his taste in painters and paintings. He's a particular fan of expressionist and impressionist work, such as that of Vincent Van Gogh, and it is fair to say that his work is influenced by these tastes. He says of these paintings, 'they're not *real*, but they capture such an energy that makes it real, and that to me is what's exciting about movies.'[5] In the same way his films are not trying to assimilate reality, but are highly symbolic and stylised in order to capture and convey the complexity of emotions within the narratives.

Burton finds drawing both satisfying and cathartic, claiming that, 'I think best when I'm drawing.'[6] His art was a way for him to create his identity and to express the emotions and feelings he had within. He describes his drawings as being part of an impulse to be seen for what he was, and one of his biggest influences as a child was 'Dr Seuss,' whose books he has described as 'beautiful and subversive.'[7]

Burton often uses his drawings to explain certain elements of his films to production designers, directors of photography and even the actors involved. For example, he has made sketches of Edward Scissorhands, the Penguin from *Batman Returns* and Ichabod Crane from *Sleepy Hollow* in order to show the kind of look he was seeking from the characters.

> **Ultimate Quote**
> 'Like most kids, I felt different... I felt like a foreigner in my own neighbourhood and in my own country' – Tim Burton[8]

Perhaps attributable to this tendency to work things out visually rather than verbally or through the written word, Burton also enjoys photography. He appreciates the fact that this visual element 'taps into your subconscious,' explaining how, 'it's a more real emotion than if I intellectualise it in my mind. I like just trying something either in a drawing or photo… It's a visual concept as opposed to thinking.'[9]

His boyhood pictures may not have been intended for show, but his films certainly are, reaching wide and often spellbound audiences. This provokes a strange reaction from their creator, who has claimed he is unable to bear watching his films in anything other than small parts until about three years after their release.[10] In part he is afraid of how they will be received, explaining that 'I love the making-of process, but I get very vulnerable at the end of it. It's like I'm afraid to show it to anybody.'[11] For Burton, the process of filmmaking must be particularly harrowing, his movies are so very personal – almost a reflection of his mind. It is hardly surprising that he is somewhat fearful of what he has displayed of himself in these films, what he has revealed to the global audience of millions. As I aim to emphasise, however, it is this very willingness to expose his interior world, and make himself vulnerable, that gives his films the impact and the lasting quality that they have.

Burton's other major boyhood passion was monster movies and horror films, especially those starring Vincent Price and based on the dark tales of Edgar Allen Poe, such as *The Pit and the Pendulum* (1961) and *The Raven* (1963), both of which were directed by Roger Corman. He also enjoyed the British 'Hammer Horror' films, the films of James Whale, such as his 1931 version of Mary Shelley's *Frankenstein*, and he also regularly watched 'The Twilight Zone' and 'The Outer Limits'.

In the realm of monster movies Burton loved the stop-motion animation work of Ray Harryhausen which can be seen in such films as *The Golden Voyage of Sinbad* (Hessler, 1974), *Sinbad and the Eye of the Tiger* (Wanamaker, 1977), *Clash of the*

Titans (Davis, 1981), and in *Jason and the Argonauts* (Chaffey, 1963), which is the first film that Burton recalls seeing.[12] His enthusiasm for the way in which these films were created was to become clear when he created his own stop-motion movies and used the technique for special effects in films such as *Beetlejuice*.

In the monster and horror films which helped him to get through his younger years, Burton found himself identifying with the monsters rather than the heroes, as the monsters tended to show passion whereas the leads were relatively emotionless. Indeed, Burton saw them as representative of suburbanites.[13] It is also the case that the monster is the outsider, the alienated; feelings that Burton was familiar with. The monster is also often misunderstood, such as in *King Kong* (Cooper & Schoedsack, 1933) and *The Hunchback of Notre Dame* (Dieterle, 1939), and again, Burton found he could easily identify with such themes. He was also attracted to horror films because of the 'grand melodramatic emotion,'[14] and we see this reflected in the emotive content of his own films.

This intensity aside, Burton's initial motivation was almost accidental. One of his first brushes with film making was down to the fact that he hadn't read a book about Houdini for a final exam at school. Because of this he filmed a little, Super 8 movie based on Houdini's escape antics, including tying himself to railroad tracks. As he recalls the story, 'It impressed the teacher and I got an A', going on to explain how this affected him, 'that was maybe my first turning point, when I said, "Yeah, I wouldn't mind being a filmmaker."'[15]

Leaving high school a semester early, Burton went on to the California Institute of the Arts after winning a scholarship. The Institute of the Arts was founded by Walt and Roy

13

Disney, and provided a training ground for animators who would go on to work for the studio – Burton being one of these. Actually, he'd only decided to follow animation as a career because at one time his parents had wanted him to become a court reporter, and he thought becoming an animator was the better option of the two.

Burton's final project in his third year at the Institute was an animation called *Stalk of the Celery Monster*. In this short we see something which would become a trademark of Burton's professional career, this being a misperceived lead character. This character appears to be Frankenstein-esque as he tortures a woman with apparent menace. However, it turns out that he is a dentist and she is his patient.

> **Ultimate Quote**
>
> 'In animation you could communicate through drawings and I was perfectly happy to communicate in that way and not in any other way'
> – Tim Burton[16]

It was on the strength of this short that the Disney headhunters chose Burton as one of the students who would join Disney. Rick Heinrichs, a fellow student and regular collaborator with Burton, says that his friend was picked because he used his film 'to tell a story and to create a complex set of relationships between a group of characters. Nobody was more surprised than Burton when he was selected.'[17]

He was added to Disney's group of talented artists in 1979, something that many would see as a dream job. However, to Burton it was like a nightmare. He was expected to be an expressive artist while at the same time conforming to the Disney style of animation in an environment not unlike a production line. He felt chained to his animation desk and has said of the time, 'I learned to sleep with my pencil in my hand sitting up at my desk so when the bosses came in I'd just *boink* [blinks awake and sits upright].'[18]

During his relatively short time working for Disney in this way Burton produced artwork for the film *The Fox and the Hound* (Berman & Rich, 1981). He also created early conceptual work for *The Black Cauldron* (Berman & Rich, 1985), none of which was eventually used. The problem was that his work wasn't your usual Disney fare, it was simply too distinctive, as anyone can tell from the look of his films (which are often formulated at an early stage through his artwork).

Strangely – considering how tortured he felt working at Disney – it would be that studio that allowed Burton to break into film directing. When it became apparent he was not able to draw such things as cute foxes, he was given more scope to work on his own projects, and due to this he created three short films (to be discussed in the following chapter). This was the pivotal move that launched his career –and the rest, as they say, is history.

Burton's time at Disney, along with his love of drawing, has meant that his films portray a highly stylised world. He communicates predominantly through imagery, which is often symbolic. He has always felt awkward with verbal communication, which is partially why he drew as a child (and continues to do so). These feelings are highlighted by a particularly symbolic dream he experienced as a child where a 'tough, purple, rubberish sea plant' was growing out of his mouth so that he couldn't speak. No matter how hard he tried to tear it away it just kept growing.[19]

Some people say that Burton has remained in touch with the 'child within', and that this element makes itself apparent in his work. However, Burton doesn't agree, objecting that, 'I really hate…that fucking "child within" bullshit.'[20] Part of his dislike of this viewpoint is that he believes we all contain aspects of both child and adult, good and bad, that we are all dualities trying to come to terms with who we are in the best way we can.

Burton's dislike of such statements also stems from his disdain of categorisation. He saw that it was very apparent in school and in the suburban environment where he lived, and, being on the receiving end as someone seen as weird and an outsider, realised also just how damaging categorisation can be. He therefore fights against it in his movies, and one way he does this is by showing how categorisation can often lead to misperception. An example of this is the giant in *Big Fish*. The townspeople are fearful of him, have categorised him as a bad, bloodthirsty, potentially human-scoffing beast. We soon find this to be completely untrue.

> **Ultimate Quote**
> 'I remember growing up and feeling that there is not a lot of room for acceptance... From day one you're categorised'
> – Tim Burton[21]

This instance further highlights the fact that Burton sees the world in a different way from the majority of people. Another example of this arises in relation to *Batman Returns*. Many people, especially parents, complained that the film was too dark. Burton didn't see it that way at all. In fact, he states that he sees films such as *Lethal Weapon* (Donner, 1987) as much darker due to the continual use of guns and the comedic touches sometimes given to killing.

There are those who criticise Burton's films for story inconsistencies and glaring problems with the narrative. However, this is because they are judging his films from an intellectual standpoint, which is entirely the wrong approach for films that have been created through passion: a passion which makes itself known visually rather than verbally or through the written word.

Tim Burton's films must be judged emotionally and symbolically before all else, something underlined by the director, who states, 'that probably means the most to me: when people get the emotional quality underneath the stupid façade.'[22] There is no room for intellectualising because Burton is not trying to communicate on an intellectual level; he is instead conducting an emotional conversation with himself on screen, releasing the feelings he has within. Yes, 'a conversation with himself' may seem a strange claim for films which reach out to millions of people, but this is truly the case. They are an extension, an evolution of the times when he was a boy and created art only for himself. He creates his films for himself; not for reward or acclaim.

> **Ultimate Quote**
>
> 'He [Tim Burton] is to me a true genius... in not just film, but drawings, photographs, thought, insight and ideas'
> – Johnny Depp[23]

So, the questions we should be asking of his movies aren't such things as 'How does the narrative hold together?' or 'Is the story consistent?'. We should be asking such things as 'In what way do they stir our emotions?' and 'How are they symbolic of the human condition?' It's clearly not what you *think* about his films that's important, but what you *feel*.

Endnotes

1. Salisbury, M. (ed.) – *Burton on Burton – Revised Edition*, p.X (Faber and Faber, 2000, UK)

2. Unknown – Biography for Tim Burton (I) (www.imdb.com)

3. Fraga, K. (ed.) – *Tim Burton Interviews*, p.162 (University Press of Mississippi, 2005, US)

4. Fraga, K. (ed.) – *Tim Burton Interviews*, p.44 (University Press of Mississippi, 2005, US)

5. Salisbury, M. (ed.) – *Burton on Burton – Revised Edition*, p.175 (Faber and Faber, 2000, UK)

6. McMahan, A. – *The Films of Tim Burton: Animating Live Action in Contemporary Hollywood*, p.20 (Continuum Books, 2005, US)

7. Fraga, K. (ed.) – *Tim Burton Interviews*, p.169 (University Press of Mississippi, 2005, US)

8. Unknown – Tim Burton

   (http://entertainment.timesonline.co.uk/article/0,,14931-1695710_3,00.html)

9. Salisbury, M. (ed.) – *Burton on Burton – Revised Edition*, p.158 (Faber and Faber, 2000, UK)

10. Salisbury, M. (ed.) – *Burton on Burton – Revised Edition,* p.146 (Faber and Faber, 2000, UK)

11. Unknown – Tim Burton

    (http://entertainment.timesonline.co.uk/article/0,,14931-1695710_3,00.html)

12. Salisbury, M. (ed.) – *Burton on Burton – Revised Edition*, p.2 (Faber and Faber, 2000, UK)

13. Fraga, K. (ed.) – *Tim Burton Interviews*, p.48 (University Press of Mississippi, 2005, US)

14. Fraga, K. (ed.) – *Tim Burton Interviews*, p.60 (University Press of Mississippi, 2005, US)

15. Unknown – Biography for Tim Burton (I) (www.imdb.com)

16. Fraga, K. (ed.) – *Tim Burton Interviews*, p.53 (University Press of Mississippi, 2005, US)

17. McMahan, A. – *The Films of Tim Burton: Animating Live Action in Contemporary Hollywood*, p.22 (Continuum Books, 2005, US)

18. Kermode, M. (int.) – Tim Burton Interviewed by Mark Kermode (II)

    (http://film.guardian.co.uk/Guardian_NFT/interview/0,4479,120877,00)

19. Fraga, K. (ed.) – *Tim Burton Interviews*, p.46 (University Press of Mississippi, 2005, US)

20. Fraga, K. (ed.) – *Tim Burton Interviews*, p.43 (University Press of Mississippi, 2005, US)

21. Salisbury, M. (ed.) – *Burton on Burton – Revised Edition*, p.87 (Faber and Faber, 2000, UK)

22. Salisbury, M. (ed.) – *Burton on Burton – Revised Edition*, p.126 (Faber and Faber, 2000, UK)

23. Salisbury, M. (ed.) – *Burton on Burton – Revised Edition*, p.XII (Faber and Faber, 2000, UK)

References

Jackson, M & McDermott, A. – Tim Burton Biography (www.timburtoncollective.com/bio)

2. A Life in Film

'All right everybody,
start your engines, this is it'
— Ben Frankenstein in *Frankenweenie*

This chapter charts Tim Burton's career in the movies, starting with his work at Disney in the early eighties and ending with the 2005 stop-motion film *The Corpse Bride*.

The Super 8 films Burton made in his youth have already been mentioned in Chapter One. The first films he made in adulthood were created at weekends, using any spare time he could grab whilst working at Disney, where he found the atmosphere severely frustrating. He and other employees who were also unhappy with the working environment at Disney made two films independently of the studio.

The first of these was called *Doctor of Doom* (1980) and was filmed on video. This black and white film featured Burton as Dr. Doom and was created with intentionally bad dubbing to give the impression of a foreign import.[1] The second film was entitled *Luau* (1982). A homage to beach-blanket films, this included song and dance routines, with Burton playing the disembodied head of 'The Most Powerful Being in the Universe.'[2] All the films that followed were made with the support of studios.

The first of three shorts he created for Disney was a homage to his favourite horror actor Vincent Price, who many will remember as the narrator in Michael Jackson's 'Thriller' video. Burton had been working on a children's book when the studio gave him sixty thousand dollars to make something of his own. So he decided to turn the story into a short film utilising both drawn and stop-motion animation.

Entitled *Vincent* (1980) it was a six minute film about a boy called Vincent Malloy who wanted to be Vincent Price. Using lyrical verse and shot in black and white, *Vincent* was narrated by Tim Burton's horror hero.

Price was the first film star that Burton had worked with and he said that 'he turned out to be a wonderful person.' Talking to Lawrence French, he went on to say, 'he gave me a lot of hope and was a great inspiration to me.'[4] This inspiration began in Burton's youth when he watched Price in various horror films and then continued into adulthood when they became friends after collaborating on *Vincent*.

> ### Ultimate Quote
> 'Tim recited the poem for me and asked me to narrate it. I was really struck by his charm and enthusiasm, so I said yes. Tim is really in love with film and is a wonderful kind of mad fellow'
> – Vincent Price[3]

This first short film of Burton's is similar in look and tone to the later *The Nightmare Before Christmas*. Two of his trademarks are apparent throughout its duration, the first being a dog and the second being a tower, which references castles. As we shall see, these two features are present in a number of his other movies.

Vincent also includes aspects which are of personal significance to Burton himself, such as Edgar Allen Poe and drawing. Thus even his first film drew upon his own personal experiences, as would his later work. *Vincent* is also typically dark and gothic. It is clearly Burton through and through and his appeal became immediately apparent when it won two awards at the Chicago Film Festival and the Critic's Prize at the Annecy Film Festival in France.

> **Ultimate Fact**
>
> After Tim Burton and Vincent Price had met for the creation of *Vincent* they remained friends right until Price's death in 1993.

The second film was entitled *Hansel and Gretel* (1982), and was a new take on the Grimm Brothers' fairy tale. It was an animated martial arts short in which the title characters end up having a kung-fu fight with the witch (played by a man). Costing $116,000, this short was made for The Disney Channel, which was still in its infancy at the time. It was written by Julie Hickson, who was also the executive producer, and produced the third and final short film Burton created while working at Disney.

This film was called *Frankenweenie* (1984) and is a take on Mary Shelley's *Frankenstein* which cost almost a million dollars. It is only one of two films that Burton wrote, the other being *Vincent*. It was also soon after *Frankenweenie* that he left Disney.

In the film, a boy's dog is killed when it is hit by a car and, taking inspiration from the original story, the boy decides to bring him back to life. This twenty-seven minute, live-action short was intended to be shown with Disney's *Pinocchio*, but received a PG rating which meant this couldn't happen. It was then not seen for a number of years until achieving a limited release on video. However, both *Frankenweenie* and *Vincent* have since been released on the special edition DVD of *The Nightmare Before Christmas* and are well worth a watch.

Right at the start of *Frankenweenie* there is an element which draws on Burton's childhood experiences. The boy in the film is showing his parents a short film that he has made, echoing Burton's own experiences of making Super 8 films in his youth. It also reflects the fact that Burton loves monster movies; the boy's film is called *Monsters from Long Ago*.

A graveyard in the title sequence of *Frankenweenie* is one of those incredibly gothic images common to Burton's work. What follows is a slightly macabre scene in a classroom, made all the more atmospheric by the use of black and white. What we also soon discover is an element of black humour. We realise that the boy, called Victor, will attempt to use electricity to bring his dog back to life, a

> ### Ultimate Fact
> Daniel Stern plays Victor's father in *Frankenweenie* and would go on to play the bungling burglar Marv in *Home Alone* (Columbus, 1990). Jason Hervey also has a small part in Burton's film and went on to appear in the popular TV series 'The Wonder Years' (1988-1993).

dog which is humorously called 'Sparky'. This mix of dark undertones with comic touches is typical of Burton's work and can also be seen in the fact that the boy's name is Victor Frankenstein, played perfectly by Barret Oliver, who went on to star in Ron Howard's *Cocoon* (1985).

Frankenweenie is also typically atmospheric, including the use of a thunderstorm which begins when Victor goes to the cemetery to dig up Sparky's body. In fact, this has a distinctly 'Hammer Horror' feel to it; a sense of the dramatic mixed with the macabre. There is also the clear feeling of a sugary sweet suburbia, the boy's actions gaining increased visual and emotional impact due to their juxtaposition with this. Such a vision of suburbia would later be taken to the extreme in

Edward Scissorhands.

Another aspect which would resurface in a later film, namely *Beetlejuice*, was the use of a book featuring very unusual instructions. In *Frankenweenie* we see Victor reading a book called *Electricity and the Creation of Life*. In *Beetlejuice* the main characters find a copy of *The Handbook for the Recently Deceased* after their untimely demise.

As with many classic horrors, the beast, the reanimated Sparky, isn't understood by the local residents, who want to kill the dog. During the following mob sequence we see an old, tatty windmill which is strikingly similar to that which is seen in *Sleepy Hollow*, even to the point of it burning down.

> **Ultimate Quote**
>
> 'His early film career was fuelled by almost unbelievable good luck, but it's his talent and originality that have kept him at the top of the Hollywood tree.'[6]

On the same crazy golf course where the windmill is located we also see a fairy tale castle, something inferred in *Vincent* and symbolically present in a number of Burton's other films. Though possibly not intentionally linked to the Disney logo (a fairy tale castle), it does seem rather apt as *Frankenweenie* was a Disney production.

Sparky saves Victor from the flames and the locals realise he isn't bad after all. At the end there is another touch of humour when Sparky and a poodle fall in love, the poodle modelling hair like that of Elsa Lanchester in *Bride of Frankenstein* (Whale, 1935). A homage is also made to James Whale's *Frankenstein* (1931) with Sparky sporting bolts on either side of his neck like Boris Karloff as the monster in that classic movie.

The internationally bestselling horror author, Stephen King, saw *Frankenweenie* and recommended it to an executive at Warner Brothers. It was then shown to the man behind the character of Pee-Wee Herman, Paul Reubens, who decided that Tim Burton, who was only twenty-six at the time, was the perfect director for his forthcoming film *Pee-Wee's Big Adventure*.[5] And that's how Burton moved from animation and shorts into the world of making feature-length movies; with a big stroke of luck.

Pee-Wee's Big Adventure (1985) had a low budget of only six million dollars, but went on to be a surprise hit at the box office, grossing forty-five million. Though the character of Pee-Wee Herman had already been well-defined by Reubens in his hit TV shows 'The Pee-Wee Herman show' and 'Pee-Wee's Playhouse,'[7] Burton still made an unmistakable mark on this movie. Paul Reubens was a member of a group of improvisational comedy actors called 'The Groundlings' who were based in Los Angeles. His alter-ego, Pee-Wee, had already appeared on such US shows as 'Letterman' and Johnny Carson's 'The Tonight Show'. Pee-Wee was a man with a squeaky voice, rouged cheeks and the mental age of a child.

The film follows Pee-Wee's search for his precious bicycle, which has been stolen despite a good deal of security. The movie begins with Pee-Wee dreaming of winning the *Tour de France* on the aforementioned bike, something which immediately informs the audience of the peddle-powered vehicle's importance. Verbal jokes and visual gags abound as Pee-Wee goes in search of his possession, going from a dinosaur park in Palm Springs to the Alamo and eventually

> **Ultimate Quote**
>
> 'It's hard for me to imagine a first movie, unless I had created it myself, that I could have related to as well as I did to Pee-Wee' – Tim Burton[8]

ending up at the Warner Brothers studio in Burbank (which seems very apt considering Burton was brought up in that location). These varied locations display the use of different genres, especially when Pee-Wee arrives at the studio. This generic blurring would also be apparent in *Beetlejuice*.

Speaking to David Breskin in 1991, Burton said, 'the most fun day I think I've ever had was on *Pee-Wee's Big Adventure* in the scene at the Alamo, with Jan Hooks, who played the guide. That was *all* improv and it was so much fun.'[9] This shows that Tim Burton enjoys spontaneous creativity without being unnecessarily restricted by script, something which he experienced again in the making of *Beetlejuice* (with Michael Keaton being a particularly spontaneous actor).

As well as improvisation, Burton also got the chance to include stop-motion in the movie, which is a fundamental part of the fingerprint he left on the film. There are two elements of this form of animation, the first being a dream sequence in which a T-Rex eats Pee-Wee's bike.

> **Ultimate Fact**
> Paul Reubens and Tim Burton attended the California Institute of the Arts at the same time, but never met while there.

The second occurs when Pee-Wee comes face to face with the truck driver, Large Marge, whose face mutates before his very eyes. Both sequences were animated by Rick Heinrichs, who acted in *Luau*, produced *Vincent*, was associate producer on *Frankenweenie*, and would go on to be production designer on *Batman Returns* and *Planet of the Apes*, as well as visual consultant on *The Nightmare Before Christmas*.

An encounter with another figure who crops up in further Burton films takes place shortly after Pee-Wee's meeting with Large Marge. At a roadside rest stop, he ends up talking to a waitress, played by Diane Salinger who went on to play the Penguin's mother in *Batman Returns* while Paul Reubens played the Penguin's father.

There is a further element in *Pee-Wee's Big Adventure* that relates to another of Burton's films. This is the skeletal reindeer which takes Pee-Wee his toast. It was taken from Burton's already devised design for the reindeer in *The Nightmare Before Christmas*, a film which Burton had also storyboarded by that time.

It was on this, Burton's first feature, that he first teamed up with Danny Elfman, who was lead singer with the cult group The Oingo Boingo Band and who hadn't previously created a film score. This working relationship would come to incorporate all bar one of Burton's feature-length films and is one of a number of relationships which have continued over large parts of his career. Burton has said of Elfman's score for *Pee-Wee's Big Adventure* that 'music is always important, but that was really the first time it was like a *character*, definitely a character.'[10]

One of the things that encouraged Burton to direct this film was the fact that Pee-Wee is an outsider. Another appealing factor may have been the blurring of reality and fiction, in that the distinction between Reubens the actor and Pee-Wee the character had become blurred through the TV show. Burton likes to explore the delineation of boundaries and indulged this interest further in both *Beetlejuice* (where generic boundaries were blurred as well as those between life and the afterlife) and also *Big Fish* (in which the reality of the main character's life was hardly distinct from his fantasy existence).

This film also gave Burton his introduction into merchandising as there was a wide range of Pee-Wee toys created. This marketing side of moviemaking was brought to the fore in the making of *Batman*, which we will investigate further in a later chapter. However, *Pee-Wee's Big Adventure* also saw Burton receiving predominantly bad reviews despite the film's good showing at the box office. Still, some of the reviewers changed their opinions in hindsight, Burton stating, 'I got the worst reviews for *Pee-Wee's Big Adventure* and then, as the years went by, I would read things from critics saying what a great movie it is.'[11]

Burton also directed two programs for television before his film career really took off. 'Aladdin and his Wonderful Lamp' (1984) was the first and was created for the 'Faerie Tale Theatre' series in the US. It featured the talents of James Earl Jones, who was the voice of Darth Vader in the original *Star Wars* trilogy, and Leonard Nimoy, who played Spock in the original 'Star Trek' series

> **Ultimate Fact**
>
> The heavy metal group Twisted Sister, who had hits in the 80s with such songs as 'We're Not Gonna Take It' and 'I Wanna Rock,' appear in *Pee-Wee's Big Adventure* performing a song entitled 'Burn in Hell.'

and starred in *Invasion of the Body Snatchers* (Kaufman, 1978). Both of these actors are sci-fi icons, so Burton was already working with big names in the realms of stardom.

A year later he directed 'The Jar' for the series called 'Alfred Hitchcock Presents.' The following year he was approached by Brad Bird, who had also worked on Disney's *The Fox and the Hound*. He was asked to create some designs for an animated episode of the Steven Spielberg television series called 'Amazing Stories.' The episode was called 'Family Dog' and was a cartoon from the point of view of a suburban family's dog. It was turned into a series by Amblin Entertainment, Tim Burton becoming its executive producer.

Burton has commented, 'I just love the idea of trying to do something from a dog's point of view. I don't know why, but I always relate to dogs.'[12] This fondness for dogs makes itself apparent in an obvious way in *Frankenweenie*. It also surfaces in *Beetlejuice*, in which a dog is responsible for the deaths of the lead characters, in *Mars Attacks!*, where one of the characters has her head transplanted onto her dog's body, and in *The Corpse Bride*, which features a skeletal dog. This love of all things canine was also seen in *Vincent*, in which Vincent Malloy fantasises about turning his pet dog into a zombie.

The film that followed *Pee-Wee's Big Adventure* in 1988 was the horror/comedy *Beetlejuice*. After that came *Batman* (1989), a film that made Tim Burton a household name. Then, with the release of *Edward Scissorhands* in 1990, Burton cemented his unmistakable style into the minds of filmgoers the world over. He was fast becoming one of only a few directors who have managed to create independently-minded and truly personal films within the Hollywood studio system, Woody Allen and Stanley Kubrick being other such directors.

> ### Ultimate Fact
>
> In 1992 director Cameron Crowe asked Tim Burton to appear in a small role in the film *Singles*. Burton agreed and his character, a director of videos for a dating agency, is referred to as 'the next Martin Scorsese' in the film.

It was becoming increasingly apparent that Burton was an auteur; a director with a style of his own, whose films could be recognised because of his distinct and very individual touch. His personal involvement was of an extent that rivalled directors such as Oliver Stone and Francis Ford Coppola, and his auteur status is also aided and abetted by his use of the same actors in more than one movie, as well as his regular use of some production team members, such as composer Danny Elfman. Part of the reason he tends to gravitate to the same people when making films is because he appreciates their passion, stating, 'you've got to work with people whose passion makes it exciting.'[13]

Burton's next big screen venture was the *Batman* sequel, *Batman Returns*, which was seen as darker than its predecessor. Then, in 1993, *The Nightmare Before Christmas* was released. It wasn't actually directed by Burton, but by long-time friend and collaborator Henry Selick. It was based on a story and characters by Burton and is a feature-length stop-motion movie.

1994 saw Burton's previous box office performances tarnished by the release of *Ed Wood*, which was praised by critics, but didn't do too well on ticket sales. That year also saw the release of Disney's *Cabin Boy* (Resnick, 1994), which was co-produced by Burton and which was a critical and commercial flop.

Burton next produced the third film in the *Batman* franchise, *Batman Forever*, which was released in 1995 and was directed by Joel Schumacher. In 1996 *Mars Attacks!* was released. Directed by Burton, it was greeted with a mixed response. That year he also co-produced *James and the Giant Peach*, which was based on the Roald Dahl story of the same name and was directed by his friend Henry Selick.

During the year after *Mars Attacks!* Burton worked on the proposed film *Superman Lives* for Warner Brothers. Nicolas Cage had already been signed up to play the hero and Burton met with the actor whose films include *Wild at Heart* (Lynch, 1990), *Leaving Las Vegas* (Figgis, 1995) and *The Rock* (Bay, 1996). They discussed focusing on the fact that

Superman is an alien and trying to understand what that would be like, which of course followed Burton's penchant for characters who suffer from alienation and are outsiders. He wanted to focus on this element above all, because he felt that of all the comic-book heroes 'he's actually the most two-dimensional'. Burton wanted to explore what it would be like 'to be somebody who's from another planet who can't tell anyone and is completely different, but has to hide it.'[14] They were even talking to Kevin Spacey, who has starred in such films as *The Usual Suspects* (Singer, 1995), *K-Pax* (Softley, 2001), and *The Shipping News* (Hallstrom, 2001), in the hope he would play Lex Luther.

> **Ultimate Quote**
>
> 'I don't want to take just anything for the sake of saying, "I'm working." I've got to like what I'm doing' – Tim Burton[15]

However, the *Superman Lives* project was pulled on the heels of a bad reaction to the fourth *Batman* film, called *Batman & Robin* (Schumacher, 1997). In Tim Burton's opinion this was done because Warner Brothers were fearful of ruining a second movie franchise after having done so with the Batman franchise and he states, 'since the overriding factor in Hollywood is fear – decisions are based on fear most of the time.'[16]

While Burton was working on *Superman Lives* he was also working on his book of illustrated, poetic stories called *The Melancholy Death of Oyster Boy and Other Stories*. This served as an outlet for the frustrations he was feeling over the Warner Brothers' project. This book was then published in 1997 and was dedicated to Lisa Marie, who was his girlfriend and muse at the time and who had also appeared in *Ed Wood* and *Mars Attacks!*, and would go on to have roles in *Sleepy Hollow* and *Planet of the Apes*.

The Melancholy Death of Oyster Boy and Other Stories contained twenty-three stories told in verse and accompanied by artwork created by Tim Burton. They have a typically Burtonesque tone which consists of both darkness and humour and the sense of alienation felt by Burton permeates the work. A reporter for the *New York Times* stated, 'inspired by such childhood heroes as Dr. Seuss and Roald Dahl, Mr. Burton's slim volume exquisitely conveys the pain of an adolescent outsider like his movies.'[17]

One of the characters from this book, a Tim Burton take on superheroes called 'Stainboy,' became the title character of a series of animated shorts on the internet in 2000. Danny Elfman was recruited for the score and Lisa Marie was the voice of Match Girl. All the animations were based on Burton's own artwork and involved the colourful characters who appeared in *Oyster Boy*.

Stainboy is quite simply a boy who leaves dirty stains on everything he comes into contact with, including a new superhero outfit he is given in one of his two stories in the book. Speaking about this character Burton states, 'Stainboy is one of my favourite characters [from the book] and in a way he's probably the perfect symbol of that whole *Superman* experience.'[18]

> **Ultimate Fact**
> Tim Burton was voted the 49th greatest director of all time by the American magazine *Entertainment Weekly* and was the youngest of the fifty on the list.

In 1998 Burton directed his first television commercial for a French chewing gum called 'Hollywood Gum.' In it a garden gnome leaves his home and hitches a ride on a garbage truck, eventually ending up, as Burton describes, 'bathing in a pool in an enchanted forest glade with a young woman who looks like Lisa Marie.'[19]

Teaming up with Johnny Depp for a third time, Burton next embarked on the feature film *Sleepy Hollow*, which was released in 1999 and met with both critical and commercial success. He followed this by directing two advertisements for Timex in 2000.

2001 saw Burton's box office appeal strengthened with the release of his re-envisaged version of *Planet of the Apes*. Tim Rothman, who was president of the Fox Film Group at the time *Planet of the Apes* was being made, said that 'Tim has that uncanny ability to walk the line between making very commercial films and yet very individualistic and distinctive films.'[20]

Two years later, in 2003, *Big Fish* was released and starred, amongst others, Helena Bonham Carter, who had become Burton's partner after they met on the set of *Planet of the Apes*. She also went on to appear in *Charlie and the Chocolate Factory* and supplied the voice to one of the characters in *Corpse Bride*, both of these films being released in 2005.

In the above films Tim Burton has created a number of trademarks that make his movies identifiable and secure the title of auteur. The first of these, which is relatively simple, but immediately lets an audience know they are watching a Tim Burton film, is his personalization of the studio logo at the start of his movies.

One of the most important trademarks, which we have already discussed at some length, is that his central characters suffer alienation and often display duality. If we take Batman as an example, we can see that he is alienated from normal society whilst struggling with the obvious duality of being both Bruce Wayne and Batman.

Another Burton trademark is the use of a symbolic castle

on a hill, which is very fairy tale-esque in its imagery. We can see this in *Beetlejuice, Batman, Batman Returns, Edward Scissorhands, Charlie and the Chocolate Factory*, and have already seen pertinent references in *Vincent* and *Frankenweenie*. Such fairy tale imagery is common to Burton's films, some of which are fairy tales in every aspect. In relation to this quality within his work Burton has stated, 'I've always liked the idea of fairy tales or folk tales because they're symbolic of something else. There's a foundation to them, but there's more besides, they're open to interpretation.'[21]

Another important aspect of all Burton's films is that there isn't an obvious hero. Some might argue that such characters as Batman are heroes, but they'd be wrong. In the case of Batman, he is a vigilante who dresses in a bat costume because he can't come to terms with the death of his parents. He is slightly mentally unstable, living a double life. He is flawed and he knows it, Burton himself saying, 'he's just a weird guy who does strange things.'[22]

Neither is Ichabod Crane from *Sleepy Hollow* a hero. He is a man too caught up in science. He doesn't believe in the supernatural, only the rational. His success in ridding the town of its headless menace is more through bumbling accident rather than any heroic traits.

People categorise the above two characters and others from his films as heroes because we're always trying to categorise everything – this is a natural tendency which Burton dislikes immensely. He doesn't portray heroes in his films, but confused, alienated people, thus subverting the Hollywood formula. These depictions make the leads more human because they are flawed, imperfect, and have difficulty coping with life and with their surroundings. They are symbolic of Burton's feelings about life and of the human struggle to understand ourselves and the world around us.

By subverting reality we see what he is trying to reveal, and see the world around us differently thanks to the juxtaposition with what is being shown on screen. For example, the scenes of suburbia in *Edward Scissorhands* are all the more powerful because they are taken to a symbolic extreme of conformity and normality.

Some people believe that Burton creates essentially live-action cartoons or animations, but this is far from the truth. Films cited in support of this argument – like *Pee-Wee's Big Adventure*, *Beetlejuice*, *Batman*, *Batman Returns* and *Mars Attacks!* – make-up only half of the feature-length live-action films Burton has directed.

Moreover, *Pee-Wee's Big Adventure* was a film over which Tim Burton had little control, the cartoonist character of Pee-Wee Herman was not of his creation, but was the creation of Paul Reubens, and therefore Burton cannot be held accountable for the tone of the character or of the film, which were both determined by a pre-established character. In the case of *Beetlejuice*, the primary element of the cartoon-like claim is the title character. Yes, Betelgeuse can be said to display cartoonist traits, including sounds to accompany his actions, but it could equally be said that this echoes the black and white slapstick films featuring such stars as Harold Lloyd and the Marx Brothers. Also, as the film was only his second after leaving the employment of Disney as an animator, it is hardly surprising that Burton may have been influenced by the style of work he created there at this point.

> **Ultimate Quote**
> 'I'm for anything that subverts what the studio thinks you have to do' – Tim Burton[23]

Batman and *Batman Returns* do not share much common

ground with cartoons, but they do with the darkly gothic graphic novels upon which they draw some of their inspiration, such as *The Dark Knight Returns* and *The Killing Joke*. Just because the characters have a partly cartoon background doesn't make the films themselves cartoonist.

The fifth and final film which some find supportive of the 'live-action cartoon' theory is *Mars Attacks!*. This, though, is more of a homage to B-movie science fiction, complete with B-movie flying saucers.

Another element to take into account in relation to all of Burton's feature-length live-action films is the fact that he didn't write the scripts for any of them, and therefore any cartoon influence he could bring would be primarily in direction rather than plot or narrative – which immediately lessens the likelihood of his films being representations of a cartoon reality. Further to this are his creative roots. They are not in cartoons, but in drawings, ones which often displayed the tortured, alienated feelings of the young Burton and so were not typically cartoonist in nature.

So, though there are elements within some of his films which could be seen as cartoonist, they didn't necessarily derive from Burton himself and they can be explained in other ways. Burton's work is actually more akin to the work of the Expressionists of Europe in the early part of the 20th Century than it is to cartoons. The Expressionists used colour for emotional and psychological depth, and imagery was often exaggerated. It is also the case that the German branch of expressionism had a darker aspect to it than others as it concentrated more on more sinister aspects of the human psyche.

In a similar fashion Burton uses colour, including the use of lighting to highlight or to cast shadows, to add emotional depth to his films. He also shows us unusual aspects of the human psyche, something most striking with such characters as Betelgeuse, who could be regarded as an expressionist exaggeration of a personality rather than a cartoonist character. His depiction of alienation also fits into this darker aspect, consider for example the young girl's depression and suicidal thoughts in *Beetlejuice* and Willy Wonka's apparent lack of concern as the children visiting his chocolate factory suffer deeply unpleasant fates.

It is also arguable in some instances that he treats subjective emotions as more important than objective observations and facts; which was another trait common to expressionism. For example, in *Big Fish* the father tells subjective stories about his life which are emotionally and not factually based. This also creates an increasingly emotionally charged atmosphere within the narrative.

This placing of subjective emotion above objective intellectualising is very apparent in Burton's approach to filmmaking. He says that intellectualising distances him from his inspiration and that he doesn't want to analyse what he does too much. Thus, even when his films aren't overtly so, we know that he has engaged in the work subjectively more than objectively.

The expressionist use of distortion and exaggeration is also clear in his work. *Beetlejuice* is filled with distortion, not just of physical, on-screen aspects, such as the Maitlands' faces when they try to look horrific, but it also conveys a sense of distortion to the audience in a number of non-visual ways. It distorts the usual Hollywood conventions in terms of leading character traits. It alters our previously held conceptions of the afterlife. It moves genre boundaries. And it also plays with traditional narrative techniques.

In the case of art, the application of this distortion and exaggeration aspect is apparent through 'intense colour, agitated brushstrokes, and disjointed space.'[24] All can be seen to varying degrees in Burton's movies. The use of colour, including black and white, is striking in *Beetlejuice*, *Edward Scissorhands*, *Mars Attacks!* and *Charlie and the Chocolate Factory*. The use of darkness and shadow is striking in the two *Batman* films and *Sleepy Hollow*.

The sense of 'agitated brushstrokes' comes in part from the alleged cartoonist nature of the minority of his movies. They have a skittish, lively feel, jumping from scene to scene.

The disjointed space can be seen in the sometimes odd, but always effective juxtapositions evident in Burton's work. This is apparent in *Beetlejuice* between the science fiction desert world and the 'real' world in which the Maitland's house exists. This feeling of the disjointed arises in *Batman* because of the blatant duality of the lead character, his divided psyche. The Batman-Bruce Wayne personality split and the character's distance from 'normal' society create a disjointed feel that permeates the whole movie. In *Big Fish* this disjointed aspect arises through the juxtaposition of the possibly fictional stories of the father and the reality experienced by his son. However, it is interesting to note that the final scenes of *Big Fish* bridge the gap and effectively weld these two fractured parts together in a secure and emotionally comforting way for the audience.

'The Scream' by Edvard Munch is a prime example of expressionist work, though it was created in 1893, prior to the 'official' beginnings of the movement. It echoes the spirits trapped in limbo in *Beetlejuice*, brings to mind the tortured psyche of Batman and that of Edward Scissorhands. It has resonances with the horror of *Sleepy Hollow* and the manic madness of the aliens in *Mars Attacks!* This effectively underlines the fact that expressionist paintings often depict emotional angst, something which is common to all Tim Burton's films, and to the man himself, as we saw in Chapter One.

It should at this point be clear to anyone who delves deeper than a quick glance at a couple of films, that Tim Burton's work cannot be equated with live-action cartoons. If they permit analysis of any kind – which is not something Burton encourages – his movies share much more in common with expressionism, which is one of his favourite art movements. The most important thing to remember in relation to Burton's work, is that it's not what the films resemble which matters, academic scrutiny is besides the point and discerning influences is irrelevant. What counts is what his work conveys in terms of its emotional content. Above all, he is concerned with the feelings he creates in the viewer. Because of this it is the audience who act as the barometer on which to judge Burton's work, and that is exactly the way he'd want it.

Endnotes

1. McMahan, A. – *The Films of Tim Burton: Animating Live Action in Contemporary Hollywood*, p.25
   (Continuum Books, 2005, US)

2. McMahan, A. – *The Films of Tim Burton: Animating Live Action in Contemporary Hollywood*, p.25
   (Continuum Books, 2005, US)

3. McMahan, A. – *The Films of Tim Burton: Animating Live Action in Contemporary Hollywood*, p.86
   (Continuum Books, 2005, US)

4. Fraga, K. (ed.) – *Tim Burton Interviews*, p.107 (University Press of Mississippi, 2005, US)

5. Jackson, M. & McDermott, A. – Tim Burton Biography (www.timburtoncollective.com)

6. Brooke, M. – Biography for Tim Burton (I) (www.imbd.com)

7. Grossberg, J. – Pee-Wee's Big Comeback? (www.eonline.com/News/Items/0,1,15304,00)

8. Salisbury, M. (ed.) – *Burton on Burton – Revised Edition*, p.42 (Faber and Faber, 2000, UK)

9. McMahan, A. – *The Films of Tim Burton: Animating Live Action in Contemporary Hollywood*, p.87 (Continuum Books, 2005, US)

10. Salisbury, M. (ed.) – *Burton on Burton – Revised Edition*, pp.140-141 (Faber and Faber, 2000, UK)

11. Salisbury,M (ed.) *Burton on Burton – Revised Edition* p.52 (Faber and Faber, 2000, UK)

12. Fraga, K. (ed.) – *Tim Burton Interviews*, p.63 (University Press of Mississippi, 2005, US)

13. Fraga, K. (ed.) – *Tim Burton Interviews*, p.8 (University Press of Mississippi, 2005, US)

14. Salisbury, M. (ed.) – *Burton on Burton – Revised Edition*, p.154 (Faber and Faber, 2000, UK)

15. Salisbury, M. (ed.) – *Burton on Burton – Revised Edition*, p.155 (Faber and Faber, 2000, UK)

16. Salisbury, M. (ed.) – *Burton on Burton – Revised Edition*, p.155 (Faber and Faber, 2000, UK)

17. McMahan, A. – *The Films of Tim Burton: Animating Live Action in Contemporary Hollywood*, p.27 (Continuum Books, 2005, US)

18. Salisbury, M. (ed.) – *Burton on Burton – Revised Edition*, p.158 (Faber and Faber, 2000, UK)

19. Salisbury, M. (ed.) – *Burton on Burton – Revised Edition*, p.161 (Faber and Faber, 2000, UK)

20. Fraga, K. (ed.) – *Tim Burton Interviews*, p.145 (University Press of Mississippi, 2005, US)

21. Unknown – Biography for Tim Burton (I) (www.imdb.com)

22. Fraga, K. (ed.) – *Tim Burton Interviews*, p.94 (University Press of Mississippi, 2005, US)

23. Fraga, K. (ed.) – *Tim Burton Interviews*, p.15 (University Press of Mississippi, 2005, US)

24. Unknown – Expressionism (www.ibiblio.org/wm/paint/tl/20th/expressionism)

References

Anderson, J. – 'Pee-wee's Big Adventure' (www.combustiblecelluloid.com/classic/peewee)

3. Beetlejuice

*'Troubled by the living? Is death a problem and
not the solution? Unhappy with eternity? Having
difficulty adjusting? Call Betelgeuse.'*

Released in America on April Fools' Day 1988, *Beetlejuice* had
a small budget of thirteen million dollars, but took thirty-two
million at the box office in just two weeks, eventually grossing
over seventy-three million dollars. It also won an Academy
Award for its makeup, created by Ve Neill, Steve La Porte
and Robert Short, and its popularity proved Burton to be
correct in his belief that audiences would appreciate a film
that broke with many Hollywood conventions.

The Warner Bros studio had wanted to call the film *House
Ghosts* due to the fact that this title was testing well with the
public. Jokingly, Tim Burton suggested the alternative title
of *Scared Sheetless* and the studio representatives actually
considered it until he made it clear he wasn't being serious.

Screenwriter Michael McDowell came up with the
original story for *Beetlejuice* with producer Larry Wilson, and
also worked on the re-writes along with Burton. He has had
more than thirty novels published in a number of genres,
including thrillers and romantic adventures. This multi-
generic background makes itself apparent in *Beetlejuice*, which

is a original blend of different genres. McDowell described the film as 'a feel-good movie about death'[1] and went on to co-write *The Nightmare Before Christmas*, one of Burton's two stop-motion feature films.

Beetlejuice turns the traditional haunted house story on its spinning head. Humans aren't trying to rid themselves of any pesky ghosts, but ghosts are trying to rid themselves of an unwelcome family of humans, especially the wife and stepmother Delia Deetz (played by Catherine O'Hara, best known for her role as the mother in the hit comedy *Home Alone* [Columbus, 1990]). Delia Deetz is a sculptor of arguably limited talents and her husband is a property developer called Charles, played expertly by Jeffrey Jones, who has starred in *Ferris Bueller's Day Off* (Hughes, 1986)

> ## Ultimate Fact
> Michael McDowell wrote a number of scripts for Steven Spielberg's 'Amazing Stories' television series, a series which also included the 'Family Dog' episode which Tim Burton worked on.

and alongside Keanu Reeves and Al Pacino in *The Devil's Advocate* (Hackford, 1997). Charles' daughter and Delia's stepdaughter is a gothic girl with a metaphorical dark cloud permanently encamped over her head. This girl, named Lydia, is played very effectively by Winona Ryder, who has appeared in films as diverse as the teen phenomenon *Heathers* (1989) and in *Alien Resurrection* (Jeunet, 1997), the fourth film in the *Alien* franchise. Burton used Ryder later, casting her opposite Johnny Depp in *Edward Scissorhands*, but *Beetlejuice* was the movie that brought her to people's attention and in it she befriends a couple of hapless ghosts.

These ghosts are of a loving, perfectly harmonious couple called Adam and Barbara Maitland. Adam is played by Alec

Baldwin, who had previously had a part in the television series 'Knots Landing' and who, like Jeffrey Jones, appeared in *The Hunt for Red October* (McTiernan, 1990). Barbara is played by Geena Davis, who many will remember as Jeff Goldblum's girlfriend in David Cronenberg's 1986 remake of *The Fly*, but is perhaps best known for her starring role in the film *Thelma and Louise* (Scott, 1991).

The couple own a hardware store and their quaint house stands on a hill overlooking the small town nearby, where the store is located. Painted white, with a turret and great view over the surrounding landscape, it is a symbolic castle, like those found in fairy tales. True to this fairy tale symbolism, the couple essentially become trapped in the house after their untimely and humorous death, then become further relegated to the attic, the castle's tower.

Ultimate Quote

'There's nothing that's just funny, just dramatic or just scary. It's all mixed together. I've always felt... that life is an incredible jumble of being funny and sad and dramatic and melodramatic and goofy and everything' – Tim Burton[2]

The mixture of dark and light evident in their final moments sets the tone for the film, which is a successfully invigorating blend of horror, humour, monster movies and even science fiction. All these genres are blurred in *Beetlejuice* just as previously in *Pee-Wee's Big Adventure*. But genres are not the only thing that's blurred in this fantasy frolic. Life and the afterlife are far from distinct as the opposing sides in the battle for possession of the house try to outwit each other. Further to this there is the blurring of the real and unreal in the use of the real town and a model Adam has created in the attic. The film therefore blends the real world with the model world, the afterlife and the science fiction desert inhabited by giant sand worms. This creates a strange kind of multi-layered reality within the movie, one which we move through relatively seamlessly.

Due to the above factors the film not only puts itself beyond generic categorization, but it also crosses the boundaries of life and death, and the real and unreal with the greatest of ease, managing to portray an afterlife unlike anything usually seen on film. Not the beautiful vision of a utopian heaven for Tim Burton, or even a torture-filled, sulphurous pit of hell. No, Burton has gone for a bland place where mediocrity and tediousness rule the day. Cross a doctor's waiting room with some council offices and you're halfway there. Add a large dose of interestingly deceased individuals and you've got it. It's a bureaucratic nightmare of pen-pushers and elevator music.

The production designer, Bo Welch, said, 'for the afterlife we wanted something vague and evasive enough to defy categorizing and invite disorientation, yet specific enough to invoke the fear that the afterlife might not be much different then real life.'[3] Welch had the perfect background to work on the generically blurring *Beetlejuice* as he'd already worked on the pop-culture vampire horror-comedy *The Lost Boys* (Schumacher, 1987).

The disorientation which Welch mentions above occurs on a number of levels in *Beetlejuice*. First, the audience feels completely confused when the Maitlands die early in the film, something described by Kevin Thomas of the *Los Angeles Times* as 'a move as shocking as it is darkly amusing, since the lethal accident is also a beautifully staged sight gag.'[5] Having

Ultimate Quote

'The movie's view is that when you die your problems aren't taken care of' – Tim Burton[4]

the lead characters die in the first few minutes of a movie is unheard of and therefore unexpected. It means that the audience are immediately thrown off course and have to adjust the way they approach this work.

This disorientation is soon heightened by the introduction of the science fiction landscape of a desert planet complete with giant sand worms. To find such a landscape in what has been dubbed a horror-comedy is unexpected. It is also shocking due to the sudden nature of our introduction to this landscape when Adam falls into it after stepping from the house.

At this point the usual formula we use to read films, one based on our viewing of numerous other treats from Hollywood and beyond, becomes evidently useless and we are left having to almost make things up as we go along. This creates a kind of freshness to the film, an invigorating sense of the new, as we joyfully wait for the next unexpected event, the next jack-in-the-box to surprise and thrill us. This is a rarity with contemporary films because we have learnt how to read them, how to spot the clues as to what will happen, who will survive and where the narrative will end up. *Beetlejuice* makes a refreshingly anarchic change, though it could also be somewhat confusing to people expecting a classical Hollywood narrative.

> ## Ultimate Quote
>
> 'After Hollywood hammering me with the concept of story structure...the script for *Beetlejuice* was completely anti all that: it had no real story, it didn't make any sense, it was more like a stream of consciousness' – Tim Burton[6]

Further disorientation of the viewer and disruption of our usual responses to a film occurs when we see Burton's portrayal of the afterlife, as mentioned above. It is not the vision of the great beyond that we have come to expect and therefore comes as quite a surprise, but one filled with humour as well as the almost terrifying thought that this could actually be what we experience when we die. This juxtaposition is highly effective in creating a sense of amusement coupled with a sense of dread.

Using disorientation in such a way means that the audience is constantly engaged with the narrative, something which is a necessity if we are to follow what is happening. In the case of many Hollywood movies you can fall asleep for a sizeable portion of the narrative and still be able to work out what is happening and even what has taken place during your nap. However, *Beetlejuice* demands our undivided attention, though this is down to fine performances, some great gags, striking visuals, and an intriguingly different plot as much as it is to disorientation.

> ## Ultimate Fact
> After an enthusiastic response to the afterlife waiting room at test screenings of *Beetlejuice*, Burton decided to include the scene near the end of the film where Betelgeuse is seated in the room and ends up having his head shrunk by a witch doctor. [7]

We also find that there are a number of other juxtapositions apparent within the film, not least that between life and death, which is especially scary because, apart from the freakish nature of some of the deceased, there's not really that much difference between the two states of being. There is also the aforementioned juxtaposition between the real and the model town. The use of this model gives the real world a strangely surreal feeling due to the fact that the two blend so seamlessly together. This feeling is aided and abetted by the other strange goings on within the house and in the deserts beyond its doors and increases the viewer's sense of disorientation throughout the film.

Another interesting juxtaposition occurs in relation to the Maitlands' death. This tragic event is contrasted with two other elements. The first is humour, the situation of their demise being tongue-in-cheek. The second is due to the fact that this tragedy takes place in what is otherwise a picturesque setting. We might expect dark clouds, rain, maybe even a storm during which the couple die. However, there are no such dark atmospherics to act as signposts informing us of what is about to happen. Instead, the death takes place on a bright and beautiful day, breaking with the usual generic conventions.

There is a further juxtaposition between the big-city types and the locals. The first are represented by the Deetzes and Otho, while the latter group are seen in the town at the start of the film and are also represented by the Maitlands. This then sets the Deetzes and the Maitlands apart on two levels; the city-country divide and the life-death divide. The person who acts as a bridge across both divides is Lydia, the alienated, depressive adolescent. Youthful characters are also given pivotal roles in *Edward Scissorhands*, *Mars Attacks!*, *Sleepy Hollow* and *Charlie and the Chocolate Factory*. It is also the case that Pee-Wee Herman could be described as a child in an adult's body and the young Bruce Wayne witnessing his parents being killed in *Batman* is highly significant to the story.

> **Ultimate Fact**
>
> Danny Elfman has not only written the scores for countless films, he also created the theme music for the immensely popular cartoon series 'The Simpsons.'

All these young characters seem to relate to the alienated

childhood of Tim Burton. He says that he must identify with the characters in a film in order to agree to direct it, and it seems safe to assume this identification is in part due to his own background.

We have already seen that the death of Lydia's ghostly friends was humorous, but there is also a great deal of humour present at other points during the film. It is evident in the afterlife waiting room for the recently deceased, which contains such people as a magician's assistant who clearly hasn't survived being sawn in half and a diver who has died in a shark attack (and the shark seems to have choked on his leg). These events clearly demonstrate a comic element mixed with the dark theme of death.

The biggest comedy set-piece occurs when the Deetzes have guests for dinner and the table of six end up becoming possessed by rhythm from beyond the grave. The Maitlands force Delia, Charles, and the four guests to dance to Harry Belafonte's 1956 song 'Day-O,' much to the amusement of the watching Lydia and audience. This amusement isn't simply due to the dance moves, but also because it is obvious that all the participants aren't in control of their actions, and are shocked, amused and worried by their sudden possession.

The humour of this situation extends beyond the enforced dance routine when the Maitlands return to their attic retreat in the hope of seeing their victims running from the house screaming in fear. What actually happens is Lydia arrives and informs them that her parents wish to meet them. Not only is this funny because of the Maitlands' failure, but it is surprising because the usual Hollywood convention would be to have people being scared by being possessed. We then see Charles becoming excited by the possibility of commercially exploiting his haunted house. This adds to the humour of the entire situation and continues to break with convention.

There are too many comic elements within the movie to discuss them all individually. However, others worth mentioning included the *Handbook for the Recently Deceased*. This book is found by the Maitlands after they have bitten the big one in the creek and is particularly amusing because it reads like programming instructions for a VCR.

Another humorous element is Otho, the interior designer with dubious talents. His somewhat camp character works in perfect comic harmony with Delia Deetz. A specific element of dialogue by Otho is also worth pointing out. Just before the 'Day-O' performance he states, 'You know what they say about people who commit suicide – they become civil servants.' This is self-referential humour in the context of the film in that it references the woman who is at the booth when the Maitlands go to the waiting room for the recently deceased, a woman who committed suicide by cutting her wrists and has become a civil servant.

As Kevin Thomas of the *LA Times* stated when the movie was released, 'By the time this irresistible treat is over it has created some of the funniest moments and most inspired visual humour and design we may expect to experience at the movies all year.'[8] All the humour in this 'irresistible treat' is a mix of dark and light tones, mixing the macabre with pure slapstick.

In relation to the Maitlands this mix of humour arises through their deaths and their activities during the afterlife, as they try to come to terms with their demise and then attempt to scare off the Deetzes, trying both gruesome and ridiculous tricks in order to achieve their aim. The mix of dark and light within the humour generated by the Deetzes and Otho comes from the mild insanity of Delia, the camp ineptness of Otho, and Charles' slightly naïve optimism.

However, this mix is topped most spectacularly by the manic character of Betelgeuse. This role is played brilliantly by Michael Keaton, who would later become Batman in the first two films of that franchise and also starred in the thriller *Pacific Heights* (Schlesinger, 1990), where he also terrorises a young couple in love. Rita Kempley of the *Washington Post* said that 'Michael Keaton is the juice that makes it go,'[9] and his performance is made even more remarkable by the fact that he improvised nearly all of his lines as the madcap bio-exorcist – an exorcist who gets rid of the living (continuing the concept of twisting the usual haunted house stories). Unusually for a director, Burton had not seen any of Keaton's work prior to casting him as Betelgeuse and says, 'I actually liked that because I felt like I was getting to know somebody for myself, freshly, and that excited me.'[10]

Keaton's character is the main source of slapstick humour throughout the film, complete with cartoonist sounds to accompany his actions, such as a *whizzing* sound when he throws of his hat.

Betelgeuse is the negative of the Maitlands' positive. These two elements combine to create a great comedy double act and without the perfect, slightly tedious nature of Adam and Barbara the bio-exorcist wouldn't have been half as fun. It is the interaction between Betelgeuse and the Maitlands, and their obvious differences of character, that help to make him the very memorable master of mirth and mayhem that he is.

> ## Ultimate Quote
> 'You show up on the set and just go *fuckin' nuts*. It was *rave* acting. You rave for twelve or fourteen hours, then go home tired and beat and exhausted... It was rave and *purge* acting' – Michael Keaton[11]

Some have complained about the blandness of the Maitlands. However, this was a necessity if Betelgeuse were to have the impact that he does. The couple are like the good cop in a good-cop bad-cop set-up, something that needs both elements in order to work. You could also describe the Maitlands as 'the straight guy' in a comedy act. They are not only perfect for each other, they're also perfect for Betelgeuse.

> **Ultimate Fact**
>
> In the original screenplay Betelgeuse was underwritten, vaguely Middle Eastern, and more evil. Burton wanted to change the tone of the character and so asked Keaton to come up with his own ideas. [12]

Betelgeuse's character has an overtly sexual nature highlighted by his repeated and lustful molestation of Barbara Maitland. He is beyond the bounds of life, but also beyond the bounds of those in the afterlife. He has a certain kind of freedom allowed by being shunned by the rest of the deceased hordes. As one critic put it, 'belching, farting, and scratching his crotch with ferocious abandon, he's the disgusting kid that every twelve-year-old boy wants to be.' [13] He does what he wants and acts how he pleases and in this sense he is akin to the Joker in *Batman*. They also share a mask of predominantly white makeup. In the case of Betelgeuse this clownish makeup along with his mad hair adds visual depth to the insanity of this crazy character. He and the Joker also share another common link, and that is alienation, something which is a very strong theme in *Beetlejuice*.

Not only is Betelgeuse an outsider, but so are the Maitlands. They feel alienated in the offices of the afterlife where their deaths have left no obvious marks on their bodies, unlike the collection of freaks about them. They also feel alienated in their own home, consigned to dwell in the attic because of the horrific humans who have moved in.

Further alienation comes in the form of the girl dressed in black. Lydia feels alone and even becomes suicidal, mirroring the feelings shared by many teenagers. She states such things as, 'Live people ignore the strange and unusual. I myself am strange and unusual,' and 'My life is like a dark room, one, big, dark room.' Both of these statements reflect Burton's feelings when growing up in Burbank, even to the extent of the second quote referencing the fact that his parents all but blocked out the windows of his bedroom.

> **Ultimate Fact**
> The character of Lydia is also known as 'Pumpkin' by her father. Pumpkins are a recurring theme in Tim Burton's films.

Feeling a lesser degree of alienation is Charles Deetz. This is due to the unwelcome activities of his wife and the interior designer with the worst possible taste, Otho.

The score for *Beetlejuice*, created by Danny Elfman on his second Burton project, is vital in helping audiences understand the film. This was proved by test screenings that were conducted with and without music. The latter tests received a negative audience response, with people not really enjoying the film on the whole. However, the results of tests with the score being played were completely the opposite. In describing why this was the case Burton has said, '…it really has to do with the fact that when you're doing a movie where people don't know what the fuck is going on the music is the guide-post, it's the tone and the context.'[14] The music helps to stabilise the disorientation that the audience is feeling and creates a backdrop which can help them follow the unusual narrative.

To create the right tone and context Elfman created a score in a minor key with an 'angular melody' played by brass instruments. This dissonance is underlined by the use of muted trumpets and suggests 'a sinister tone to the music.'[15] However, this sinister aspect is offset by the pace of the music, which is often fast and dance-like. The bright quality is juxtaposed with the darkness of the dissonance, suggesting the mixture of comedy and horror which is apparent on screen, and therefore acting as a perfect companion to the action.

> **Ultimate Fact**
> Only $1 million of the $13 million budget for *Beetlejuice* was spent on the film's effects.[16]

It is the music that tells the audience which elements of the film are playful and which are more serious. The music also adds to the mood, giving it additional depth and impact. Without the score the film would lose much of its strength, and the tones of the film would no longer be so clearly contrasted. So Elfman's skills are vital for enjoying and understanding *Beetlejuice*, almost playing the part of a narrator in that to a degree the music informs the audience of what is happening. With such an unconventional and groundbreaking film, a 'guide-post' element such as this was vital to the success of the movie.

The lighting works in a similar way to the music. It enhances the mood of the movie and its power cannot be underestimated. The opening 'perfect couple' scenes of the film are bright with natural light, adding a cheerfulness to the action that unfolds before us. Once Delia has made her mark on the house it takes on darker tones, almost like a coffin, which is rather apt.

There are also other important uses of light, such as when the Maitlands' afterlife 'case-worker', Juno, gives them a brief history of Betelgeuse. The character's faces are up-lit and this has the effect of deepening the sense of foreboding, partly because this lighting effect relates to times as children when ghost stories were told around camp fires or with torches held beneath our chins. This lighting effect is accompanied by Elfman's music and the two combine to create a greater depth of atmosphere.

> **Ultimate Fact**
> There is a considerable amount of 'fan-fiction' on the internet which deals with every aspect of 'the pageant world of Betelgeuse'.[17]

As well as Danny Elfman, there are a number of other cast and crew members who worked with Burton on projects other than *Beetlejuice*. As far as the cast goes, we've seen that Michael Keaton went on to play Batman, Jeffrey Jones reappeared in *Ed Wood* and *Sleepy Hollow*, Catherine O'Hara supplied one of the voices for *The Nightmare Before Christmas*, Winona Ryder played one of the title roles in *Edward Scissorhands*, and Sylvia Sydney helped save the world in *Mars Attacks!* Production designer Bo Welch worked with Burton again on *Edward Scissorhands* and *Batman Returns*, cinematographer Thomas Ackerman had previously worked on *Frankenweenie*, and visual effects consultant Rick Heinrichs had acted in *Luau*, worked on *Vincent* and *Frankenweenie*, and would also go on to work with Burton on a number of his other films.

Special effects appear throughout this film and utilise a number of different techniques, including the use of mirrors and stop-motion animation. This style of animation was used by Burton in both *Vincent* and *Pee-Wee's Big Adventure*, and he went on to work on three stop-motion feature films. In *Beetlejuice* it is used on three notable occasions. The first is in animating the sand worms on the desert planet. The second is when Betelgeuse himself becomes a large snake in order to terrify the Deetzes. And the third use is when Delia's sculptures come to life in the climax of the movie. On each occasion the stop-motion is effective and has more of a presence than many computer generated effects.

The first of these effects concerning the sand worms is especially interesting because the beasts reference two cult films. They are reminiscent of the sand worms in David Lynch's science fiction epic *Dune*, released in 1984. They also remind older viewers of the alien in Ridley Scott's 1979 science fiction horror *Alien*. This is largely due to the fact they have an outer mouth and a far more deadly inner mouth.

Another, more obvious, film reference occurs when Betelgeuse drags a housefly down to his lair, which is situated in Adam's model of the town. As he pulls the housefly down it repeats the phrase 'help me' in a high pitched voice. This is a direct reference to the final scenes of the original black and white version of *The Fly* (Neumann, 1958). This has humour taken in isolation, but is heightened by the fact that Geena Davis starred in the remake of the film.

Janet Maslin of the *New York Times* wasn't particularly taken with the film and neither was critic Roger Ebert. Maslin felt the actors were 'limited by the stupidity of their material.'[18] However, this is hardly a valid criticism, when both Keaton and O'Hara improvised much of their performances, and also part of the point of the Maitland's characters is that they *are* limited. This limitation is 'part of the theme' according to Burton,[19] and is present in both their lives and their deaths.

In life the Maitlands were limited by plainness, by their own straight-laced personalities. In death they also find their personalities limiting in that they have trouble coping with trying to scare off the Deetzes because they are too nice.

Death brings its own problems, because of their entrapment within their home for one hundred and twenty-five years. These limitations are purposeful and symbolic of the kind of limits Burton experienced in his suburban childhood.

The Maitlands also display the same sort of alienation that Burton felt as a boy. As he says, 'if you've ever felt out of place you'll plug into the ghost's awkwardness.'[20] In fact, what the ghosts experience could be seen as the ultimate form of alienation, one in which the world cannot see you and completely ignores you – similar feelings which Burton felt when trying to create an identity for himself through his drawings as a child.

There are those who complain about certain inconsistencies within the film. There is the fact that when Betelgeuse pulls a housefly into his lair in the model town the fly is suitably large in comparison with Betelgeuse, but when he eats a beetle it is strangely as small as it would be if he were human sized. Barbara talks without the use of her mouth or tongue after the Maitlands have mutated their faces to show Juno how horrific they can be. Lydia goes downstairs to find out what is happening immediately after her father and Otho have removed the model town from the attic and yet when she reaches the ground floor dinner guests have arrived and the model is already fully in place, too much time having passed between her departure from upstairs and her arrival downstairs. Adam drives a model car which wouldn't have an engine. Betelgeuse is already dead and yet has to go to the waiting room with little sign of being chewed by a sand worm. Finally, if people stay as they were when they died then how can there be skeletons in the afterlife?

Criticism of these inconsistencies seems to be nit picking, after all, what film hasn't got its problems? Burton doesn't worry about such minor details, stating, 'part of the joy of life is in the flaws.'[21] It is also the case that audiences were happy to ignore any such problems within *Beetlejuice* and were still thoroughly entertained by this bizarre movie. Burton himself admits that his films do sometimes contain holes, but how much does this matter as long as they communicate and connect with the audience? Very little – judging from the box office takings; in fact one reviewer remarked that *Beetlejuice*'s very success was 'no doubt due to its unconventional structure and sprinklings of dazzling genius.'[22]

Some critics complain that in Burton's films the characters aren't changed by events which have taken place, which conforms to the Hollywood formula. However, this isn't the case with *Beetlejuice*. Two of the characters appear different by the end of the film in comparison with their previous personas. Firstly, Delia Deetz seems to have lost the edge of her insanity and though she is still sculpting, she has come to accept the Maitland's idea of interior décor, something which was not the case during the rest of the movie.

> ### Ultimate Quote
> 'I feel very good about being part of a project that has broken some rules and is at the very least innovative, imaginative, creative – just plain funny'
> – Michael Keaton[23]

The second character to have changed is Lydia. She has spent most of the film being a depressive, black-clad teenager. However, by the end of the film she has brightened considerably. She is shown to be happy, with friends at school, and doing well in her studies.

It is also of note that the lighting returns to the natural light which was seen in the opening scenes of the film. This creates a sense of circularity, especially when coupled with the fact that we see the Maitlands decorating their house, an activity they were indulging in at the start. The film has come full circle and the harmony within the house has been restored.

On an emotional level *Beetlejuice* makes audiences feel thrilled and excited by its blend of genres and by breaking with usual Hollywood conventions. We are gripped by the often rapid change of imagery, finding the film both funny and frightening, silly and serious. The exuberance of the on-screen festival of sights and sounds is infectious, making us feel invigorated by the experience of watching something completely different from the usual Hollywood fare. As Desson Howe of the *Washington Post* says, 'the joy of *Beetlejuice* is it's completely bizarre.'[24] This bizarre quality arises from its difference to other mainstream movies, its wacky characters and extremely strange situations. It is this bizarre quality that helps to make the movie both highly entertaining and memorable.

Endnotes

1. Salisbury, M. (ed.) – *Burton on Burton – Revised Edition*, p.54 (Faber and Faber, 2000, UK)

2. Fraga, K. (ed.) – *Tim Burton Interviews*, p.116 (University Press of Mississippi, 2005, US)

3. *Beetlejuice* – DVD, Production Notes, Behind The Scenes (Warner Home Video, 1999)

4. *Beetlejuice* – DVD, Production Notes, Behind The Scenes (Warner Home Video, 1999)

5. Thomas, K. – 'Gleeful Grand Guignol of *Beetlejuice*' (*Los Angeles Times*, 30th March 1988, US)

6. McMahan, A. – *The Films of Tim Burton: Animating Live Action in Contemporary Hollywood*, p.61
   (Continuum Books, 2005, US)

7. Salisbury, M. (ed.) – *Burton on Burton – Revised Edition*, p.66 (Faber and Faber, 2000, UK)

8. Thomas, K. – 'Gleeful Grand Guignol of *Beetlejuice*' (*Los Angeles Times*, 30th March 1988, US)

9. Kempley, R. – 'Beetlejuice' (*Washington Post*, 30th March 1988, US)

10. Fraga, K. (ed.) – *Tim Burton Interviews*, p.64 (University Press of Mississippi, 2005, US)

11. Fraga, K. (ed.) – *Tim Burton Interviews*, pp.12-13 (University Press of Mississippi, 2005, US)

12. Fraga, K. (ed.) – *Tim Burton Interviews*, p.12 (University Press of Mississippi, 2005, US)

13. Breese, K. – Beetlejuice (www.filmcritic.com, 2005)

14. Fraga, K. (ed.) – *Tim Burton Interviews*, p.61 (University Press of Mississippi, 2005, US)

15. McMahan, A. – *The Films of Tim Burton: Animating Live Action in Contemporary Hollywood*, p.199 (Continuum Books, 2005, US)

16. Salisbury, M. (ed.) – *Burton on Burton* – *Revised Edition*, p.61 (Faber and Faber, 2000, UK)

17. Breese, K. – Beetlejuice (www.filmcritic.com, 2005)

18. Maslin, J. – 'Ghosts And Extra Eyeballs' (*New York Times*, 30th March 1988, US)

19. Fraga, K. (ed.) – *Tim Burton Interviews*, pp.73-74 (University Press of Mississippi, 2005, US)

20. Fraga, K. (ed.) – *Tim Burton Interviews*, p.11 (University Press of Mississippi, 2005, US)

21. Fraga, K. (ed.) – *Tim Burton Interviews*, p.59 (University Press of Mississippi, 2005, US)

22. Rosenbaum, J. – Beetlejuice (http://onfilm.chicagoreader.com/movies/capsules/839_beetlejuice)

23. Fraga, K. (ed.) – *Tim Burton Interviews*, p.13 (University Press of Mississippi, 2005, US)

24. Howe, D. – 'Beetlejuice' (*Washington Post*, 1st April 1988, US)

4. Batman

*'Did you ever dance with the devil
in the pale moonlight?'*
– Jack Napier/the Joker

Batman's relationship with the general public didn't begin with its release in 1989. A phenomenon since the famous 1960s TV series, the general public were to be assaulted by a huge amount of hype, merchandising and gossip. This was created in part by the Warner Brothers studio, whose subway and bus shelter posters advertising the film were often stolen by fans. The hype was aided by the merchandising, with items such as T-shirts featuring the Batman logo and toys of the Caped Crusader spreading pre-release excitement for the film at a virtually unprecedented level. When asked about this merchandising Burton replied, 'I'm very afraid of this kind of marketing stuff. It kind of destroys the movie sometimes.'[1]

Gossip played a big hand in making *Batman* the phenomenon that it became, Burton stating, 'so much has been written about this picture that is simply untrue. I almost feel like I'm on a parallel planet.'[2] The controversial casting of Michael Keaton in the lead role also created a huge stir. Many saw Keaton as a comic actor and feared the film would go down the same road as the 1960s TV show, especially after his extremely funny slapstick performance as Betelgeuse. However, Burton had no reservations about using Keaton in the movie, stating, 'He's got that look in his eyes...*that guy you could see putting on a Batsuit.*'[3] It is also the case that Keaton wouldn't have even read the script if Tim Burton hadn't been attached as director.[4]

> ### Ultimate Fact
> The movie took ten years to finally come to the big screen, passing through the hands of a number of writers and directors, including Ivan Reitman, who was the director of the 1984 hit *Ghostbusters*.

The casting of Jack Nicholson as the Joker met with the opposite reaction to that of Keaton as Batman. Alex Ben Block, then editor of *Show Biz News*, said that 'With Nicholson part of the package it raised it to a new level.'[5] This was true not only of the film itself, but also of the hype, many seeing Jack as the perfect actor for the part, including Burton himself.

Each of the above elements served to create a massive buzz about the movie well in advance of it actually coming to the big screen. Kim Basinger, who played Bruce Wayne's love interest, Vicki Vale, stated, 'This isn't a film, it's an event.'[6] Some people were so keen to get even the slightest glimpse, they bought cinema tickets simply so they could go and see the trailer for the film, which acted as a mouth-watering appetiser.

With two soundtrack albums, one featuring the score by Danny Elfman and the other songs by Prince which would appear in the movie, warehouses full of merchandise, fans up in arms about Keaton's casting, fans equally enthralled by the prospect of seeing Jack Nicholson as the Joker, and people everywhere wondering if the film could possibly live up to the hype, it was finally released in the US on the 21st June 1989.

Batman became an immediate box office sensation and was one of the highest grossing films in Warmer Brothers' long moviemaking history. It became the first film to break the hundred million dollar barrier in only the first ten days of its release. It was the biggest hit of the year and eventually earned over $500 million worldwide. *Batman* was

> ### Ultimate Fact
>
> Fifty thousand letters from fans protesting about the casting of Keaton flooded into the studio. Furious fans tore up publicity material for the film, Warner Brothers' stock slumped, the *Wall Street Journal* covered the crisis on page one, and, worst of all, Adam West, who'd played the camp Batman in the 60's TV show even thought he'd make a better choice than Keaton.

a true blockbuster in every sense and put Burton firmly on the map. Many even drew parallels between him and George Lucas, whose third film had been the huge hit *Star Wars* (1977). It also began the Batman franchise, which still continues today, the latest offering coming in 2005 with the release of *Batman Begins* (Nolan).

In creating *Batman*, Burton was heavily influenced by two particular graphic novels. One was Frank Miller's *The Dark Knight Returns* and the other was entitled *The Killing Joke*, written by Alan Moore and illustrated by Brian Bollard. In fact, when meeting with potential licensees for the film, Burton would hold up *The Killing Joke* and state, 'This is what I want the movie to look like.'[7]

A dark and moody film, *Batman* centres around two main characters with personality disorders. Batman and the Joker are like two sides of the same coin. The former is an introvert,

> **Ultimate Fact**
>
> Twenty-eight Batsuits were used in the making of the movie and cost $250,000. They were created by casting a soft rubber mould over Keaton's body.[8]

the latter an extrovert. Batman is limited until he puts on his mask, the Joker has a permanent, grinning mask and has a certain, manic freedom of behaviour not unlike that of Betelgeuse. Batman is mentally damaged and the Joker is physically disfigured. Batman is a force for the good and fights crime, while the Joker is a force for evil and creates crime. Batman has a split personality and the Joker is intensely single-minded.

Bruce Wayne's parents were killed before his eyes when he was a boy. He has found it hard to cope with this childhood trauma and this has led to a split personality. One half is the respectable, wealthy society man, and though quirky, he's not particularly unusual, merely eccentric. The other half is in shadow, wanting to hide in the darkness and conceal his face. He is Batman: the Dark Knight. Batman is the part of him which seeks to silence the feelings he has concerning the deaths of his parents. This side of his personality is an outlet for the release of inner pressure. Without it you suspect Bruce Wayne wouldn't be quite as sane as he appears to be.

Bruce is basically a mixed-up individual, more human than many superheroes and virtually the opposite of Superman, who was from another planet, virtually indestructible, super strong and the owner of a pair of X-ray eyes. Batman is simply a human who chooses to put on a Batsuit rather than booking in to see a psychotherapist. He needs gadgets in order to traverse the city and evade his adversaries. He requires body armour because, unlike Superman, he isn't impervious to bullets. 'Lets face it, you're not exactly normal,' comments Vicki Vale in an amusing use of understatement which underlines how strange this man is.

A small scene which highlights Bruce Wayne's edgy personality occurs in Vicki Vale's apartment after the Joker has joined the couple with henchmen in tow. Bruce states, 'You wanna get nuts? Come on, let's get nuts,' as he uses a poker to smash a vase. This is very Betelgeuse-esque and gives us a brief glimpse of the anger within the character, allows us to see that he is close to the edge, an edge he may have fallen from a long time previous if it weren't for the emotional outlet of his alter ego.

The split personality which is highly pronounced in Bruce Wayne's character reflects the fact that we all have various parts to our personas, various interior struggles and life situations that we try to come to terms with. In relation to this subject Tim Burton has said, 'This whole split personality thing is so much a part of every person that it's just amazing to me that more people don't consciously understand it... no one is one thing.'[9] We are all made up of different aspects, some of which are discordant and dark, and Batman is the ultimate symbol of this element of what it is to be human.

> **Ultimate Fact**
> The notes that accompany the gas mask given to Vicki Vale were actually written by Tim Burton himself.

We can see from what we know about Burton's past and his continuing feelings of alienation that he could identify somewhat with Bruce Wayne/Batman. This character was the source of his main interest in doing the film, as is evident from the way in which Burton invested his emotion as he delved into Batman's mythology and uncovered a vision of the Caped Crusader far more gripping than Adam West's camp portrayal in the 1960s television show.

The portrayal of a dark, mysterious and melancholy Batman was described by the Caped Crusader's creator, Bob Kane, as 'the way I created Batman in 1939.'[10] Kane was a consultant on the film, which returns to the original vision of the lead character. For the first year or so of Batman's existence he wasn't accompanied by Robin, the 'Boy Wonder', and so the movie also remains true to this fact. Batman is portrayed relatively alone and isolated, his only friend being his butler, Alfred Pennyworth, expertly played by Michael Gough who said of Burton, 'I liked working with him because he gives you the problem, he explains how it works, and says "Now play with it"... and that's exciting.'[11]

In truth, Robin's absence from the movie wasn't actually down to his absence in Batman's early adventures, but was due to the fact that Burton and writer Sam Hamm couldn't find a suitable place for him in the film. Burton says, 'We just couldn't figure out how to slip Robin into the story structure. Since we were dealing with the duel of Batman and the Joker, Robin seemed irrelevant.'[12] This was a wise move, as Robin's presence would have detracted from the story, which has a foundation so personal and specific to the two main characters. It is also the case that Robin was left out of the sequel, *Batman Returns*, to be discussed in Chapter Six.

> ## Ultimate Quote
> 'The film is like the duel of the freaks. It's a film about two disfigured people. That's what I love about it' – Tim Burton[13]

The mythology surrounding the reasons for Bruce Wayne's need to become Batman were dealt with in the DC Comics featuring the character, and the film stays true to this when the young

Wayne sees his parents murdered. This mythology meant that, as with *Pee-Wee's Big Adventure*, Burton had to create a film centred around pre-established characters and background, something which meant he had to stay within certain boundaries and couldn't have complete creative freedom. It also means that his emotional attachment wasn't as great

> **Ultimate Fact**
>
> Sean Young, who had previously starred in David Lynch's sci-fi epic *Dune* (1984), was originally cast as Vicki Vale, but had to be replaced at the last minute after a riding accident during pre-production.

in this film as in the majority of his other work.

The criminal Jack Napier, who soon becomes the Joker, is a psychotic personality with obvious single-mindedness. He is both self-obsessed and crazy, the latter quality accentuated after he is disfigured by acid. With his new mask he is freed of any previous misgivings or interior boundaries which previously stopped him giving in to his darker urges and takes on the new identity of the Joker. Like Betelgeuse, he does whatever he wants, follows every one of his urges without the usual restrictions we place on ourselves and with complete disregard for the restrictions society attempts to place on us.

The Joker is brilliantly played by Jack Nicholson. His natural ability to play such a psychotic character was evident in Stephen King's *The Shining* (Kubrick, 1980). The performance is scarily convincing as Jack lets loose and really makes the role his own.

The Joker's behaviour has a certain childlike quality to it. This can be seen in his bright optimism, his lively nature which implies a joy in being alive, and in his playfulness. This childlike aspect is highlighted very simply when Vicki Vale receives a gas mask while waiting at a restaurant table in Gotham City's museum. The notes with it simply read 'urgent' and 'put this on right now'. The way in which they are written is a childish scrawl and it is obvious from what we have already seen of the Joker that this is supposed to be his writing.

We also see an example of the dark humour evident in the film during the scene where the Joker and Vicki Vale are at the restaurant table. He states, 'I am the world's first fully-functioning homicidal artist,' a statement which is humorous in isolation, but made especially so when taking into account his destruction of works of art within the gallery, his destruction of his previous girlfriend's good looks in the name of art and his hope that Vicki Vale will suffer the same fate.

> ### Ultimate Fact
> While shooting *Batman* in England, Burton met a German painter called Lena Gieseke, whom he married early in 1989 during post-production on the movie.

An interesting use of imagery in the film occurs when Jack Napier's acid scoured hand rises from the water outside the Axis chemical factory in the first portion of the film. This is akin to the classical shot of a zombie's hand rising from the grave. It represents the fact that Jack Napier is dead, but will rise again in a new form. As he himself states, 'I've been dead already, it's very liberating.' This liberation comes in the form of a complete breakdown of interior boundaries so that he does whatever he feels like doing, as previously mentioned.

Wayne and Napier's characters are not only opposite sides of the same coin, their fates have also been entwined since the day when Bruce saw his parents murdered. Jack was the killer and therefore created Wayne's need to become Batman. He created his nemesis long before they would eventually come face to face. In turn Batman created the Joker at the Axis chemical factory when Jack fell into the vat of chemicals. In fact, this is highlighted clearly in some of the dialogue during the final showdown in the church tower. The Joker says, 'You made me,' to which Batman responds 'I made you, you made me first.'

So, if Napier hadn't killed Dr. Wayne and his wife he wouldn't have fallen into the vat because Batman would not have existed and couldn't have caused him to do so. He also wouldn't have had to face Batman when he became Gotham's crime lord and wouldn't have died in a final showdown between the pair of freaks.

This showdown between good and evil has resonances with those seen in many westerns, such as *High Noon* (Zinnemann, 1952). The twist that adds to the darkness of this film is that the showdown doesn't take place at midday, but midnight. The contrast is clear, one occurring in bright, warm sunshine, and the other taking place in the cool darkness of night.

The showdown also has links with classic fairy tales. Like Cinderella, Vale loses a shoe, one which her rescuer, her knight in dark armour, sees on the stairs of the church tower. It is in this tower that we discover two further fairy tale images. Firstly, there is that of the princess trapped in a tall, dark tower. Secondly, there is also the imagery of Beauty and the Beast dancing together made clear when the Joker states, 'It's as though we were made for each other, beauty and the beast. Of course, if anyone else calls you beast I'll rip their lungs out,' this dialogue also containing the typically dark humour evident in this movie.

The images of the beautiful Vale and the disfigured Joker in the bell tower also bring to mind *The Hunchback of Notre Dame* (Dieterle, 1939). However, in both that movie and the more classical Beauty and the Beast story the beast is misunderstood, whereas in *Batman* we understand the beast perfectly, we are aware of the murderous intent hidden behind the Joker's leering grin.

One scene mentioned above deserves closer inspection: the scene where Jack Napier falls into the vat of acid. When watching this event we are left with a question in our minds; did Batman lose his grip on the criminal or did he let him go intentionally? There is no real answer to this, Burton preferring to leave the situation ambiguous, thus creating a degree of additional darkness and mystery in relation to the winged wonder.

The above two characters are clearly extremes, but we are also shown a less extreme example of an unusual personality trait. This is displayed by Vicki Vale, who has a bat fetish, this being the reason she is drawn to the reporter's story of a bat man on the prowl in Gotham City.

We also see a character being undone by his jealousy. This is the crime boss Grissom, played by Jack Palance. His jealousy in regards to the affair his partner, Alicia, played by Jerry Hall, is having with Napier causes him to send Jack and his cronies to Axis chemicals, which in turn causes Jack to fall into the acid before returning for his bullet-ridden revenge.

An interesting event occurred on set between Palance and Burton during the first day of shooting. Jack was supposed to walk out of a bathroom, but didn't appear when Burton called 'Action'. He explained to Palance what was required of him and then tried again, the actor still not appearing on cue. So Burton went back to the actor to reiterate his instructions and Palance started breathing heavily before grabbing Burton and screaming 'Who are you to tell me what to do? I've done over a hundred movies!' Burton's reaction is best given in his own words: 'Palance scared me to death – I literally saw white and left my body… I absolutely freaked out and one of the producers had to calm everybody down.'[14] Considering the stresses of such things as budget and expectation, this can't have been a good way to start shooting the film.

Some have criticised Burton for concentrating too much on Jack Napier/the Joker in comparison with Bruce Wayne/Batman. The balance between these characters

> **Ultimate Fact**
> Burton first met Prince on set in the Batcave.

may seem in the Joker's favour because he is flamboyantly expressive, an extrovert and colourfully dressed, which puts him in stark contrast to Batman, who dresses in black and is an introvert. The Joker's prominence in comparison with Batman is also caused by the fact that the grinning crime boss has a horde of henchmen, whereas Batman acts alone. Thus the Joker leaps off screen with a huge grin on his face while Batman hides in the shadows behind him, watching in silence.

Another reason why the Joker stands out so much is down to Gotham City and its inhabitants. Both are dark and colourless, lacking in vibrancy. The Joker is the opposite of this, being bright and full of energy. This clearly helps him stand out like a sore, acid-scarred thumb.

The criticism about this perceived character imbalance is similar to that levelled at Burton in relation to the treatment of the Maitlands in *Beetlejuice*. However, as was pointed out in Chapter Three, their relative blandness was accentuated by Betelgeuse and was also entirely necessary in order for the Maitland-Betelgeuse relationship to have impact. The same can be said for the Batman-Joker relationship. It works because they are opposites, and are distanced from each other. Both characters are better defined by this difference and are given additional depth by it.

Further depth is created by Anton Furst's set design, which is visually enthralling and won him an Academy Award. The cityscape draws us in, the dark skyscrapers towering to either side joined by bleak gangways. The streets are like a dismal prison, the walls to either side entrapping the citizens in a place rife with crime as City Hall tries to bring some order and sense of pride to the sorry inhabitants.

Furst's fantastical and impressive gothic set was built at Pinewood Studios in England, partly so that Burton could escape some of the hype surrounding the film, which was concentrated in the US. Giving Batman his own city to prowl was a masterstroke. To have placed him in New York or another contemporary city would have been to take him out of his true environment and to create a specific timeline in the film. His darkness is complemented by Gotham City, as it is clear the atmosphere of the city could have helped form the person he has become. By giving Batman his Gotham City in which to roam the whole film is given additional depth. It also becomes more of an experience for the viewer; we are transported beyond our own reality, though remaining close enough to realise how near we are to such a dark vision.

The set is one of only a few examples of such memorable cityscape designs seen in the movies. Others include the dingy streets in Ridley Scott's science fiction classic *Bladerunner* (1982), and in the city shown in Terry Gilliam's *Brazil* (1985). Such visions of distopia become implanted in our minds and the sensations of enclosure and dread they evoke remain with us long after having viewed the films.

The dismal view of Gotham City was partly down to

Sam Hamm's script, in which he described it as 'if hell had sprung up through the pavements and kept on going.'[15] Part of its power is in its comparison with contemporary American cities. We see the built-up similarities, but find an all-pervading darkness in Gotham which makes the cityscape intensely atmospheric.

Vincent Canby of the *New York Times* noted that Gotham City is 'an expressionist world,'[16] and this does ring true as the city certainly has a sinister feel, generated by the angst present in the people inhabiting its dark streets, and its exaggerated appearance. The same elements of expressionism are also seen in the painting that the Joker spares before meeting Vicki Vale in Gotham's museum. This is a piece of art by Francis Bacon and displays a striking use of darkness and light, just as Tim Burton's films do.

Another memorable aspect of set design is Bruce Wayne's huge and impressive mansion. It is symbolic of a fairy tale castle upon a hill and the same symbolism was also evident in *Beetlejuice* and later presented itself in *Edward Scissorhands*, *Big Fish*, and *Charlie and the Chocolate Factory*. This mansion is also symbolic of Bruce Wayne's public persona. It is a rambling building filled with many rooms, a place in which you could easily become disorientated and lost. This reflects Wayne's psyche in that he seems muddled and disorientated at times, his mind rambling and filled with corridors in which he can lose himself, not least in memories of the past. 'Some of it is very much me

> **Ultimate Quote**
>
> 'The Gotham City created in *Batman* is one of the most distinctive and atmospheric places I've ever seen in the movies' – Roger Ebert[17]

and some of it isn't,' says Wayne to Vicki Vale in relation to the mansion, but also with implied reference to the Batcave beneath.

The Batcave is symbolic of Wayne's dark side, the hidden side. It is filled with shadows and concealed beneath the mansion, just as Batman is concealed beneath the everyday persona of Bruce Wayne. It is a place where he can indulge his need to come to terms with the loss of his parents, where he can leave his other life behind, donning his costume to find release.

> ### Ultimate Quote
> 'I loved the extremes, the operatic quality of the characters... I loved that basic good verses evil, night fable, *Phantom of the Opera* stuff'
> – Tim Burton [18]

Unlike Burton's previous two features, *Batman* didn't employ stop-motion animation for effects purposes. Instead we see the use of models and even of traditional, hand-drawn animation techniques. The former is most obvious when the Batwing is hit by the Joker's bullet and crash lands in front of the church. The latter is evident at two points in the film which come near the beginning and the end. The first is the animated silhouette of Batman as he walks in from a balcony overlooking the city streets and is the first shot of the character. The second is when the Joker falls from the church tower, his form an animation as he plummets to his doom.

Even though there is no stop-motion, another early trademark of Burton's makes itself apparent in a scene outside City Hall. A group of criminals posing as mime artists approach and are predominantly dressed in black and white striped clothing. Betelgeuse also dressed in black and white stripes and the use of black and white can also be seen in *Batman Returns* on one of the Penguin's umbrellas.

Batman also saw the introduction of something which

would become equated with Burton's films, and this is the alteration of the studio logo in the opening titles of the film. Burton claims he was one of the first people to do this, believing that as 'the titles always help to set the mood of the film' they are extremely important.[19] This was especially the case with *Batman* because he wanted to show how different the film was from the TV series.

Other Burton trademarks present in *Batman* include the use of dark humour, the portrayal of alienated characters, the use of disfigurement, both mental and physical, and the use of symbolism common to fairy tales.

Danny Elfman's score is the perfect accompaniment to the visual spectacle of this film. It is filled with dark and sinister tones, unlike the score for *Beetlejuice*, which also contained a great amount of playfulness. There is also a clear use of triumphant music at the end when Batman is victoriously standing atop one of Gotham's skyscrapers and the Bat Signal is used for the first time.

The story behind the origins of Elfman's score is an interesting one. He was on a plane and ideas suddenly started coming to him. Because of this he kept darting to the toilet in order to record these ideas, causing the flight attendants to suspect he was either feeling unwell or taking illegal substances. When he arrived home he was almost in a panic due to the fact that the noise of the plane interfered with the taped notes he'd made, but eventually managed to figure out what he'd said after repeatedly listening to the recordings.

The use of Prince's music alongside Elfman's score meant that two different soundtrack albums were available, as mentioned earlier. Burton liked Prince and even went to see him in concert at London's Wembley stadium twice during the shooting of the film. However, he wasn't happy about the use of the pop songs and didn't think they worked in the film, though this wasn't to do with the tunes themselves, but with their integration into the movie. Prince had originally been commissioned to provide only two songs, but was inspired to create much more work. The marketing team for the film saw this as a great opportunity to boost publicity for the film and Burton was encouraged to include Prince's work in the movie.

This is the least personal of Burton's films while also being the least emotionally charged. Burton says, 'It's the movie that I feel more detached from than the others.'[20] Along with the fact that *Batman* was as much about marketing and hype as it was about the film, and the fact that central characters were already well established before Burton became involved, there were other elements which created distance between the man and his movie. These include the fact that he felt ill during the entire shoot, was under extreme pressure due to public expectations and the huge budget he was working with, and there were also the constant rewrites that the script went through on almost a day to day basis. This latter aspect was most keenly felt by Burton, who felt as if the script was unravelling and somewhat out of his control.

One criticism which could be related to the constant script changes is concerned with the scene when Vicki Vale is led to the Batcave by

> ### Ultimate Fact
> In the summer of 1989 Tim Burton went for a long drive in the desert in order to escape the Batmania which had gripped America. He went into a roadside diner in the middle of nowhere and a waitress came over to take his order. Looking up, he discovered she was wearing a Batman pin.[21]

Alfred. She shows no sign of real surprise at discovering Bruce Wayne and Batman are one and the same. However, there is an argument that Vale could have already known the truth as she had already been given a number of clues as to Batman's identity. These include Bruce Wayne hanging upside down like a bat after they'd slept together, her seeing that the Batcave was out of the city and in the general direction of Wayne's mansion while also seeing Batman's distinctive profile when previously taken to the Batcave, and, ultimately, being led down into a series of caves by the gentile butler (who may have even told her for all we know). So, though it's a valid criticism, it can be deflected through careful explanation.

Three particular plot holes have also been pointed out as follows. Firstly, why doesn't the mayor seem to be affected by the Joker tampering with Gotham's cosmetic products when people such as the news reporters are? Secondly, why don't the hordes of revellers in the streets attack the Joker and overpower him when he releases his toxic fumes in the carnival scenes? And finally, where did the Joker's henchmen appear from in the scenes at the top of the church tower?

The first and second questions are easily answered. In regards to the first, it is possible that Mayor Dent still had products left over from prior to the Joker's prank. In relation to the second question, it is obvious that the crowds don't attack because they're not wearing gas masks and would therefore probably die if they didn't try to make their escape. The third question, however, doesn't have an answer and so does appear to be a flaw in the film's narrative – though the appeal of comic book plots is rarely diminished by their occasional lack of continuity.

But to return to the first and second questions, there is

an interesting point to make in relation to both. This is that the Joker uses the vanity and greed of Gotham's residents against them. His actions of tampering with the cosmetics and handing out free money takes the weaknesses of the people and uses them to his own evil advantage.

Despite the criticisms, *Batman* is a visually stunning film with great performances from all its cast. Ultimately, its popularity wasn't just down to hype, something which is borne out by the fact that it remains a favourite with fans even to this day.

The struggle between Batman and the Joker – between good and evil – captured audience's imaginations, as did the imposing presence of Gotham City. The clear alienation of the two main characters marked this film out as a clearly identifiable Tim Burton movie, along with the use of dark humour and dark atmospherics. The success of *Batman* also made Tim Burton a household name and gave him more power within the Hollywood studio system, power which he would use to make his next, much more personal film, *Edward Scissorhands*.

Endnotes

1. Spillman, S. – 'Will Batman Fly?' (*USA Today*, 19th June 1989, US)

2. Elliot, D. – *Tim Burton: The Man Behind 'Batman'* (www.timburtoncollective.com/articles/bat5)

3. Salisbury, M. (ed.) – *Burton on Burton – Revised Edition*, p.72 (Faber and Faber, 2000, UK)

4. *Batman* –Two-Disc Special Edition DVD, Disc Two, Shadows of the Bat: The Cinematic Saga of the Dark Knight pt.2: The Gathering Storm (Warner Brothers, 2005)

5. Spillman, S. – 'Will Batman Fly?' (*USA Today*, 19th June 1989, US)

6. Spillman, S. – 'Will Batman Fly?' (*USA Today*, 19th June 1989, US)

7. *Batman* —Two-Disc Special Edition DVD, Disc Two, Legends of the Dark Knight: The History of Batman (Warner Brothers, 2005)

8. Spillman, S. – 'Will Batman Fly?' (*USA Today*, 19th June 1989, US)

9. Salisbury, M. (ed.) – *Burton on Burton – Revised Edition*, p.72 (Faber and Faber, 2000, UK)

10. Spillman, S. – 'Will Batman Fly?' (*USA Today*, 19th June 1989, US)

11. *Batman* —Two-Disc Special Edition DVD, Disc Two, Shadows of the Bat: The Cinematic Saga of the Dark Knight pt.2: The Gathering Storm (Warner Brothers, 2005)

12. Elliot, D. – *Tim Burton: The Man Behind 'Batman'* (www.timburtoncollective.com/articles/bat5)

13. Salisbury, M. (ed.) – *Burton on Burton – Revised Edition*, p.80 (Faber and Faber, 2000, UK)

14. Fraga, K. (ed.) – *Tim Burton Interviews*, pp.162-163 (University Press of Mississippi, 2005, US)

15. Salisbury, M. (ed.) – *Burton on Burton – Revised Edition*, p.75 (Faber and Faber, 2000, UK)

16. Canby, V. – 'Nicholson and Keaton Do Battle in *Batman*' (*New York Times*, 23rd June 1989, US)

17. Ebert, R. – Batman (http://rogerebert.suntimes.com/apps/pbcs.dll/article?AID=/19890623/REVIEWS/906230301/1023)

18. Elliot, D. – *Tim Burton: The Man Behind 'Batman'* (www.timburtoncollective.com/articles/bat5)

19. *Batman* —Two-Disc Special Edition DVD, Disc One, Director's Commentary (Warner Brothers, 2005)

20. Salisbury, M. (ed.) – *Burton on Burton – Revised Edition*, p.102 (Faber and Faber, 2000, UK)

21. Easton, N. – 'For Tim Burton, This One's Personal' (*The Los Angeles Times*, 8th December, 1990, US)

References

Benson, S. – 'Batangst in Basic Black' (*Los Angeles Times*, 23rd June 1989, US)

Carr, J. – 'Batophilia Strikes' (*The Boston Globe*, 23rd June 1989, US)

Collins, A. – 'Batman: Special Edition' (www.empireonline.com/athome/movies/review.asp?id=11301)

Jackson, M. & McDermott, A. – 'Tim Burton Biography' (www.timburtoncollective.com)

McMahan, A. – *The Films of Tim Burton: Animating Live Action in Contemporary Hollywood*, p.205 (Continuum Books, 2005, US)

Unknown – BOF Interview: Mark S. Reinhart (www.batman-on-film.com/mreinhartinterview)

5. Edward Scissorhands

*'Who's handicapped? My goodness,
don't be ridiculous, you're not
handicapped you're...exceptional'*
– Joyce speaking to Edward

Edward Scissorhands saw Tim Burton gaining full control over
one of his films for the first time, thanks in no small part to
the huge success of *Batman*. It was released in 1990 and had
a modest budget of only twenty million dollars. It was well
received by critics and moviegoers alike. It also marked the
beginning of Burton being taken seriously as an artist.

The script for the movie was commissioned while Burton
was still involved with pre-production on *Beetlejuice*. Novelist
Caroline Thompson was introduced to Burton by the agent
that they shared, who believed they'd get on well together. In
fact, they built up such a rapport that not only did Thompson
write the screenplay for *Scissorhands*, but she also went on to
write the screenplay for *The Nightmare Before Christmas*, worked
on *The Corpse Bride*, and even dated Burton's long-time
collaborator Danny Elfman.

Edward Scissorhands is a bittersweet fairy tale about a boy
with huge scissors for hands who wouldn't look out of place

in a horror movie. Dressed in black like the pivotal character in *Beetlejuice*, Lydia, and also like Batman, Edward is found in a mansion upon a hill, the symbolic fairy tale castle which we have already seen referenced in the previous two films. Another link with *Beetlejuice* and *Batman* comes with the obvious use of disfigurement, which makes itself apparent not only in Edward's unusual hands, but also in the scarring he bears due to these hands. In

> ### Ultimate Fact
>
> The idea behind *Edward Scissorhands* came from a drawing Burton had done a long time before the film was eventually produced. It was linked to a character who wanted to touch, but couldn't, who was both creative and destructive.

Beetlejuice we saw numerous recently deceased characters who were physically disfigured. In *Batman* the Joker was physically disfigured and Batman was mentally so.

Mental disfigurement is also apparent in the tragic life of Edward Scissorhands. His inventor/creator, played by Tim Burton's hero and muse, Vincent Price, died before he had the chance to finish his creation. This left Edward all alone, an orphan, just like Bruce Wayne. The character played by Price is akin to a kind of Doctor Frankenstein figure. He is an inventor whose greatest achievement is Edward.

When speaking about casting Price in this role Burton stated, 'His role probably had a lot to do with how I felt about him in terms of watching his movies and how he was my mentor, so to speak, through his movies.'[1] Burton found himself identifying with the films he watched as a boy, many of which starred Price in horror roles, some of which were based on work by Edgar Allen Poe. Finding little in common with his parents, he found his inspiration in the movies and this is how Price came to occupy the role of a kind of mentor.

It is therefore fitting that he should play Edward's creator as Edward could be seen as an on-screen representation of Burton in many ways.

This latter point is highlighted through Edward's link to the character Vincent from Burton's short film of the same name. Both Vincent and Edward have a gothic look and are young. It is also the case that in the rhyming narrative of *Vincent* it is stated that the character wants to share his home with 'spiders and bats' and wanders 'dark hallways alone and tormented.' Both of these aspects can be seen to be reflected in Edward's existence.

The link between these characters is especially pertinent as the two films they appear in are the most personal to Burton. Some have said that Vincent is a depiction of the director as a boy. Therefore Edward could be said to be the depiction of Burton as a teenager, and, as we shall see, the depiction of Burton as a man can be found in *Big Fish* to a degree.

> ### Ultimate Fact
> Michael Jackson wanted to play the part of Edward, but wasn't offered the part. Both Tom Cruise and Tom Hanks were also considered for the role, the latter choosing to star in *Bonfire of the Vanities* (De Palma, 1990) instead.

The tragic nature of this story is underlined with significant strength when Edward's creator shows him the hands which he is supposed to have instead of scissors and then has a heart attack. The hands are then shown shattered on the floor, a symbol of his shattered dreams of being like normal people and fitting in, being accepted.

It is also the case that during the course of the movie three people tell Edward they know of doctors who may be able to help his condition, to give him hands. However, none of these offers bares fruit and Burton says that this is one of his favourite aspects of the film. He states, 'They might as well be saying "have a nice day."'[2] In this sense Burton is clearly of the belief that insincerity is an everyday part of our culture. The statement of 'have a nice day' is not one usually filled with genuine feeling, and he sees the offers to help Edward as similarly lacking in sincerity. This rather pessimistic view is no doubt derived from Burton's upbringing in a bland and judgemental suburban environment and his view of modern America.

Edward's home is dark and dingy, and this is placed in juxtaposition with a stylised view of suburbia. Both are accentuated by their close proximity and obvious difference. Suburban normality is contrasted against the gothic and expressionist home in which Edward dwells, one filled with a sinister atmosphere and with the angst of the lead character. Edward has tried to express himself, to create an identity by indulging in topiary, shaping bushes into wonderful animals, like his huge sea monster, for

> **Ultimate Quote**
>
> 'With *Scissorhands*, Burton reached a high point of poetic lyricism that is all the more remarkable when viewed against the brutality and literalness which characterises many offerings in contemporary cinema.[3]

example. He has also notably sculpted a hand and we can presume this is symbolic of his longing to be complete, while also symbolising both his wish to touch the world and for the world to touch him. His use of visual expression rather than verbal echoes the same traits evident in Burton himself.

There was a clear divide between Bruce Wayne's mansion and Gotham City in *Batman*, though both displayed an element of darkness. In *Edward Scissorhands* the hilltop mansion-suburbia divide shows a use of both darkness and light. The mansion is dark and gloomy, the only colour apparent in Edward's topiary creations which are vibrantly green, something that echoes the vibrant creativity of the character. The suburban environment, which stands in purposefully stark contrast, is a mix of soft, pastel colours. This gives it a kind of 50s retro feel, one which carries with it a sense of a quieter, more innocent America that is often portrayed prior to the hippy revolution in the 1960s. Such portrayals can be seen in the ever popular series 'Happy Days' (1974-1984) and in films like *Back to the Future* (Zemeckis, 1985) and *Pleasantville* (Ross, 1998). As Derek Malcolm of *The Guardian* pointed out regarding Burton's view of suburbia, it 'is a world waiting for someone to astonish it with passionate unorthodoxy, and Edward is just the man to do it.'[4]

> **Ultimate Fact**
>
> Academy Award winning special effects expert Stan Winston created Edward's hands and went on to design the makeup for The Penguin in *Batman Returns*.

The duality created by the mansion-suburbia juxtaposition creates a strong visual boundary between Edward's world and that of society beyond. Other examples of duality present in the movie include the slightly sinister appearance of Edward compared with his quiet nature, and the early niceness of the suburban inhabitants compared with the nastiness which becomes apparent towards the end of the movie.

Further to the above there are dualities within Edward's character. As Burton says, 'the character is both simple and complicated...both creative and horrifically clumsy.'[5]

With hands like scissors, Edward cannot touch anything or anyone with tenderness while he also stands out as different and is labelled by the suburban world as strange. Thus he tries to create identity through creativity, a creativity that holds the promise of possible acceptance by those he comes into contact with. As already stated, this longing for identity and the creation of it through artistic means, echoes the early life of his real life creator, Tim Burton.

Edward's feelings of longing for acceptance and love are coupled with feelings of loneliness, all of which are very successfully portrayed by Johnny Depp in his first role in front of Burton's camera. With wild dark hair and a tendency to wear black, Johnny's Edward could be seen as a representation of Tim Burton. However, he is much more than that. He is a representation of all of us who seek acceptance and love, looking to make our mark on the world despite our shortcomings. Edward is representative of us all as he tries to come to terms with himself, his past, and his place in the world.

> **Ultimate Fact**
>
> Johnny Depp's film debut was in the 1984 movie *A Nightmare on Elm Street* (Craven) in which he played a victim of Freddie Kruger, a character who used blades as fingers.

In this way a broad spectrum of viewers can identify with Edward, and feel for him when they see his longing and his awkwardness. We can empathise with the character and therefore want him to find happiness and be successful in finding a place in the world. This empathy creates interest in what will occur on screen whilst also creating an emotional link to the quiet Edward whose eyes communicate a depth of character far beyond words.

Edward's character is one of 'the innocent others' who suffers from alienation. In this way he shares a common bond with Pee-Wee Herman, the Maitlands from *Beetlejuice*, the orphaned Bruce Wayne and other filmic characters like ET. We can see why the audience feels a fondness for this outsider who needs love and care, when our natural reaction to such a vulnerable character is one of protection and nurturing.

Another important aspect in relation to the depiction of Edward is Depp's own feelings about the character. He had been starring as Officer Tom Hanson in a US TV cop show called '21 Jump Street' (1987-1989) and was quite a heartthrob, something which didn't sit well with Depp. He states about the time prior to when he first received the script for *Scissorhands* that he was 'dumbfounded, lost, shoved down the gullets of America... TV boy, heart throb, teen idol, teen hunk. Plastered, postered, postured, patented, painted, plastic!'[6] This clearly shows his dislike of the position he found himself in − he intensely disliked the direction his career was taking. Then, out of the blue, the script for *Scissorhands* was sent to him by Depp's new agent, an event which he has described in interviews as a 'godsend'.

> ### Ultimate Fact
> At the time of filming *Edward Scissorhands* Johnny Depp, who was twenty-seven, was engaged to co-star Winona Ryder.

Depp was 'obsessed' with the story after reading the script instantly and was so deeply affected that he wept. Though he was convinced he wouldn't get the part due to his clean-cut, teen idol role on TV, Tim Burton hadn't seen his previous work and, luckily for Depp, offered him the part. Depp has said 'This role for me was not a career move. This role was freedom. Freedom to create, experiment, learn and exorcise something in me. Rescued from the world of mass-product, bang-'em out TV death by this odd, brilliant young guy who had spent his youth drawing strange pictures.'[7]

Two things are apparent from the above statement. Firstly, Depp took a fairly heavy load of emotional baggage coupled with a great deal of affection and desire to the role. This increases the emotional content of Edward's characteristics, partly because Depp himself had felt a similar sort of isolation while trapped in his TV role. The second element which is apparent from Depp's words is his admiration of Burton, something which has no doubt had some bearing on their fruitful partnership in the world of cinema.

Because of Depp's identification with Edward he plays the part perfectly. In a performance which is almost a throwback to the era of silent movies, he plays the gothic outsider with style and grace. As one critic for the *LA Times* wrote at the time, he 'translated the script's emotions with such transparency that it is the freak who seems real and all the human denizens of the comical flatland suburbia below who seem false or grotesque.'[8]

In the film Edward's affections are directed toward the daughter of Peggy, who is the kindly Avon lady that takes him into her home. This character is played by the soft-voiced Dianne Wiest who many will remember as the mother in *The Lost Boys* (Schumacher, 1987) and who said of *Scissorhands*, 'the movie is just different. There is something pure about it.'[9] Her daughter, Kim, is played by Winona Ryder, who we have already seen as Lydia in *Beetlejuice*. Because our fondness and empathy towards Edward is already established by the time the pair meet we feel sorry for him when witnessing his awkwardness. Many audience members will also identify

> **Ultimate Fact**
>
> *Edward Scissorhands* was Vincent Price's last film role before his death in 1993.

with the clumsiness of a youth clearly besotted. We also hope that somehow Edward can win the love of this girl that initially sees him as some kind of freak. This is one example of misperception in the movie, one which is slowly overcome as Kim gets to know Edward better and sees beyond his obviously surprising appearance.

When Peggy first goes to the dark mansion where Edward lives we see another small example of misperception, something that Burton noted in some of the horror films and monster movies he used to watch as a boy when the monster's intentions or motivations were misunderstood. In the case of this movie we see that Peggy is a little fearful of Edward when she first sets eyes on him in a shadowy attic room, his gothic appearance and stainless steel hands creating the impression that he is possibly going to harm her. The audience are also unsure as to the shadowy stranger's motivations at this point, but Edward is soon revealed as nothing but a quiet, creative and relatively helpless boy in need of help, though his appearance is somewhat threatening. Even this visual element is quickly softened as we come to know him. This occurs with an almost imperceptible ease and speed due to some great acting from Depp, and due to the simplicity of the character's behaviour, which transmits his vulnerability with such great clarity that he is made all the more endearing.

> ## Ultimate Quote
> 'Edward is not a human being, he's not an android, he's not an alien. To me he was like a newborn baby, with that kind of innocence' – Johnny Depp[10]

Peggy's family are kindly accepting of Edward, as are most of the local residents, including Joyce, played by Kathy Baker, who is sexually attracted to the newcomer. However, there is one local resident one who is unwilling to accept the unusual stranger. She is akin to a wicked witch figure in this fairy tale and is the overly religious Esmerelda, who sees Edward as the product of evil and the representative of Satan. The princess figure is clearly Kim, and it is upon her return home from a trip with friends, including her boyfriend, Jim, that things begin to change for the worse for Edward, though this change is gradual. It is also centred around Kim's boyfriend, who displays the typical traits of a 'jock', these being intolerance and a lack of acceptance of anyone who is different from the norm. Here we are presented with the age old divide between the quiet creative types and the outgoing sporty types, reflecting also the introvert-extrovert balance between Batman and the Joker, and the quiet-loud divide between the Maitlands and Betelgeuse.

If Esmerelda is the witch and Kim is the princess many may presume that Edward is the prince. However, this is not the case. Edward is really the misunderstood monster. He is the beast that longs for love and acceptance, that hopes to become just like everyone else – by getting hands. And like most such monsters the end result is not a good one. His downfall is almost a foregone conclusion once this monster role is realised, for rarely is a monster able to exist in such an environment of normality, predictability and relatively passionless calm. This downfall is linked to his affection for Kim. Her boyfriend uses this to his advantage in getting Edward to help break into his parents' house.

Kim and Jim's use of Edward to help break into the house isn't vindictive on anyone's part, they are simply utilizing his talents for their own gain. However, it is their abuse of his innocence and his feelings for Kim that cause Edward to get in trouble with the law for breaking and entering. This creates a great deal of misunderstanding, the community turning on him and Peggy and her husband presuming Edward was trying to steal in order to fund the opening of a beauty salon. The beast is now revealed in his true nature, as the misperceived, tortured individual who finds his difference creates a negative response from those around him. The neighbours are soon gossiping, soon avoiding Peggy's family and Edward, unwilling to associate with the monster in their midst.

Like Frankenstein's monster, Edward cannot cope with everyday life and needs guidance in order to survive in the 'real' world. He doesn't know how to handle his feelings towards Kim and her boyfriend. The former feelings are those of love and the latter are those of hatred, two poles of emotion that cause a confusing and powerful mix in the gothic lead character.

Kim starts to fall for the monster like Beauty with the Beast. The family remains firmly in support of Edward and his place in the community, and because of this they are shunned by everyone.

Danny Elfman's music adds an intensely atmospheric feeling to a particular scene during the darker second half of the film. Kim goes out into the garden while Edward is carving a fantastic ice sculpture. She dances in the ice chippings that fall through the air like flakes of snow as the fairy tale music plays and we are captivated by the beautiful simplicity of the scene. But then there is a sudden change of tone, both through the narrative and the score.

Edward accidentally cuts Kim's hand and Jim witnesses this, becoming abusive and somewhat violent towards the monster in suburbia, the music reflecting this unfortunate turn of events. Edward, unable to control his feelings or convey them in a normal manner, then goes on a kind of rampage through the suburban landscape, hacking at topiary figures he'd previously created, venting his feelings in the only way he knows how.

The misperception of Edward reaches it peak when he saves Kevin, Kim's younger brother, from being run over by Jim and his friends. He cuts the boy's face accidentally and this is taken as an attack by onlookers. Jim attempts to fight him, but is cut by the beast who must now flee with a mob at his back, much like the dog, Sparky, in *Frankenweenie*. This mob scene is partly a homage to James Whale's 1931 film *Frankenstein* in which a mob also chases after the beast in order to destroy it.

As with *Batman*, a final showdown between good and bad occurs from a location high above the homes of the ordinary people, in this case in the dark mansion where Edward was conceived. He fights with Jim, surprisingly killing him with a stab of his hand, the young jock then falling from a great height into the garden below, not unlike the Joker falling from the church tower.

This killing in the finale is said by some to be a mistake. This is due to the fact that audience members have not been prepared for such violence on Edward's part. However, this kind of disorientation is apparent in *Beetlejuice* and Edward's actions can be justified by his strength of feeling for Kim and the fact that he is essentially backed into a corner by Jim and the mob, and, like any wild beast in such a situation, he will fight for his life, an element of his character which creates a juxtaposition with his more innocent nature.

Deepening the tragedy of the story are Kim's three, parting words to Edward: 'I love you.' This makes her departure from the mansion and their permanent separation even sadder than it might otherwise have been. Their love can never blossom, Edward will forever remain alone in the shadowy depths of the big, dark house, a solitary figure, incomplete, unfinished and unloved in the silence. The heartfelt sadness of Edward's predicament is made all the more intense by the fact that we know he will live for an immensely long time because he wasn't born, he was created. With only the distant love of Kim to keep him warm during long, cold nights, Edward resorts to carving ice sculptures of her as he remains the misunderstood beast in his castle on a lofty hilltop, a situation echoing Batman's poignant solitude at the end of that film as he stands atop a Gotham City building.

Here we find that the usual 'happily ever after' of a Disney fairy tale has been dispensed with. Instead this is replaced by an ending more suited to the sort of fairy tale tradition which originally included such things as the ugly sisters in Cinderella being so desperate for the shoe to fit that they made their feet bleed as they tried to put it on. Symbolism played an important role in these fairy tales and was used to represent often violent human emotions such as greed and jealousy. In *Edward Scissorhands* the human aspects that are portrayed include a longing for identity and acceptance, love, and, ultimately, loneliness. We can all identify with these elements and they are strengthened by the simplicity of the lead character and such things as the mansion in which he lives, its vastness and darkness serving to accentuate Edward's isolation and loneliness.

The popularity of *Edward Scissorhands* derives from the fact that not only does the film manage to be entertaining whilst also exploring the depths of human nature, but it also achieves this with an impressive degree of gentleness – something rarely seen in contemporary cinema. We all understand the struggle to feel complete and to be accepted by those around us and because of this we find that Edward is representative of us in some ways.

Burton says of the ending, 'It's not a happy ending, it's not a sad ending. To me it's more of a symbolic ending. Some things work out and some things don't.'[11] Such an ending is more realistic than most Hollywood films, which seem to require happy endings and neat resolutions to life's problems. Instead we are shown an important insight, one which wouldn't be amiss in a fairy tale: life doesn't always reward the good hearted and things don't always work out for the best.

Another symbolic element of the movie relates to Edward's scissor hands. Scissors are cutting devices and the owner of this particular set of unusual hands cuts through the mediocrity of ordinary life, his creativity transforming the environment.

Further symbolism occurs in relation to Peggy's attempts to cover Edward's scars and dress him in appropriate clothes for suburbia. She is attempting to make him more normal, hoping she can cover up his

> **Ultimate Quote**
> 'What is remarkable about *Edward Scissorhands* is how rapidly an audience sated with slashings and slayings will take this jagged child to its heart.'[12]

abnormality to some degree in order for him to more easily fit into society. However, it is clear that he cannot be made normal simply by changing his outward appearance because his difference is as much interior as exterior, if not more. The symbolism therefore equates to the idea that it's what's inside each of us which defines us more than how we look.

As previously mentioned, Burton used Danny Elfman for the third time to create the score for *Edward Scissorhands*. Elfman not only successfully captures the fairy tale spirit of the movie, but also its gentle playfulness. This latter element occurs in the vision of a neighbourhood where gossip is rife and the women are left alone when their husbands go to work, leaving all at the same time and with a smartly choreographed movement of cars on the driveways and streets.

Not only is this depiction of suburbia typical of Burton, but we also find certain trademarks of the director in the movie. Snow is a common element in his work, as is the inclusion of a hilltop house or castle. The juxtaposition of dark and light and alienation of the lead are also apparent in a great many of Burton's films. There is also one other small aspect which recurs a number of times and this is the inclusion of a dog, as seen in *Frankenweenie* and *Beetlejuice*. In *Edward Scissorhands* we see Edward dejected and rejected by most of the suburban community as a dog comes up and sits beside him, the kindly aspect of the character's personality coming to the fore when he cuts the hair from the hound's eyes.

> **Ultimate Quote**
> 'I got the chance [with this film] to do what I wanted to do completely' – Tim Burton[13]

However, there is one important difference with *Scissorhands* when compared with Burton's other films bar *Ed Wood*. This is the lack of special effects. These are few and far between, limited to Edward's makeup and his dark, towering home.

This, of all the feature-length films already discussed, is the most personal to Tim Burton and one of the most emotional for the audience. There is a visual circularity in the movie as it begins and ends with the elderly Kim telling her granddaughter a bedtime story. This echoes the minor circularity evident in *Beetlejuice*, which starts and ends with the Maitlands decorating their house in bright daylight.

The personal element of this film is apparent through a number of factors. These include Burton's identification with the main character, who is almost an exaggerated form of Burton in his youth. Anchoring this is Edward's feelings of alienation and his inability to communicate with others other than through creativity, both of which were strong elements of Burton's childhood.

This identification of Burton with Edward means that the latter is depicted with a true fondness and love which transmits itself to the audience. This is partially achieved through Edward's naivety and partly through his vulnerability, something accentuated by his quiet and kind nature. In this way he has childlike

> **Ultimate Quote**
> 'Edward Scissorhands isn't perfect. It's something better: pure magic.' Rolling Stone[14]

qualities and our natural urges with regards to children are concerned with protection and hope. Such feelings are bestowed upon Edward. We hope he will succeed, that he will find happiness despite his obvious disfigurement.

Ultimately, when he doesn't succeed, we feel saddened while at the same time marvelling in his creativity. We remain hopeful that he finds inner peace and a degree of happiness knowing that Kim cared for him, finding warmth in her parting words of 'I love you'.

Endnotes

1. Salisbury, M. (ed.) – Burton on Burton – Revised Edition, p.98 (Faber and Faber, 2000, UK)

2. Fraga, K. (ed.) – Tim Burton Interviews, p.73 (University Press of Mississippi, 2005, US)

3. Andac, B. – Tim Burton (www.sensesofcinema.com/contents/directors/03/burton)

4. Malcolm, D. – 'Unkind Cuts in Shining Suburbs' (*The Guardian*, 25th July 1991, UK)

5. Easton, N. – 'For Tim Burton, This One's Personal' (*The Los Angeles Times*, 12th August 1990, US)

6. Salisbury, M. (ed.) – *Burton on Burton* – *Revised Edition*, p.IX (Faber and Faber, 2000, UK)

7. Salisbury, M. (ed.) – *Burton on Burton* – *Revised Edition*, p.XI (Faber and Faber, 2000, UK)

8. Wilmington, M. – 'Soft-Hearted Fairy Tale of an Outsider' (*The Los Angeles Times*, 14th December 1990, US)

9. Green, T. – 'Wiest Finds it Hard to let go of *Edward Scissorhands*' (*USA Today*, 17th December 1990, US)

10. Easton, N. – 'For Tim Burton, This One's Personal' (*The Los Angeles Times*, 12th August 1990, US)

11. Fraga, K. (ed.) – *Tim Burton Interviews*, p.69 (University Press of Mississippi, 2005, US)

12. Mars-Jones, A. – 'A Cut Above; Tim Burton's *Edward Scissorhands*' (*The Independent*, 26th July 1991, UK)

13. Halpern Smith, L. – 'Look, Ma, No Hands, or Tim Burton's Latest Feat' (*The New York Times*, 26th August 1990, US)

14. Travers, P. – 'A Cut Above the Rest' (*Rolling Stone*, 10th January 1991)

References

www.imdb.com

Jackson, M & McDermott, A. – Tim Burton's Filmography (www.timburtoncollective.com/bio)

Scott, R. 'Pointed, Poignant' (*The Times*, 10 September 1994, UK)

6. Batman Returns

*'I am the light of this city
and I am its mean, twisted soul'*
— Max Shreck

The second film in the *Batman* franchise came three years after the first and was released in 1992. It had a lot to live up to, especially considering the box office takings of the first movie, which was an absolute smash. However, there was nothing to worry about and the film's $45 million budget was surpassed on the opening weekend in the US. In fact, *Batman Returns* beat *Batman's* record-breaking $42 million opening, reaching an astounding $47.7 million and creating another Burton blockbuster.[1]

This success was partly due to the good reception the first film received, partly the associated hype, and partly because Tim Burton had remained the director. His influence on the film was greater than it was in relation to *Batman* thanks to the success of that movie. In creating *Batman*, Burton had to bow to pressures from the studio, which made him take such decisions as including the songs by Prince. With *Batman Returns* he was given a greater freedom as he'd proved his calibre as a good director, one underlined by the critical and commercial success of *Edward Scissorhands*.

The film marked an important change in the comic book franchise. The following two films (*Batman Forever* and *Batman & Robin*) would be directed by Joel Schumacher as the studio went for a lighter feel, following complaints from fans that *Batman Returns* was too dark (though Burton produced *Batman Forever* in 1995). Not everyone agreed, though, and some feel that *Batman Returns* was the last great Batman film.

The latest in the series, *Batman Begins* (2005) was directed by Christopher Nolan and starred Christian Bale as the caped crusader. It is a prequel, exploring the character's past prior to the older series of films. The idea of doing a prequel was actually Michael Keaton's and he came up with it during negotiations to star in the third movie. He says that during these negotiations he said, 'You know, I'm not into this, but you know what would be interesting? A kind of prequel.'[2] He decided not to play Batman for a third time because he read the script and thought that it wasn't very good. Not only would *Batman Returns* be Keaton's last big-screen outing as the winged wonder, it would also be the last of three roles he would play in Tim Burton films.

The original script for *Batman Returns* was intended to be a direct sequel to the first film. There were clear examples of continuity other than the use of the same lead character and these included fragments of the destroyed Batwing being sold in shops, new revelations about Jack Napier's past, and even Bruce Wayne proposing to Vicki Vale. However, Burton

> ## Ultimate Fact
> By the time *Batman Returns* was released Burton's marriage to the German painter Lena Gieseke, who he'd met while filming *Batman* in the UK, was over and Tim had fallen in love with the model Lisa Marie, who would go on to have roles in a number of his films.

hoped to avoid such obvious links with the first movie, preferring to take this follow-up in a new direction. Burton said that 'There was a lot of pressure to get me to do *Batman Returns*, but I couldn't say yes until something inside me got real excited about it. I don't go by money… I just need the clarity and excitement in myself.'[3] So it wasn't until the script was altered to suit his vision of the film more closely that Burton finally accepted the role of director, despite having said at the time of *Batman's* release that he didn't want to do a sequel.

There was an attempt by Burton to write Robin into the script, but to no great extent. Ultimately, he didn't feel right about Batman being partnered with someone else, feeling that the character's psychology dictated that he worked alone, something which works well on screen. Burton's judgement proved well founded as Robin would have interfered not only with the shadow-dwelling character of Batman, but also with his love-hate relationship with Catwoman.

There are no huge special effects in the film, no massive explosions or particularly big chase scenes. There is also none of the stop-motion animation used in *Vincent*, *Pee-Wee's Big Adventure* and *Beetlejuice*, as well as the two feature films he made entirely in this format – namely *The Nightmare Before Christmas* and *Corpse Bride*.

One of the most notable elements of the film is the Penguin's makeup, designed by Oscar-winning effects artist Stan Winston, who won an Academy Award for his work on *Edward Scissorhands*. Burton is also due some credit however, as the Penguin's grotesque appearance was actually based on one of his early sketches of the character.

The digital effects which were used for the penguins and bats in this movie also received Academy recognition, gaining a nomination for visual effects supervisor Michael Fink in the category of Best Visual Effects. Anyone interested in sound production might also care to note that *Batman Returns* was the first film to be made in Dolby Digital, which added to the sound effects and the score of the movie.

Anton Furst, who was the production designer on *Batman*, couldn't work on this later film due to contractual reasons. Sadly he committed suicide three months after *Batman Returns* began principle photography. Despite the fact that much of Furst's set remained stored in England where the first movie had been shot, *Batman Returns* was filmed in Los Angeles. Production designer Bo Welch, who had worked with Burton on *Beetlejuice*, created the new set, one which contributes to the dark and oppressive feel of Gotham City. It is highly atmospheric with its gloomy buildings and walkways, its narrow, snow-covered streets, and mix of gothic and art deco architecture. In this setting the events of *Batman Returns* are perfectly placed, especially in relation to the Penguin's snowbound lair in the 'Arctic World' part of the city zoo.

The opening scenes of this film are concerned with the Penguin's experiences as a child and immediately introduce us to a number of themes and trademarks which are typical of Tim Burton. The first is the alteration of the film studio's logo, the studio being Warner Brothers in this case. The second is the use of snow, something also seen in *Edward Scissorhands*, *The Nightmare Before Christmas*, *Sleepy Hollow*, *Charlie and the Chocolate Factory* and *Corpse Bride*. The third is the repeated use of actors, the two actors playing the Penguin's parents having appeared in *Pee-Wee's Big Adventure*, the father being of special note as he was Pee-Wee himself, AKA Paul Reubens.

The fourth and final Burtonesque element in the initial

scenes is the most personal to the director. This is the rejection and abandonment of the Penguin by his parents. The same can be seen to varying degrees with the character of Lydia in *Beetlejuice*, whose parents ignore her. Bruce Wayne is also abandoned by his parents, though not intentionally, and the same goes for Edward Scissorhands. We also find Richie Norris being rejected by his parents in *Mars Attacks!* and Will Bloom being estranged from his father in *Big Fish*, a situation very similar to that of Willy Wonka in *Charlie and the Chocolate Factory*.

This treatment of the child-parent relationship is hardly infrequent in Burton's films, and such variances on this theme are no doubt linked to Burton's own estrangement from his parents, even while living with them in Burbank, California. By using his films as vehicles for exploring parent-child relationships, Burton creates something he can truly identify with, an emotional investment which shows clearly on screen and adds essential depth to his visual feasts.

A further theme that is clearly apparent in all three films, and one which has been noted previously, is that of disfigurement. In *Batman Returns* it is not only evident in Bruce Wayne's psyche, but also in the villain he must confront, as it was in the

> ## Ultimate Fact
>
> The production team were determined to use King Penguins for the film, but the only tame ones in captivity were in a bird sanctuary in England. They were flown to the US in the refrigerated hold of a plane and were then given a refrigerated trailer and a swimming pool with over half a ton of ice a day, as well as fresh fish.

first movie of this franchise. However, the villain here is not the madcap extrovert that the Joker was. Instead we are confronted with the Penguin as an adult, disfigured physically with flipper-like hands, but also disfigured mentally through his abandonment by his parents. He is no extrovert, on the contrary, he has been hiding away in the sewers and in the city zoo for years, brooding on the sorry state of his life until the time arrives for him to find his parents. He is twisted by circumstance and the leader of the Clown Gang, who wreak havoc throughout Gotham City. Danny DeVito plays the Penguin in the first of three roles he has had in Tim Burton's movies, the others being in *Mars Attacks!* and *Big Fish*.

Unlike the first film, in *Batman Returns* there is not merely one villain, but two – the second being the character Max Shreck. He is played with customary style and menace by Christopher Walken, who went on to star as the Hessian horseman in *Sleepy Hollow*. Shreck is a powerful businessman and, like many powerful businessmen in the movies, is a little short on scruples. He is responsible for a great deal of the pollution which Gotham City has been suffering from, but, as the Penguin says, he's a 'well respected monster.' He is also responsible for manipulating his flippered friend for his own ends, namely to have an ally as mayor, one he can use like a puppet.

The use of the name Max Shreck is an inspired choice. An actor called Max Schreck played the first movie vampire in the film *Nosferatu, eine Symphonie des Grauens* (Murnau, 1922). The Shreck in *Batman Returns* is like a vampire wanting to suck the blood from Gotham. He wants to suck the energy out of the city, to build a power station intended to draw energy from the city and store it up rather than to generate new energy. So, though it's electricity and not blood, Max Shreck really does want to suck Gotham City dry.

There is one other main character who is neither good nor bad. This is Catwoman, played by Michelle Pfieffer in a black cat-suit which leaves little to the imagination. She is not a straight villain, she is a secretary who has been resuscitated by cats and is out for revenge and a bit of flirtatious fun with Batman.

Though the part of Catwoman had already been cast, the actress Sean Young went to Warner Brothers dressed as the character. She had originally been cast as Vicki Vale in the first film before breaking her arm in a horse riding accident and being replaced by Kim Basinger. Because of this she felt she should have been chosen to play Selina Kyle and made this fact known on talk shows in the US, even appearing on the Joan Rivers Show in a Catwoman

> **Ultimate Fact**
> Annette Bening was originally cast as Catwoman, but was replaced by Michelle Pfieffer when she became pregnant.

outfit. However, Burton was dismissive of the issue stating, 'She's screaming "Hollywood system" and I'm saying "no, artistic choice."'[4]

The tone of the film, as with its predecessor, is dark, both visually and in its narrative. This was said by Desson Howe of the *Washington Post* to bring the movie '...closer than ever to Bob Kane's dark, original [comic] strip.'[5] Part of the reason why this film is darker than *Batman* is because it lacks the sense of fun that the Joker's character brought to the screen, even if his humour was by and large of the dark variety (something which should come as no surprise in a Burton film). Without such a character the film loses a great deal of the light-hearted content, despite the numerous quips made by Catwoman and the Penguin.

The narrative of the film is set in the run-up to Christmas. The usual atmosphere of this time of year is one of festivities, but this expectation is undermined by the crime wave which is taking place in Gotham. This accentuates the besieged nature of the city. We know what Christmas should be like, but see the city plagued by crime at a time which should be filled with goodwill.

This further darkens the tone of the movie, though it could also be said to be an amusing take on what Christmas is really like, including the painful family relationships which come to the fore at that time of year (something especially apparent in regards to the Penguin and his quest to find his parents).

The dark feel of the movie is also added to in a very literal sense by the fact that both Batman and the Catwoman dress in black, the Penguin dresses predominantly in black, and the city is in darkness thanks to the fact that it is winter and most of the events occur after night has fallen. This mood is further accentuated by Danny Elfman's score – as atmospheric as always – adding a sense of dread and doom to the scenes of a city under inches of snow and under siege by the Clown Gang.

Last, but by no means least, there is the bitterness of the Penguin and the powerful callousness of Max Shreck, who has no qualms about committing murder. He is directly responsible for the emergence of Catwoman when he pushes his secretary, Selina Kyle, from a high window. As with Jack Napier (the Joker) in the first film, Max unwittingly creates his own nemesis, the person who will bring about his doom.

The perceived darkness of this film drew a lot of criticism

both from reviewers and parents who took their children to see the movie, criticism which upset Burton. This is because he didn't see *Batman Returns* as overly dark in tone, objecting that, 'What is perceived as light and dark is completely open to interpretation.'[6] As Burton also points out, the prevalent attitudes of many Hollywood films are arguably 'darker' than anything he produces, with their light-hearted approach to violence being particularly offensive.

Opinion is also divided in relation to the humour evident or otherwise in the film. Some critics stated such things as 'the shock here is the remarkable lack of any humour.'[7] Others said things like 'the follow-up to the blockbuster of summer '89 is faster and funnier.'[8] The film appeared to divide critics and audiences alike, reminding us how difficult it is to conceive of objective judgements within artistic fields. However, one thing that nearly everyone seemed in agreement with was Pfieffer's great performance as Selina Kyle and the steamy Catwoman.

Selina goes from being a mousy woman lacking in self-confidence, one without a date or a social life, to being the proverbial 'cat's whiskers'. She becomes much tougher and dislikes the weaknesses of the fairer sex. This more assertive, violent side is clarified when she states, 'Life's a bitch, now so am I,' a comment which shows there is at least on occasion humour evident in the film. 'I don't know about you, Miss Kitty, but I feel so much yummier,' she says after making and then donning her new outfit, as she adopts a far more overtly sexual persona.

It is clear that Selina's split personality means she is presented as a person with a dual nature. In *Batman* the duality was limited to the lead character, but in *Batman Returns* it not only extends to Catwoman, but also to the Penguin and Max

Shreck, who both have public personas and darker sides which are revealed in private. This duality reflects the fact that we all have different sides to our personalities which are often defined by our public and private lives. This is also the case when it comes to Burton himself. Burton is intensely private, but has to don a public face when publicising his movies and attending premieres and award ceremonies.

> ### Ultimate Quote
> 'I like their duality. And the thing that I really liked about *Batman* as a comic book property was that they're all fucked-up characters' – Tim Burton[9]

It is interesting that Denise Di Novi, who was Burton's co-producer up until and including *Ed Wood*, developed a spin-off film called *Catwoman* (Pitof, 2004). It starred Halle Berry, took twelve years to reach the big screen after the release of *Batman Returns*, and was completely slated by critics and audiences alike. She explained that the reasons why she pursued this project was because she 'saw what a powerful icon the Catwoman character was' – unfortunately without Burton on board the film lacked originality, style and substance.[10]

To return to the question of duality: in the first Batman movie Bruce Wayne had a romance with the photographer Vicki Vale. In *Batman Returns* there is a relationship with two sides to it, displaying the duality present in the main characters. Firstly, there is the growing attraction between Selina Kyle and Bruce Wayne. There is also the more openly sexual and violent relationship between Catwoman and Batman.

These two elements entwine towards the end of the movie when the two characters realise each other's alternative identities while living out their day-to-day roles. With the common ground of a dual nature, both see a possibility that a relationship could work, that they would understand each other better than other people could. However, Catwoman is more feral than Batman, who is limited by moral boundaries. Therefore a partnership of bat and cat could never truly work.

An important aspect of this film in relation to the communication between Batman and Catwoman, as well as between these characters and the audience, is the use of the actor's eyes. Due to the masks of their costumes it is vital they portray their feelings through the way they look at each other and the world about them. Keaton proved adept at this in the first film and Pfieffer proved his equal in this movie. In Keaton's eyes you can see a haunted look, the ghosts of his parents and the memory of their untimely death still lingering in his mind. Pfieffer's eyes portray her angst, her disillusionment, and her anger with the world. This use of such a typical means of conveying feelings and emotions – through the 'windows to the soul' – is very effective in letting the audience see into the psyches of these characters.

> ## Ultimate Quote
>
> 'Batman is not a crime-fighting superhero but a reclusive neurotic who feels he has to prove himself to a society he does not really inhabit' – Roger Ebert[11]

Burton also uses eye contact to a great extent in *Edward Scissorhands*, Depp successfully using his very expressive eyes to underline Edward's innocence and vulnerability, something made all the more vital due to the character's limited speech. Eyes are also important in *Planet of the Apes*, especially in relation to the apes themselves because the makeup acts like a mask, leaving the eyes as a vital means of communication.

We also see the use of the eyes in *Charlie and the Chocolate Factory*, both in the hope twinkling in Charlie's and especially in the mild madness and reminiscing of Willy Wonka, Depp again proving his ability to convey feelings in such a way.

In the case of the above films the eyes were an important element of the acting, but the rest of the actor's faces could also be seen, even though they were not 'real' faces in the case of *Planet of the Apes*. However, the audience's gaze in *Batman Returns* is specifically drawn to the eyes of Batman and Catwoman due to their masks and so it makes this aspect of their character definition all the more prominent.

At the core of the main characters is a sense of otherness, as is the case with many of Burton's films. Bruce Wayne is a rich introvert who resides beyond the city in his dark mansion and dresses up as a bat to fight crime. Selina Kyle has her darker, wilder side unlocked by Shreck's murderous intentions and operates beyond the law in her cat costume. The Penguin hides from society in the sewers and when he is revealed his disfigurement sets him apart, along with his limited stature. Shreck himself has this sense of otherness due to the fact that he is mega-rich, something which alienates him from the everyday people of Gotham City.

This alienation of the lead characters is an accentuated take on the otherness many of us have felt in our lives. Each of us has at times felt different from other people or out of place, and can therefore empathise with these characters to a degree, though their extreme natures does put them beyond the bounds of our experiences.

Critic Roger Ebert points out in his review of *Batman Returns* that there is a theory that in a franchise such as this it is the lead villain which gives each film its 'flavour.'[12] The energy of *Batman* was created by the vibrant character of the

Joker, but the feel of *Batman Returns* reflects the salaciousness and bitterness of the Penguin. The sexual nature of the Penguin arises through innuendo, behaviour and direct sexual references, though not in the humorous and light-hearted way in which Betelgeuse made them. The Penguin makes such comments with black bile dripping from his lips and comes across as a malicious pervert.

This sexual theme is continued in the character of Catwoman, as has been mentioned. This is not only through her skin-tight costume, but also through her interactions with Batman, there being a clear sexual chemistry between the two of them which she underlines not by kissing him, but by licking him.

The bitterness of the Penguin is reflected in the winter chill which grips Gotham City and the revenge-motivated Selina who dislikes weakness in women as much as she dislikes men who take advantage of this. This combines with the openly warped sexuality and creates an underlying feel to the film as far as character psychology is concerned.

As well as duality and alienation there is another element that *Batman Returns* has in common with the first film. This is the fact that the title character is seen less than the lead

> ### Ultimate Quote
> 'When I was on set doing it every day, that movie became my total reality. Going outside the studio became the biggest fantasy. In fact, picking up my laundry was probably the most mind-blowing experience the whole time we were making this movie' – Tim Burton[13]

villain, especially early on. However, Bruce Wayne is not a man who likes the limelight, whereas the Penguin is obliged to take centre stage as he conducts his campaign to become the mayor of Gotham City. Batman hides in the shadows as the Penguin has to come out of the sewers and face the brightness of camera flash bulbs. So, as the Joker's vibrant personality made him stand out like a sore thumb in *Batman*, the Penguin's quest to find his parents and then run for public office make him stand out in *Batman Returns*.

It has been noted that Bruce Wayne and the Penguin, whose real name is Oswald Cobblepot, are linked by this shared experience of losing their parents whilst still young. However, the way in which this arises for each character defines their adult life. Wayne's were killed by criminals and to cope with the loss and find some sense of justice he dresses up and fights crime. Cobblepot's parents abandoned him and this gave rise to an intense bitterness not just towards them, but to the society that allowed this to happen, one which he perceives as having labelled him as unfit to be a part of it, its ideas of normality being instrumental in his parent's decision to set him adrift in a basket and leave him to die in the sewers.

The fact that the Penguin not only blames his parents, but also society for his predicament is made clear by his plot to take all of Gotham's first born sons and drown them in the sewers. He states in the film that, 'I was my parents' number one son, but they treated me like number two.' This is exactly what he intends to do with the city's first born, wishing to metaphorically 'flush' them down the sewers just like his parents did with him.

So, these characters share a common bond, but developed different ways to deal with the circumstances which life brought upon them. This last point is important because it reflects what Burton believes about life (evidenced in earlier films such as *Edward Scissorhands*): that it isn't always within our control, that both good and bad things happen to us which we can do little about.

Another common bond between Bruce Wayne and Oswald Cobblepot is the fact that their alter egos are named after a species of animal, and the same is true of Selina Kyle. In fact Selina and Oswald owe their survival to the animals their alternative selves are named after, Selina having been given the breath of life by cats and Oswald having been reared by penguins in the city zoo.

The end of the film shows the Penguin being abandoned by his gang, his surrogate family. At the beginning he was abandoned by his parents, his real family, so a minor example of postmodern circularity is created.

Also at the end of the film we see Batman discouraging Catwoman from killing Max Shreck despite the fact that she points out he may get away with his crimes, stating, 'The law doesn't apply to people like him, or us.' Batman says that she is wrong on both counts, but we have seen him kill members of the Clown Gang, which is murder as they haven't been tried or found guilty of any crime in a court of law. In a further example of the conflicting elements within his psyche, which adds depth and interest to the character, Batman can be seen as a hypocrite in this case and no better than Catwoman.

The finale of the film involves the discovery that Catwoman has to be killed nine times before she dies, following the myth about cats having nine lives. She is killed eight times and then her continued existence is alluded to when Bruce Wayne sees her shadow on a Gotham City wall. Her existence is then confirmed in the final shot of the movie when she rises into view.

When the end credits roll we are left with a resounding sense of the atmosphere which the film created, as well as having witnessed some satisfying conclusions. However, as with many Burton films, the ending is left open to a degree, with Catwoman still roaming the snow-laden city streets. The same openness is evident in *Beetlejuice*, with the title character surviving, though with a shrunken head. In *Edward Scissorhands* the title character remains in his dark mansion. In *Sleepy Hollow* Ichabod Crane and co. are beginning a new life in New York at the end and in *Mars Attacks!* the world has to be rebuilt and a new stability found. *Ed Wood* only concerns the early part of the title character's career, leaving us wondering what he went on to do. *Planet of the Apes* finishes on a cliffhanger and *Charlie and the Chocolate Factory* leaves us wondering what new choccy treats Wonka and Charlie will invent together. Thus, with the conclusion of *Batman Returns* the director's stamp is finalised and we leave the theatre assured that we have seen not just any film but a Tim Burton film.

Batman Returns is a 'love it or hate it' film to a large degree, the critics split down the middle in relation to their opinions. There are those who feel it is overly dark and humourless and others who see its darkness as part of its brilliance, one mingled with a good deal of humour. However, it certainly added to Burton's reputation for consistent brilliance as a director.

Endnotes

1. Thomas, P. – Batman Returns (15)

    (www.empireonline.com/athome/movies/review.asp?id=116102)

2. Otto, J. – Interview: Keaton and Bale (http://filmforce.ign.com/articles/624/624398)

3. Fraga, K. (ed.) – *Tim Burton Interviews*, p.93 (University Press of Mississippi, 2005, US)

4. Salisbury, M (ed.) *Burton on Burton – Revised Edition*, p.104 (Faber and Faber, 2000, UK)

5. Howe, D. – 'Batman Returns' (Washington Post, 19th June 1992, US)

6. Salisbury, M. (ed.) – *Burton on Burton – Revised Edition*, p.83 (Faber and Faber, 2000, UK)

7. Thomas, P. – Batman Returns (15)

        (www.empireonline.com/athome/movies/review.asp?id=116102)

8. Travers, P. – Batman Returns (www.rollingstone.com)

9. Salisbury, M. (ed.) – *Burton on Burton – Revised Edition*, p.103 (Faber and Faber, 2000, UK)

10. Stax – An Interview With Denise Di Novi

        (http://filmforce.ign.com/articles/527/527604p1)

11. Ebert, R. – Batman Returns (http://rogerebert.suntimes.com)

12. Ebert, R. – Batman Returns (http://rogerebert.suntimes.com)

13. Fraga, K. (ed.) – *Tim Burton Interviews*, p.93 (University Press of Mississippi, 2005, US)

References

Brundage, J. – 'Batman Returns' (www.filmcritic.com)

www.imdb.com

McMahan, A. – *The Films of Tim Burton: Animating Live Action in Contemporary Hollywood*

        (Continuum Books, 2005, US)

7. The Nightmare Before Christmas

'There's no reason I can find,
I couldn't handle Christmastime.
I bet I could improve it too,
and that's exactly what I'll do'
– Jack Skellington, The Pumpkin King

The Nightmare Before Christmas is a feature-length stop-motion animation, and was the first of its kind to be produced by Disney. Unlike all the other films discussed in this book it was not actually directed by Tim Burton because of his commitment to *Batman Returns*. His long-time friend Henry Selick took on the mantle of director. The two of them had worked together as animators at Disney in the early 1980s and Burton had shown him the original sketches at that time. It is also of note that Selick helped to create the look of music channel MTV with a number of stop-motion commercials.

Even though Burton himself wasn't at the helm, the film was based on a three-page poem and sketches which he had created in 1982, and he also oversaw much of the production design and musical composition. The script was written by Caroline Thompson, who penned *Edward Scissorhands* and who would go on to write the screenplay for *Corpse Bride*.

The musical content was as important as the look of the movie as ten songs are contained within the narrative, all of them written by Burton's most frequent collaborator Danny Elfman, who has said that writing them was one of the easiest jobs he's ever had.[1] The once member of 80s band Oingo Boingo also provided the vocals for the main character, Jack Skellington. He even included a reference to the Oingo Boingo song 'Tender Lumplings' in one of this movie's musical numbers, the line 'tender lumplings everywhere' appearing in the piece entitled 'This is Halloween.'

This was the third Burton film in a row set at Christmas and follows in the footsteps of seasonal ghost stories like *It's a Wonderful Life* (Capra, 1946) and *A Christmas Carol*, of which there have been numerous film and TV adaptations, including the modern take on the tale entitled *Scrooged* (Donner, 1988), starring Bill Murray. Such films have helped to

> ### Ultimate Quote
> 'This was an opportunity for us to be in business with Tim Burton and to say, "We can think outside the envelope. We can do different and unusual things"' – David Hoberman, President of Walt Disney[2]

create a tradition of Christmas shows with a supernatural touch produced for children, an example being *The Muppet Christmas Carol* (Henson, 1992). *The Nightmare Before Christmas* adds to this group of films, enriching it with a new tale to hold both children and adults spellbound.

Nightmare cost $18 million and took $51 million at the box office in the US. Disney released it in 1993 under its Touchstone adult branch and only acknowledged it as a Disney film nearly a decade later when, in 2001, they turned the Haunted House ride in Disneyland into a *Nightmare Before Christmas* ride. The movie wasn't particularly pushed on the promotional front and the studio allowed Selick and Burton to have full creative control, partly due to the relatively small budget. Because the idea for the film had been created by Burton when he was working for the studio they owned it and, as Henry Selick has stated, 'used it as a carrot on a stick.'[3] The chance for Burton to do this film was used as a way to get him to once again work for the studio, though he never doubted that he'd eventually get the chance to make it, having said, 'I decided to bury it, but always with that feeling that I would do it some time.'[4]

The film has distinct resonances with Burton's earlier Disney short *Vincent*, not only because it was created in the same format and he came up with the initial idea at roughly the same time, but also because the style of animation is similar in look and in its dark atmospherics, especially in Halloween Town. This is strengthened by the appearance of a cat which is akin to the one at the start of *Vincent*. Another cat bearing a strong resemblance is also to be seen in *Corpse Bride*.

One further common factor between this film and *Vincent* is the use of rhyming narration, something which brings to mind many children's tales, especially nursery rhymes, and therefore keys into a childhood element most audience members will be familiar with. This is heightened by the fantastical nature of the story, something also reflected in many children's stories, not least in fairy tales. As this is a Tim Burton production it is distinctly different in tone from the usual Disney fairy tales, but harks back to the darker, original tales, Burton stating that it was 'German Expressionism combined with Dr. Seuss.'[5] This expressionist element is clear in nearly

> ### Ultimate Fact
> *The Nightmare Before Christmas* was inspired by Clement Clarke Moore's 19th century children's book *The Night Before Christmas*.

every film he has had a hand in making and is usually shown both in the angst of his lead characters and in the gothic visuals.

The film contains a good deal of imagery which would be at home in a tale by Roald Dahl, and Burton's leaning in this direction made him the perfect director for *Charlie and the Chocolate Factory*. It also may be no coincidence that Henry Selick went on to direct Dahl's *James and the Giant Peach* (1996), which is similarly a fantastical tale utilising songs and elements of darkness. It was co-produced by Burton and Denise Di Novi, who also produced *Nightmare*. Unsurprisingly, Selick also used stop-motion animation for this feature after saying of *The Nightmare Before Christmas*, 'that's what I like about it the most: The fact that it's handmade.'[6]

The two main locations of Halloween Town and Christmas Town display Burton's love of juxtaposing light and dark. Halloween Town contains gothic darkness and is somewhat dismal, filled with nightmare and horror characters such as zombies, vampires and even a werewolf. There is little laughter and the tonal quality is reminiscent of such locations as Gotham City and those seen in *Sleepy Hollow*. The opposite qualities can be found in Christmas Town, which is filled with colour and brightness, and because of this juxtaposition the qualities of each town are highlighted and accentuated.

One interesting note in relation to the horror characters in Halloween Town is that three in particular reference other films. The first of these creates a link with *Beetlejuice* and is seen near the start when we see a character with a head like one of the snakes on the film's desert planet, acting as a small homage to Burton's second full-length flick. There is also a hunchback, referencing *The Hunchback of Notre Dame*, and a beast that looks like the title character from *The Creature from the Black Lagoon.*

The inclusion of a hunchback also references Burton's love of misunderstood monsters, like Jack in this film. He wants to create a Christmas people will enjoy, but his attempt fails and he is seen to be sabotaging the festive season, which was not his intention at all. He is therefore misperceived by the general public as a monstrous skeleton ruining Christmas.

There are a myriad of other Burton trademarks in this film. These include the use of a full moon, something referenced in *Ed Wood* by Wood and his friend Lugosi and also seen in Burton's other feature-length animation, *Corpse Bride*. There is also the use of pumpkins and scarecrows, both seen in *Sleepy Hollow*, and skeletons, which are used in *Corpse Bride*. There are witches in Halloween Town, and we also see them in *Sleepy Hollow* and *Big Fish*. However, the most common visual trademark is that of a graveyard, seen in the majority of Burton's films.

All of these particular elements add to the dark visual tone of this movie as they're linked to old, classic horror films as well as to tales of ghosts and ghouls we were told of as children, especially in the case of Halloween's own bogie man, Oogie Boogie. The imagery Burton employs creates a bond with a great tradition of children's literature and film. At the same time as drawing on this tradition this movie also adds to it with a new story filled with fairy tale and fantasy qualities.

Three other visual touches in the movie are clearly

> ## Ultimate Fact
>
> A skull resembling Jack Skellington's head can be seen atop the carousel hat that Betelgeuse wears. Jack also makes an appearance in *James and the Giant Peach* as the pirate captain, Mr Centipede even saying 'A skellington!' when first seeing him.

Burtonesque. The first is the use of snow, seen in *Edward Scissorhands*, *Batman Returns*, *Sleepy Hollow*, *Charlie and the Chocolate Factory* and *Corpse Bride*. This addition is a necessity in a narrative sense as Christmas and snow go hand in hand like Halloween and pumpkins, and it also adds to the fantasy element of the tale.

The second additional Burton touch is the use of a dog, in this case a ghost dog called Zero. Dogs can also be seen in *Beetlejuice*, *Edward Scissorhands*, *Mars Attacks!* and *Corpse Bride*, and all take major parts in the narratives with the exception of *Scissorhands*. A dog was also a lead character in Burton's short *Frankenweenie*. In this case Zero is a companion to Jack and also acts as a warped version of Rudolf with his glowing, red nose helping to guide the Pumpkin King's sleigh through the night of Christmas Eve.

The third element is common to his earlier work, and this is the use of black and white stripes. In *The Nightmare Before Christmas* we see examples of this in the loudhailer the mayor of Halloween Town uses to announce a town meeting

> ### Ultimate Fact
> The punk rock band Blink 182 included a reference to *The Nightmare Before Christmas* in their song 'I Miss You,' released in 2003, ten years after the film's release. These lyrics are, *'We can live like Jack and Sally if we want, where you can always find me, we'll have Halloween on Christmas, and in the night we'll wish this never ends.'*

after Jack arrives back from Christmas Town. There are also numerous characters in Halloween Town who wear striped items of clothing. Such uses of stripes, especially black and white ones, can be seen in *Beetlejuice*, *Batman*, and *Batman Returns*.

We also find Burton using young people in key roles. In

the case of this movie there are Lock, Shock, and Barrel, three trick-or-treat children with an intense sense of mischief and mayhem. However, they differ from other youngsters in Burton's films because they are not a force for good, unlike Masbath in *Sleepy Hollow* and Richie Norris in *Mars Attacks!*, as examples. These trick-or-treaters are disliked because of their 'trick' mentality, which is why they are called in to catch Santa. This terrible trio also look after Oogie Boogie.

Oogie Boogie is like Betelgeuse, the Joker and the Martians in *Mars Attacks!* He is a character without scruples who enjoys the freedom of having no moral boundaries and who doesn't care what's right or wrong. He displays a distinct insanity, one which, through comparison, shows us that the rest of Halloween Town's inhabitants aren't mad, but are merely obsessed with Halloween and all its dark associations.

Oogie was loosely based on a character who appeared in Betty Boop cartoons and whose voice was provided by Cab Calloway. 'I remember seeing these Betty Boop cartoons, where this weird character would come out. I didn't know who it was, but it would do this weird musical number in the middle of nowhere,' said Burton on the subject.[7] Oogie is the villain of the piece, the evil character that we'd all be booing and hissing at if this were turned into a pantomime. His nasty playfulness is suited to this children's seasonal tale and well matched with the well-meaning inhabitants of Halloween Town, who are harmless and simply seek to make 31st

> ### Ultimate Fact
> The animators used a computer program to check Jack Skellington's mouth movements and created frame by frame posters of William Shatner's tirade as the evil half of James T. Kirk in 'Star Trek' to study every aspect of his facial movements.[8]

October a memorable night in the only way they know how; with as many frights and scares as possible.

At the heart of this story is Jack Skellington, a character feeling unsatisfied with his role in creating Halloween, a character looking for new experiences and finding them in the discovery of Christmas. Also part of the story's warm heart is Sally, who is extremely fond of Jack, The Pumpkin King, while also understanding his dissatisfaction. Both her voice and that of the trick-or-treater Shock were provided by Catherine O'Hara, who also played Delia Deetz in *Beetlejuice*.

The characterisation of Jack is done with great style considering he has a skull for a head with no eyes in his sockets. Such a lack of facial features with which to create expressions must have been quite a challenge for the animators, but they rose to it and succeeded in making Jack as expressive as any other character, something partially done by altering the size and shape of his eye sockets to suit his mood.

> **Ultimate Fact**
> To get the entire range of emotions needed one hundred and fifty interchangeable heads were made for Jack Skellington. [9]

His character displays further Burton trademarks within the film. Jack, whose voice is provided by Danny Elfman when singing and Chris Sarandon at other times, suffers from alienation in Halloween Town, feels distanced from the activities and sole purpose of the town. Sally also suffers from alienation as her creator, Dr Finkelstein, keeps her locked in his home. Therefore both Jack and Sally display the same trait – alienation – as do all of Burton's lead characters.

Jack also displays creativity in his planning of Halloween and then in his take on Christmas. Creativity is to be found in all of Burton's main characters and often defines them. We can see this in the case of Betelgeuse, who is defined by his bio-exorcist creativity. It is also clearly evident in the case of Edward Scissorhands, whose creativity makes him stand out from the suburbanites and defines him in that environment.

In regards to Jack Skellington, his creativity also defines his role. Due to his boredom with Halloween he finds an outlet in the newly discovered festivities of Christmas, something which he clearly relishes after the frustration he'd been feeling at going through the same routine year on year. We can understand this boredom of repetition, all of us having been bored by classes at school or jobs in which we feel as though we're just going round in circles. Therefore both children and adults can identify with Jack's excitement at discovering Christmas and at the prospect of trying something new. We empathise with the character, an empathy made all the stronger when we see his good intentions backfire and he is wrongly perceived as a skeleton ruining all the joy of Christmas. When we reach this point in the story we feel sorry for Jack while also being amused by the gruesome presents he's delivered to unsuspecting households. These two emotions create an interesting mix and follow Burton's common use of juxtaposing such things as horror and humour, as seen in *Beetlejuice* and *Sleepy Hollow*.

> ### Ultimate Fact
> The voice for trick-or-treater Lock is provided by Paul Reubens, who played The Penguin's father in *Batman Returns* and was the star of *Pee-Wee's Big Adventure*.

Characters such as the stitched-up Sally and the trick-or-treat children could have happily been at home in Burton's 1997 book of rhyming stories and accompanying artwork

The Melancholy Death of Oyster Boy and Other Stories (Faber). A quick flick through this work not only underlines the clear similarity between the stop-motion animation and Burton's drawings, but also the style of darkly humorous storytelling, something evident in all of his work.

Sally herself creates a strong link with the character of Edward Scissorhands. She is not human, a creation made by creepy Dr. Finkelstein, and Edward was also a creation. Both of these characters also found themselves living high above the surrounding landscape in dark and somewhat foreboding homes, something seen in all of Burton's films in various guises and also reflected in Jack Skellington's home, which is a tower.

This creator-created link between Sally and Edward can also be seen in a different way in *Batman* and *Batman Returns*. In the first movie Batman, the alter-ego of Bruce Wayne, was created by Jack Napier and his alter-ego, the Joker, was in turn created by the actions of Batman. In the sequel the Penguin was created by the heartless actions of his parents and Catwoman was born of the murderous intent of rich businessman Max Shreck.

In the case of Sally, we see that she is roughly stitched together, like a reject toy doll. Burton identified with this character because she represents 'the feeling of not being together and of being loosely stitched together and constantly trying to pull yourself together.' You can extend this to the sentiment of coming apart at the seams, something which Sally does quite literally when escaping from Dr. Finkelstein's home. She creates another link with Catwoman, whose outfit displayed a large amount of obvious stitching, Burton saying, 'I was into stitching from that Catwoman thing, I was into that whole psychological thing of being pieced together.'[10]

Another thing Sally's character brings to mind is the fact that we all consist of different parts; different emotions and different aspects of our personalities. It reflects Burton's use of duality in some of his main characters, something which stems from his assertion that none of us are just one thing. Sally displays this sentiment, is made up of a number of parts, though this multifaceted nature is on the outside as well as within in her case.

Jack and Sally create a love story central to the narrative, one which is also evident in many of Burton's films, including his other stop-motion movie, *Corpse Bride*. However, though we can see that Sally is fond of the Pumpkin King, Jack doesn't return these feelings until the end of the film, so preoccupied is he with his take on Christmas festivities.

His enthusiasm is contagious. The songs, their energetic choreography, his words and actions, all combine to underscore the creativity and vibrancy in his character. This allows us to understand his role as the head of Halloween Town. We see why the other residents would look up to him and feel lost without his motivation and input. He is like a beacon of brightness in the otherwise drab and dreary surroundings.

> **Ultimate Quote**
>
> 'Growing up in Burbank, I responded to the holidays, especially Halloween and Christmas, because they were the most visual and fun in some respects' – Tim Burton[11]

Jack's ultimate failure to make Christmas his own is also reflected by Ed Wood's failure in the movie business. This kind of bittersweet ending is also seen in both *Batman* films to a minor degree, but especially in *Edward Scissorhands*, *Mars Attacks!*, *Planet of the Apes* and *Big Fish*. The reason for such endings is Burton's understanding that in life some things work out and some things don't.

Another character displaying a common Burton trait is the mayor of Halloween Town, who has a very apparent duality. It is clearly highlighted by the mayor's two faces, which he switches between depending upon his mood and the circumstances. Such duality was also evident in the case of Bruce Wayne/Batman and Selina Kyle/Catwoman, both characters effectively having two faces, one which is human and one which is a mask. The mayor also displays a Burton reuse of actors, his voice being provided by Glenn Shadix, who also appeared in *Planet of the Apes* and later provided a voice for *The World of Stainboy*.

Also evident in this film is Burton's darkly orientated humour, which has been touched upon already. It can be seen especially in Jack's take on Christmas, which is tainted by his Halloween background. The children's presents are far removed from the normal kind and include such things as smashed up toy cars, bats as hats and a shrunken head. One of these presents resembles the desert snakes in *Beetlejuice* as it curls around the base of a Christmas tree and then gobbles it up. We also see Jack in a Santa Claus outfit, his skull face grinning from behind a large, white beard in an amusing undead version of the portly and jovial 'Ho, ho, ho' man.

Two of the presents create a link between this film and *Batman Returns*, which Burton was working on at the same time. These presents are a yellow toy duck with wheels, referencing the Penguin's duck vehicle, and an evil cat doll whose head is akin to the symbol for Max Shreck's corporation. We also hear part of the *Batman* score when searchlights pan the night sky trying to locate Jack and his sleigh.

One interesting aspect of this film, and one that makes it stand out from any other film Burton has been involved with, is the fact that no adults are clearly portrayed. People like the policeman taking reports of the terrifying Christmas presents and the news reporter telling people about a skeleton making a mockery of Christmas have their heads obscured, and another policeman's face is too dark to see as he sits in a squad car. This avoidance of adulthood and normality helps to keep the story firmly rooted in the fantastical.

> **Ultimate Fact**
>
> Henry Selick's favourite sequences in the film are a wide shot of Lock, Shock, and Barrel entering their clubhouse, those involving Oogie Boogie, and Sally following Jack through the graveyard.[12]

After over a decade since the release of *The Nightmare Before Christmas* new audiences, mainly made up of children, are still being attracted to it, as retailer Will Marston can vouch due to the continuing popularity of action figures from the film. This is due to the movie's childlike energy and wonderment, both of which are encapsulated in the song 'What's This?' which is sung by Jack. This song is filled with a vibrant enthusiasm, injected with amazement by the lyrics. These feelings can be found like a rich vein of gold running through the movie's narrative and are directly connected with Jack and his excitement at having discovered Christmas, his excitement reflecting that of children all around the world at this particular time of year.

The continuing popularity of this film among children is also due to the 'Dahlesque' darkness apparent in Halloween Town, its inhabitants and their take on Christmas. As can be seen in many popular children's stories, there is an element of scariness, something which the young love and which is part of the attraction of such programs as the BBC series 'Doctor Who'. Children like the thrill of this darkness combined with the energy of the narrative and *The Nightmare Before Christmas* balances its mild horror with Jack's enthusiasm perfectly, the two elements combining to create a film that children and adults adore.

The animation technique of stop-motion is particularly loved by children, but also has resonances with adults due to its use for special effects in classic movies such as *Jason and the Argonauts* (Chaffey, 1963) and *Clash of the Titans* (Davis, 1981), two films which feature the work of Ray Harryhausen, a man highly regarded by Burton himself. Burton fans will have already seen the use of stop-motion animation for special effects in *Beetlejuice*, where it was effectively used to make the fantastical live and breathe on the screen. *The Nightmare Before Christmas* in its entirety is alive with this same energy, one which has got a handmade immediacy. This immediacy is a quality that Burton likes and is the reason behind his general avoidance of using too many computer generated effects as they don't possess the same feeling, but have a certain thinness to them.

As with *Beetlejuice*, *Batman*, *Planet of the Apes* and *Charlie and the Chocolate Factory*, the possibility of a sequel has been discussed. As we know, only one of the above films (*Batman*) actually did spawn a follow-up. In the case of *The Nightmare Before Christmas*, Henry Selick was approached by Disney in the spring of 2002 in order to do a sequel, but Burton said he wasn't ready to do one.[13] There may not be a film sequel, but there has however been a sequel to the computer game '*The Nightmare Before Christmas*: *The Pumpkin King*'. Its follow-up is named '*The Nightmare Before Christmas*: *Oogie's Revenge*,' and is set after the events portrayed in the movie.

There are numerous small touches that add greatly to the stunning visual quality of the animation. These include such things as Jack's collar, which is shaped like a bat, the mayor's tie, which is a spider, and Jack's sleigh, which is shaped like a coffin. These and other touches not only add to the scenes, but they add to the overall darkness and creepiness of Halloween Town with a glorious subtleness. Because of these elements and the overall appearance of the movie it has attracted a good deal of praise. Critics have stated, '*Night* is a visual splendour,'[14] and, 'each and every creation is realised to delicious perfection.'[15] The glorious visual element is coupled with a relatively simple, but well constructed plot and songs which combine to create a 'delectably ghoulish fairy tale'[16] which has a distinctively Burtonesque aesthetic.

The continuing popularity of this movie probably has something to do with its message. It is about staying true to yourself, despite failures, despite misunderstandings. Through Jack's failure to bring seasonal goodwill the film also tells us that not everything in life will work out the way we want it to. This is an important message, especially for children who are often force fed 'happily ever after' endings that give them a false perspective on life. *The Nightmare Before Christmas* presents something more real, though woven into a fantastical narrative.

This is a beautifully made film with an extremely high standard of craftsmanship and production. The engaging narrative is coupled with engaging visuals to draw in adults and children alike. *The Nightmare Before Christmas* is a wild ride in a realm born out of Burton's mind, and it's damn good fun!

Endnotes

1. Fraga, K. (ed.) – *Tim Burton Interviews*, p.101 (University Press of Mississippi, 2005, US)

2. Fraga, K. (ed.) – *Tim Burton Interviews*, p.98 (University Press of Mississippi, 2005, US)

3. Epstein, D.R. (int.) – Henry Selick

> (www.ugo.com/channels/filmTv/features/henryselick)

4. Salisbury, M. (ed.) – *Burton on Burton – Revised Edition*, pp.116-117 (Faber and Faber, 2000, UK)

5. Busack, R.V. – Skellington Crew

> (www.metroactive.com/papers/metro/10.26.00/nightmare-0043)

6. Epstein, D.R. (int.) – Henry Selick

> (www.ugo.com/channels/filmTv/features/henryselick)

7. Salisbury, M. (ed.) – *Burton on Burton – Revised Edition*, p.123 (Faber and Faber, 2000, UK)

8. Busack, R.V. – Skellington Crew

> (www.metroactive.com/papers/metro/10.26.00/nightmare-0043)

9. Andac, B. –Tim Burton (www.sensesofcinema.com/contents/directors/03/burton)

10. Salisbury, M. (ed.) – *Burton on Burton – Revised Edition*, p.123 (Faber and Faber, 2000, UK)

11. Salisbury, M. (ed.) – *Burton on Burton – Revised Edition*, p.124 (Faber and Faber, 2000, UK)

12. Epstein, D.R. (int.) – Henry Selick

> (www.ugo.com/channels/filmTv/features/henryselick)

13. Epstein, D.R. (int.) – Henry Selick

> (www.ugo.com/channels/filmTv/features/henryselick)

14. Berardinelli, J. –The Nightmare Before Christmas

> (http://movie-reviews.colossus.net/movies/n/nightmare)

15. Wood, D. –The Nightmare Before Christmas (1993)

> (www.bbc.co.uk/films/2000/12/04/the_nightmare_before_christmas_1993_review)

16. Maslin, J. – 'Infiltrating the Land of Sugar Plums' (*New York Times*, 9th October 1993, US)

References

Marston, W. –Tim Burton: A Discussion (www.lollipopanimation.com)

8. Ed Wood

*'Greetings my friend. You are interested
in the unknown, the mysterious,
the unexplainable. That is why you are here'*
– Criswell

Edward D. Wood Jr. was the director of numerous films, many of which he also wrote. He was also a man of vision, even if it wasn't always 20/20. Born in 1924, Wood grew up in Poughkeepsie, NY, and his first directorial experience was *The Sun was Setting* in 1951. He was never successful and never broke into the Hollywood studio system. Burton is almost the director Wood could have been if only he'd had the talent and maybe this is what first attracted Burton to the project, one he directs with an obvious fondness for the B-movie king.

Ed Wood the film couldn't be more different from the title character's movies if it tried. It was beautifully filmed, Burton taking his usual care over well executed shots. It was well funded, unlike Wood's cheap flicks. It was liked by critics, though it was Burton's first commercial failure at the box office, something which seems rather apt as it reflects Wood's own lack of commercial success during his career. And it was made within the Hollywood studio system, Burton one of only a handful of directors who have managed to make personal films within the warm folds of this privileged clique. The studio in this case was Touchstone, Disney's adult branch, Burton returning to the studio he first worked for, one which gave him total creative autonomy due to the relatively small budget.

Ed Wood is also brilliantly acted. The lead characters of Wood and his actor friend Bela Lugosi are played by Johnny Depp and Martin Landau respectively, the latter winning an Oscar for Best Supporting Actor and both receiving much praise from critics. 'Depp is terrific in a hilarious, heartfelt performance,' stated Peter Travers of *Rolling Stone*[1] while Desson Howe of the *Washington Post* said that it was probably the most assured performance of Depp's career.[2] Landau also received such praise as 'a brilliant performance,'[3] and, 'both verbally and physically, he's simply astounding.'[4]

There are a number of cast members that Burton had previously worked with who appear in *Ed Wood*. Jeffrey Jones starred in *Beetlejuice* and would go on to have a role in *Sleepy Hollow*. He plays Criswell, a man who claims to have the power of foresight. Lisa Marie would go on to have parts in *Mars Attacks!* and *Planet of the Apes*, and stars as Vampira in this movie. And we can't forget the already mentioned Johnny Depp, Burton's most utilised acting talent, who enjoyed his second live-action role for Burton in this film.

In *Ed Wood* Depp's acting is intentionally of the 'gee-whiz' kind, in a fashion not dissimilar to Ewan McGregor's portrayal of the young Edward Bloom in *Big Fish*. In the case of *Ed Wood*, this style of acting compliments the 'hammy' nature of the films Edward Wood made during his career and makes his character an extension of these works. The movie blends the real Edward D. Wood Jr. with the works of fiction he created. These two elements of fact and fiction become inseparable, something reflected by the fact that his first film, *Glen or Glenda*, starred himself in a role which reflected his own fetish of dressing in women's clothes.

Wood says to Bela Lugosi that *Glen or Glenda* is about how people '...have two personalities; the side they show to the world and then the secret person they hide inside.' This is not only a reflection of the introverted Bruce Wayne and Edward Scissorhands, it also reflects the director himself – Burton being a private person who reveals himself to the world primarily through his movies and the personal touch he brings to them, especially in the cases of *Edward Scissorhands* and *Big Fish*.

> ### Ultimate Quote
> 'To me it almost doesn't matter what Tim wants to film – I'll do it, I'm there because I trust him implicitly – his vision, his taste, his sense of humour, his heart and his brain' – Johnny Depp[5]

As with all of Burton's films, there were a number of regular crew members present on this production, such as editor Chris Lebenzan and costume designer Colleen Atwood. There were also two others who would not work with Burton again after this film, but who had already taken part in the creation of a number of his previous projects. Tom Duffield had been the art director on *Beetlejuice* and *Edward Scissorhands*, and the supervising art director on *Batman Returns*. Cinematographer Stefan Czapsky had filled the same role on *Edward Scissorhands* and *Batman Returns*.

Another notable absentee from Burton's future movies would be Denise Di Novi. She and Burton would go their separate ways in relation to co-productions of Burton's movies, the two of them having produced *Edward Scissorhands*, *Batman Returns*, *The Nightmare Before Christmas*, and, of course, *Ed Wood*. However, they did go on to produce *James and the Giant Peach* (1996), which was directed by Burton's long-time friend – and director of *The Nightmare Before Christmas* – Henry Selick.

There was also a name which was surprisingly missing from *Ed Wood's* credits: Danny Elfman. Though he had worked on all of Burton's other films, in this instance Elfman didn't create the score. The director chose Howard Shore instead, his style being more suited to the less fantastical nature of this biopic when compared with Burton's other work. It was also more apt when coupled with the use of black and white stock, Elfman's tunes being far more colourful and vibrant.

Along with regular faces there are also a number of unique Burton touches evident in the film. These include the personalisation of the studio logo at the start of the film, which, in this case, has been created in black and white to correspond with the stock used for filming. There is also the use of a fake graveyard in the movie, something seen in *Frankenweenie*, *Beetlejuice*, *The Nightmare Before Christmas*, *Batman Returns* and *Corpse Bride*. The graveyard opening sequence of *Ed Wood* is actually borrowed from the

> ### Ultimate Fact
> Tim Burton got the art department and other members of the crew who hadn't seen Edward D. Wood Jr.'s films to watch them. He also gave them a UK documentary hosted by Jonathan Ross, one which he felt captured the 'true spirit' of Wood and his friends.

opening titles of the real Edward Wood's sci-fi/horror *Plan 9 From Outer Space* and we see it again during the course of Burton's movie when Wood makes the aforementioned film.

We also see Burton's use of stop-motion animation effects in the title sequence, in relation to the tentacle of a giant octopus. However, most of the effects used in this film are achieved through effective make-up, specifically that of Martin Landau. It is this make-up that won the film its second Academy Award, this Oscar double further distancing Burton's film from Wood's, who never received such acclaim. However, Wood did win a much less prestigious brace of awards. These were Golden Turkeys, the first being for the worst picture in the history of cinema for *Plan 9 From Outer Space* and the second being for worst director of all time.[6]

The use of black and white for this film harks back to Burton's first two studio shorts, *Vincent* and *Frankenweenie*, both of which were also shot with this film stock. It also ties in with the fact that the period of Wood's career this movie deals with occurs in the 1950s, a time when black and white was still the predominant type of film used for the cinema. It was also the cheapest stock to use and therefore Burton reflects the type of movies Wood made, which were on shoe-string budgets. These limitations in budget are also evident from the far from state-of-the-art effects Wood uses in his movies, the fact that his budgets are always very small, and the clear problems he has with raising finds. These elements are part of what defines Wood's B-movie creations.

Another thing that defines these early films, and part of the reason why he was able to get funding, is the use of washed-up horror actor Bela Lugosi. He was an actor who Wood greatly admired and one who was able to help open doors for the director purely by having his name attached to projects, though this help was minimal, many seeing Lugosi as long past his prime.

The relationship portrayed between Edward and Bela is

extremely touching. They are entirely supportive of each other and have faith in each other's talent despite the fact that few others do. Ed still sees Bela as the star he once was, whereas others see him as a washed up old fool with a drug problem. Bela sees Ed as a capable writer and director, which is far removed from the majority view. With their mutual support their dreams of working in the movies are allowed to stay alive and even advance when Ed manages to embark on further projects despite the complete failure of *Glen or Glenda*.

The bond between Wood and Lugosi is akin to that between Burton and Vincent Price. Lugosi is Wood's on-screen mentor who he then gets to meet in real life and persuades to do the narration for *Glen or Glenda*. Price was Burton's on-screen mentor and he managed to meet with him and convince him to narrate the short film *Vincent*. Further to this is the fact that Price and Burton continued to have a friendship right until Price's death, just as Wood and Lugosi did.

This link is no doubt one of the reasons Burton took on this project. This director-actor friendship would have had a distinct resonance with Burton, as did the father-son relationship in *Big Fish*, providing him with the personal connection he requires before agreeing to direct a script. However, there was also another relationship which created an additional bond between Burton and the movie. This was Burton's friendship with production designer Anton Furst, who worked on *Batman* and then committed suicide while Burton was working on *Batman Returns*, which Furst wasn't able to work on. Burton felt a correlation between this relationship and that of Wood's with Lugosi, something which added considerably to his emotional link with the on-screen relationship when coupled with the Vincent Price connection.

Wood and Lugosi talk about early horror films, mentioning the mythic and poetic qualities of the movies, qualities helped by such things as castles and full moons. These qualities are evident in numerous Burton films, a full moon is used very effectively in *The Nightmare Before Christmas*, for example. Burton clearly appreciates the horror atmospherics which held him transfixed to TV screens when a boy and continue to do so now he's an adult. Also, because of his love of old horror movies, Burton would have been familiar with Lugosi's work.

Another element personal to Burton is made clear in a small piece of dialogue spoken by Patricia Arquette's character, Kathy O'Hara. She states, 'You should feel lucky, Eddie's the only fella in town who doesn't pass judgement on people,' when speaking to Vampira. This statement reflects Burton's belief that people are generally too judgemental, something he experienced first hand when growing up in Burbank. This anti-judgemental sentiment is also apparent in Burton's use of a misunderstood monster in *Frankenweenie* and *Edward Scissorhands*. This theme is also seen in *Big Fish* when the son eventually understands his father after having previously passed an incorrect judgement on him.

Another thing this simple statement by Kathy reflects is that Burton has not created a moralistic film with *Ed Wood*. It would have been all too easy to pass judgement on the title character, but Wood is portrayed with kind fondness. He isn't mocked and even his habit of cross-dressing is introduced without ridicule. As one critic notes, 'The laughter that comes from seeing Wood in a dress is secondary to the understanding that comes from seeing how the clothes bring Wood a serenity he can't find otherwise.'[7] It is clear that this habit calms Wood, that he is at his ease when in women's clothes.

This promotion of non-judgemental attitudes that is present in both the narrative itself and in Burton's filmic approach, is also apparent when Wood tells Kathy he enjoys dressing in women's clothes. This occurs while they are trapped on a House of Horror ride at a fairground, and Kathy accepts this part of his character without judging him, in a moment which toys playfully with horror conventions. If such a ride would have broken down in a horror movie it would have been a scary scene filled with tension, but Burton manages to create a touching moment between these two characters.

Tim Burton hasn't used this film as a form of ridicule, but has created an affectionate window into the life of a fellow director, one who was empowered by his creative visions, just as Burton is. *Ed Wood* isn't a celebration of bad movies, it's a celebration of tenacity, courage, vision and drive. It also shows that there is something about Wood's films that deserves note, and this is their honesty.

> **Ultimate Quote**
>
> 'When people are open and not judgemental I just find that really beautiful and great and somewhat rare' – Tim Burton[8]

They remain true to Wood's creative vision and, despite lacking in quality, manage to capture a certain reality of film production which is glossed over and edited out of the

> **Ultimate Quote**
>
> 'There's a sincerity to them [Wood's movies] that is very unusual, and I always found that somewhat touching; it gives them a surreal, weirdly heartfelt feeling' – Tim Burton[9]

majority of films. This is done to create the suspension of disbelief, to allow the audience to believe in what is taking place on screen. This does not occur when watching Wood's movies. What the audience actually experiences is the opposite; a suspension of belief. We cannot believe in what we are being shown in such work as *Plan 9 From Outer Space*. However, the clarity of the film's constructed nature gives it a kind of raw honesty.

Wood's constant enthusiasm and optimism in the face of adversity create an empathetic bond with the audience because we have all had to try and overcome obstacles in our lives. At the same time you feel a little sorry for him because he is so deluded about his ability and the quality of the films he is making. Burton has stated, 'I think most people have some delusion in their lives,'[10] in relation to this aspect of Wood's character. This, like the overcoming of obstacles, creates further empathy with Wood.

In a sense Ed lives in a world of fantasy, a world confined to his own head, in a mind which causes him to see only what he wants to see. This creates a link with Edward Bloom in *Big Fish*, who spins a past filled with fantastical stories he has created in his mind based on the real events of his life.

Wood is driven by a desire to make movies and his continuing efforts to do so despite the odds being stacked against him is incredibly endearing. It is also an element of his personality which creates a common bond with his directorial hero Orson Welles. Ed successfully wrote and directed his own films, even if they themselves weren't successful. He trod in Welles' footsteps, but would always remain in the shadow of the big man's talent, his own talent going unrecognised apart from in a negative way.

Wood has a definite charisma, one predominantly created by his overriding sense of optimism and determination. It is this charisma that caused his entourage of oddballs to remain at his side despite the failures of his career. It is also this charisma that causes the audience to be further drawn to the character, to engage with him and hope he'll overcome the problems he encounters. Our support for Wood is also furthered by the quality of the script and by Depp's acting, for these factors combine to build a character which we can't help but care for, while at the same time sharing in his disappointment and frustration.

> **Ultimate Quote**
>
> 'When you're making a film it's like doing a painting: you have this weird sense of power and energy, and you feel – and you should feel – like you're making the best movie ever made' – Tim Burton[11]

Because we know the genuine belief and motivation behind Wood's work it seems cruel when a Hollywood producer takes *Glen or Glenda* to be a practical joke. We have seen that Ed is open, honest, and uncomplicated, and this further endears us to both him and his quest to make it in the movie world.

Ed is completely convinced of his own talent and when he goes to the premiere of *Plan 9 From Outer Space* we can see he is totally enraptured by his film, one which we know is a low-grade, B-movie creation, having witnessed parts of its development. As with all of his work, he knows the lines off by heart. This shows how in love with his films he really is, that he has invested a great deal of himself in them. Because of this the audience can't help but feel for him in the light of the truth; that his attempts to be recognised as a big screen director would be in vain, at least during his lifetime.

Wood is also convinced of the talent of Bela Lugosi and the other people he has gathered about him. He cannot understand why the world has yet to realise he has great talent. In Edward's mind he is a great director and screenwriter, someone who deserves to rank alongside people like Orson Welles, who he meets late in the narrative.

Wood does have times of self-doubt, but these are short lived. They create a realism to his character. His optimism cannot be constant and is at these infrequent moments juxtaposed with this doubt, something which accentuates both aspects. Also juxtaposed in the film is the vibrant, bright nature of Wood with the much more dour Lugosi. This serves to highlight how energetic Wood is, making his enthusiasm for his movies more pronounced.

We see Wood's doubt and disappointment after a bash to raise money for his new project, *Bride of the Atom*, fails completely. This doubt is portrayed purely through his facial expression, an element of acting that Depp is highly adept at, as was seen when he played *Edward Scissorhands* and would also be seen when he starred as the introverted Willy Wonka in *Charlie and the Chocolate Factory*.

The low-budget director shares a common bond with nearly all of Burton's lead characters in that he is alienated. The Hollywood studio system both mocks and ignores this outsider. Despite this he continues to try and make his name in the movies, forever striving to achieve the Western ideal of success, and though he is continually confronted by rejection, his hopeful smile remains.

When speaking about the American ideal of winning and

success, Burton has said that because this film celebrates cinema's greatest loser it is 'therefore a political statement.'[12] What he of course means is that the film shows how important it is to try and follow your dreams and your creative vision. Success isn't the be all and end all, what matters is the journey you take and staying true to yourself while taking it.

Burton also implies that success is subjective. Wood *was* successful because he managed to get his visions into film while staying true to himself, something that *Glen or Glenda* clearly underlines. In this respect Wood's films bare a resemblance to Burton's in that the latter makes a similarly wholehearted and personal investment with every movie that he makes, demonstrating a sensitive and thoughtful nature in the process. Both are utterly committed visionaries.

As well as the alienation apparent in the character of Ed, there is also a somewhat flawed nature. This, like the alienation, is common to Burton's main characters. In *Beetlejuice* the Maitlands were too nice and Betelgeuse too nasty. In *Batman* Bruce Wayne needed the outlet of dressing as a giant bat in order to cope with the death of his parents. In *Edward Scissorhands* Edward is incomplete and too innocent. In *Ed Wood* Ed is overly optimistic. It is also the case that Bela Lugosi has a drug addiction. Thus the two main characters display personality flaws and this makes them more real because we all have weaknesses of one kind or another. This is partly why audiences identify with Burton's characters; because they display traits common to all our experiences. Burton doesn't create heroes for the big screen, he creates people who are struggling both with themselves and the positions they find themselves in, usually through no fault of their own.

This latter point is important because this is more realistic than most Hollywood movies. They will often portray a character's destiny as being in their own hands, whereas this is often not the case in reality. Ed Wood has no real control over his destiny. He cannot make himself become a good director and screenwriter however hard he tries. He will never become the next Orson Wells because he hasn't the talent. Basically, Burton again shows that life is not intrinsically fair, that success doesn't always come to those who seek it out and the good or earnest do not always win the day.

This realism relating to the human condition actually links into Burton's fairy tale sensibilities due to the fact that it touches on what it is to be human. It also creates a juxtaposition with the fact that *Ed Wood* is about making movies, about fiction and unreality. This juxtaposition of realism and unreality serves to heighten the humanness of Wood's character, his flawed nature and alienation.

> ### Ultimate Quote
> 'One of the things I liked about Ed, and I could relate to, was being passionate about what you do to the point of it becoming like a weird drug' – Tim Burton[13]

His character shares a further bond with many of those appearing in other Burton films. This is the duality clearly evident in his habit of cross-dressing. Sometimes he is dressed as a man, sometimes as a woman. We also see duality in the character of Edward Bloom in *Big Fish*, his younger self seen both active and living the adventure of life while his older self is dying and restricted to his bed. Moreover there is the duality of the factual Bloom and the fictional, something also evident in *Ed Wood*. The events portrayed are based on fact, but the creations of Wood are fictional.

In this film the use of humour is particularly Burtonesque, and particularly dark, in that we laugh at Wood's usually unfailing optimism and the following lack of success. At one point the humour also references the film itself, a colour blind character stating that he likes the grey dress when asked if he likes the red or green one. This is a typically post-modern example of self-referencing, with the script poking fun at the fact the film is shot in black and white.

In fact, this movie is possibly the most postmodern of all Burton's films – though *Mars Attacks!* admittedly comes close – as it is about Hollywood and the movie-making process, even if only on an extremely low budget level, and this is self-reflexive.

The film also displays a minor example of circularity because it begins and ends with Criswell, the mentalist, in his coffin. This circularity is another postmodern aspect of the movie, but also reflects the use of Criswell at the beginning and end of *Plan 9 From Outer Space*, even to the extent of using some of the same opening lines. It is also the case that Criswell used a coffin from which to address the public on one of the programs he appeared in.

Not only is there a selected cast and crew listing for this film at the end of the chapter, but in tribute to Wood there is also a list of his credits. These help to underline the fact that Burton's work concentrates solely on Wood's early career and ends on a rather optimistic note despite the director's eventual drunken demise in obscurity (though this optimism is in line with Wood's character).

What we have in *Ed Wood* is a movie which portrays this main character with the kind of charm befitting Burton's sensibilities, a charm which is reminiscent of Burton's depiction of Edward Scissorhands. A director renowned for his bad movies has been given the Burton touch, one that allows us to see Wood's qualities, ones which aren't evident on the whole when you watch his films.

At the last count we are confronted with one final irony. As one critic has noted, thanks to Burton's film Edward D. Wood Jr. is now better known than many of the other directors of his era.[14] The characteristics that endeared him to screenwriters Scott Alexander and Larry Karaszewski and to Tim Burton have caused Wood to grow in reputation rather than diminish, something which is sure to also happen in regards to Burton himself.

Endnotes

1. Travers, P. — Ed Wood (www.rollingstone.com)

2. Howe, D. — 'Ed Wood' (*Washington Post*, 7th October 1994, U.S.A.)

3. Ebert, R. — Ed Wood (http://rogerebert.suntimes.com/apps/pbcs.dll/article?AID=/19941007/REVIEWS/410070301/1023)

4. Hinson, H. — 'Ed Wood' (*Washington Post*, 7th October 1994, U.S.A.)

5. Salisbury, M. (ed.) — *Burton on Burton* — *Revised Edition*, p.XII (Faber and Faber, 2000, UK)

6. Unknown — Plan 9 From Outer Space (www.play.com)

7. Travers, P. — Ed Wood (www.rollingstone.com)

8. Kermode, M. (int.) — Tim Burton Interviewed by Mark Kermode (III) (http://film.guardian.co.uk/Guardian_NFT/interview/0,4479,120877,00)

9. Smith, G. (int.) — Tim Burton Interviewed by Gavin Smith (http://minadream.com/timburton/EdWoodInterview)

10. Pratt, D. — Ed Wood (www.hollywoodreporter.com/thr/reviews/review_display.jsp?vnu_content_id=1000724187)

11. Smith, G. (int.) — Tim Burton Interviewed by Gavin Smith (http://minadream.com/timburton/EdWoodInterview)

12. Smith, G. (int.) — Tim Burton Interviewed by Gavin Smith (http://minadream.com/timburton/EdWoodInterview)

13. Salisbury, M. (ed.) — *Burton on Burton* — *Revised Edition*, p.134 (Faber and Faber, 2000, UK)

14. Bezanson, D. — Ed Wood (www.filmcritic.com)

9. Mars Attacks!

'Ack, ack-ack, ack, ACK ACK.
Ack ack ack, ack-ack, ack, ack, ack-ack, ACK-ACK!'
– Martian Leader's address to Planet Earth

The initial inspiration for *Mars Attacks!* was a set of fifty-five 'Topps Trading Cards' which featured colourful Martians in various situations, surely making Burton's film one of the strangest in regards to its inspiration. The original cards were withdrawn from circulation in the decade they were released (the 60s) due to parental complaints about the violence depicted on them, but were then reissued in 1994. In fact, one of the reasons Burton decided to go ahead with the project was because he 'just liked the anarchistic spirit' of the Martians.[1]

Though this $75 million film didn't do well at the US box office thanks in part to a lukewarm reception from critics, it did considerably better in Europe, where the fun poked at the American establishment couldn't cause any offence. However, upon its release on video *Mars Attacks!* gained a great deal in popularity in the States, especially amongst a younger audience. This factor can be said to reflect the film's cartoonist violence and the alien's clear hilarity when conducting their destruction of earth and its citizens. Such 'fun' violence can be seen in such things as 'The Itchy and

Scratchy Show,' which often appears in episodes of 'The Simpsons'.

One thing of note in regards to this violence is that Burton claimed he dislikes light-hearted killing in the movies, something which he stated in defence of the darkness in *Batman Returns*. The fact that *Mars Attacks!* is packed to the rafters with such killing does seem to place the director in a rather hypocritical position. However, as the scenes of violence in this film are in no way realistic, but are instead cartoonist, this removes it from everyday life and therefore from the types of depictions Burton was referring to.

> ### Ultimate Quote
> 'It almost seemed like we had done a kind of a *Mad* magazine version of *Independence Day*'
> – Tim Burton[2]

Released in December 1996, *Mars Attacks!* followed in the alien footsteps of that year's summer blockbuster, *Independence Day* (Emmerich), which was another invasion movie with disaster movie qualities. The films were at the opposite ends of the spectrum, *Mars Attacks!* taking nothing seriously and *Independence Day*, though displaying a good deal of humour, being far more earnest. *Mars Attacks!* does not show a great deal of sentimentality and nor does it wallow in patriotism, unlike *Independence Day*, the film's very title being a huge clue as to this aspect of its narrative.

A simple moment in Burton's film underlines this difference. One of the characters waves an American flag and this would have been a patriotic moment in *Independence Day*. However, the character is zapped by the Martians without ceremony or a whiff of patriotism in *Mars Attacks!*

The films did share some common ground other than the obvious aspect of alien invasion. One of the correlations is

The Maitlands entering the bureaucratic afterworld where dark humour abounds

When Betelgeuse appears at the film's finale he has bat ears, hinting at future films

The use of stop–motion animation: the sandworms which bear a resemblance to creatures in *The Nightmare Before Christmas*

The terrible duo of Delia Deetz and Otho

Batman is played by Michael Keaton and displays two traits common to
Burton characters; alienation and a dual persona

We see Michael Keaton in one of three lead roles and the use of stripes,
which often feature in Burton's early films

The impressive Gotham City which displays both gothic and expressionist influences, like many other locations in Burton's films

Jack Nicholson as the Joker is prominent due to his extroverted nature, while Batman hides in the shadows

The Bat Signal introduced at the end of the first movie is put to good use in *Batman Returns*.

Michelle Pfeiffer as Catwoman, who displays an overt sexuality, something not seen in many other Burton films

Danny DeVito as the Penguin, in one of Burton's trademark graveyard scenes

Two Burton trademarks in *Mars Attacks!*: a dog and a severed human head

The alien ambassador prepares to address congress – and then to laser it to oblivion

Burton's once partner, Lisa Marie, makes an appearance as a freaky alien in female disguise

The severed heads of Pierce Brosnan and Sarah Jessica Parker kissing in *Mars Attacks!*, showing dark humour and an unusual sexual attraction

Ichabod Crane is alienated in the superstitious community and his companions are young, showing the use of young people in pivotal roles

The lopping of heads in *Sleepy Hollow* was cathartic for Burton after spending a year on a *Superman* film which then fell through

The Hessian finally reclaims his head and becomes autonomous

The windmill in *Sleepy Hollow* was a homage to his earlier short entitled *Frankenweenie*, and was also part of the gothic setting of the film

Danny DeVito plays circus owner Calloway who also happens to be a misunderstood monster – a werewolf

The Hand-i-matic which Ed Bloom sells is reminiscent of Edward Scissorhands' hands

Big Fish contains a strong fairy tale element, something which creates a link with a number of other Burton movies, such as *Edward Scissorhands*

Burton's long-term partner Helena Bonham Carter as the witch in whose eye people can see their demise

Willy Wonka, played by Johnny Depp

The Buckets' run-down and slanted house, reflecting the same expressionist style used in *Beetlejuice*, the *Batman* films, *Sleepy Hollow*, and *Big Fish*

Willy Wonka's chocolate factory where things are not as sweet as they may at first seem

The all-singing, all-dancing Oompa-Loompas in the Nut Sorting Room

Bonejangles putting his all into a good old knees-up in the underworld

The 'head' waiter in *The Corpse Bride*

The maggot living inside the Corpse Bride's head is a clear use of Burton's zany humour

The view from Victor's perspective as he walks into the Land of the Dead

The raised dwelling which is a regular motif in Burton's work

the use of a number of narrative strands which take place in different locations. In both cases these are used to build a picture of how all-encompassing the invasion is, allowing the audience to see the scale of what is taking place.

Another link between the two films is that of iconographic landmarks being destroyed. In this the difference between the movies is made very, very clear. In *Independence Day* landmarks like the White House are destroyed with utmost seriousness. In *Mars Attacks!* the highly amused aliens do high fives when bowling over the stone figures on Easter Island and carve Martian faces in the place of the president's faces on Mount Rushmore, both clearly humorous parodies of the usual devastation in such films.

These actions fit perfectly with the tone of this modern, B-movie style, zap-fest of a science fiction flick. Its tongue is firmly stuck in its cheek right from the start, when we see typical 1950s flying saucers approach the earth after taking off from Mars, Danny Elfman's strange score adding a quirky oddness with its eerie tones and weird voices.

The B-movie heritage is clear from the beginning, the saucers being reminiscent of those in Edward D. Wood Jr.'s cult film *Plan 9 From Outer Space* (1956), an extremely apt parallel considering the last film Burton directed before this one was *Ed Wood*.

We are immediately confronted not only with Burton's trademark of changing the studio logo, but also his habit of reusing actors. We see Jack Nicholson returning to the Burton fold after playing the Joker in *Batman*, and in *Mars Attacks!* he appears in two roles, the first being the President of the United States which he plays with a great sense of ineptness. In his second role he plays a Las Vegas businessman whose lust for money hilariously takes precedence over the fact that a bunch of aliens with a twisted sense of humour are invading the planet.

Other regular Burtonites include Lisa Marie, who also appeared as Vampira in *Ed Wood* and would go on to have a roles in *Sleepy Hollow* and *Planet of the Apes*, and Sarah Jessica Parker of 'Sex in the City' fame, who'd also starred in *Ed Wood*. We also see Danny DeVito in the second of three roles in Burton films, the first being as the Penguin in *Batman Returns* and the third being as Amos Calloway in *Big Fish*. Finally, there is the reappearance of Sylvia Sydney, who played Juno, the Maitland's case worker in *Beetlejuice*. In *Mars Attacks!* she brings an equally dry humour to the part of an old lady who inadvertently helps to avert alien occupation of our planet.

As well as regular actors, there are two members of the crew who are of special note. These are editor Chris Lebenzon and costume designer Colleen Atwood. This movie was the fourth Burton film that Lebenzon had worked on and he would go on to work on four others, so this makes *Mars Attacks!* the halfway point in his working relationship with the director. However, he not only shares a close relationship with Burton, but also with English director Tony Scott, for whom he has also edited eight films, including *Top Gun* (1986), *Crimson Tide* (1995) and *Enemy of the State* (1998).

Colleen Atwood was also at the 'halfway stage' of her working relationship with Burton with this film. She'd already worked on *Edward Scissorhands* and *Ed Wood*, and would go on

> **Ultimate Fact**
>
> Screenwriter Jonathan Gems first introduced Tim Burton to Lisa Marie at a go-go bar in New York during the Christmas of 1992 and they fell for each other straight away.

to work on three more of Burton's visual treats, including *Planet of the Apes*. She has also been costume designer on *The Silence of the Lambs* (Demme, 1991), *Gattaca* (Niccol, 1997) and the visually stunning *Memoirs of a Geisha* (Marshall, 2005).

As well as those mentioned above, there are a whole host of others whose appearance in this movie make it a truly star-studded affair. There's Pam Grier, who played the title role in Quentin Tarantino's *Jackie Brown* (1997), Rod Steiger, who has starred in a whole host of movies, taking the role of the title character in *Al Capone* (Wilson, 1959), Martin Short, who many will remember from *Innerspace* (Dante, 1987), Michael J. Fox, who starred in Spielberg's *Back to the Future* trilogy, Glenn Close, who's appeared in countless films but is perhaps best known for her roles in *Fatal Attraction* (Lyne, 1987) and *Dangerous Liaisons* (Frears, 1988), Annette Bening, who gave a stunning performance as Carolyn Burnham in the 1999 smash *American Beauty* (Mendes), Jack Black, who was great alongside John Cusack in *High Fidelity* (Frears, 2000), and even the singer Tom Jones appearing as himself – not forgetting the cameo appearances from those such as blaxploitation icon Jim Brown.

Some of the film's humour is generated by the treatment of the characters played by these big movie stars. For example, 007 Pierce Brosnan, who plays White House advisor Professor Donald Kessler, is decapitated. However, his head is kept in working order and seeing a star depicted in such a way is highly amusing. It also both funny and surprising to see stars like Michael J. Fox and Jack Nicholson zapped to kingdom come by egg-headed freaks from outer space. Our expectations are that the big names will survive by and large, due to the usual Hollywood offerings in which the stars inevitably survive whatever is thrown at them (consider, for example, Arnie surviving a nuclear blast in *Predator* [McTiernan, 1987]).

The aforementioned Professor Donald Kessler is a character of special note as he helps to anchor the film in the science fiction genre while also adding a great deal of weight to the film's parody of the genre. Unlike the scientists in *Forbidden Planet* (Wilcox, 1956), *Alien* (Scott, 1979), *Independence Day*, and a host of other science fiction films, Kessler thinks he knows what he's talking about, but the audience know better and are able to snigger at the clichés relating to Kessler's conclusions about the aliens because we realise they're completely wrong. The stereotypical role of 'educated man of science,' personified by Spock in 'Star Trek' (Roddenberry, 1966-1969), is turned on its decapitated head in a very successful and amusing way.

In *Mars Attacks*, Kessler makes the statement, 'Logic dictates that given their extremely high level of technical development they're an advanced culture, therefore peaceful and enlightened.' This type of opinion is presented in a quite a few science fiction films, but thankfully Burton doesn't adhere to it. I say 'thankfully' because the statement is not logical at all. We as a race are advancing at a terrific rate technologically, but our society and intelligence is not. We could therefore become highly advanced without ever improving on any other cultural or biological level, just like the Martians in this movie.

Some, like critic Roger Ebert, have stated that the aliens in this film are dumb.[3] This isn't really the case. What is true is that they are merely immature, preferring childish behaviour to that of mature adults. Maybe this is their form of 'enlightenment' – they've realised that a happy and fulfilling life means following the 'child within'. Or maybe this is Burton's way of mocking the concept of an inner child, something which it has been claimed he utilises in his movies, but which Burton denies and despises.[4]

There is one plotline which involves Donald Kessler that highlights the bizarre nature of this film and its twisted humour. This is the love story between Kessler and TV presenter Nathalie Lake. This is no ordinary love story between two people, it's a love story between a severed head and a dog-woman. It encapsulates the tone of the movie and the fact that it is not supposed to be taken seriously on any level. It is also hammed-up to quite some extent, which adds to audience amusement as the heads of these two characters pout at each other. Furthermore, it introduces the theme of disfigurement, something seen in *Beetlejuice* when the title character has his head shrunk, when the Maitlands alter their appearance in order to look scary, and in relation to most of the recently deceased. Disfigurement has been discussed in relation to *Batman*, *Batman Returns*, *The Nightmare Before Christmas* and *Edward Scissorhands*. However, as in *Beetlejuice*, the disfigurement in *Mars Attacks!* is used to comic effect.

> ## Ultimate Quote
>
> 'You want to make him [Tim Burton] happy. If he asked you to stand on your head and shoot flames out of your heels you would just do it and you wouldn't even ask why' – Sarah Jessica Parker[5]

The twisted humour seen in this love story is also evident throughout the film and reflects Burton's penchant for black comedy, something seen in all of his films. We see it in the actions of the humans as they struggle to retain a sense of normality despite suffering such inconveniences as having their heads cut off and then having them surgically attached onto the body of a dog. The aliens provide a rich vein of humour with their somewhat psychotic, trigger happy nature. They're like NRA members high on some mind blowing, head expanding drug; happy to toy with the little humans whose planet they have targeted to be the butt of their bad taste, but very funny jokes.

The Martians are entirely computer generated, but this works well with these creatures as it adds to their otherness, a quality which Burton likes to portray in all of his movies. The way in which they have been created serves to highlight their quirkiness and alien nature.

This film was the first one in which Burton plumped for fully computer generated effects, and would also be the last to date. He had originally intended the aliens to be stop-motion, but after having a team of animators from the UK working on the project for a while Burton realised it would prove too expensive and too time consuming to do the entire movie in this way. Due to this a test reel was created by Industrial Light and Magic (a visual effects company owned by George Lucas' Lucasfilm company), who were based near the *Mars Attacks!* production offices in San Francisco. Burton was suitably impressed with the work to give the go ahead for all the effects to be done in such a way.[7]

> **Ultimate Quote**
>
> 'There was something about the computer medium that seemed to work with these characters, because they were all the same, because they had a certain quality in the movement' – Tim Burton [6]

Danny Elfman wrote the score for the film and there is an element of spookiness which is perfectly matched to the skeletal appearance of the Martians' faces, their homicidal cartoonist 'Tom and Jerry' approach to life, and to the odd movements of Lisa Marie when playing an alien in freaky female disguise.

The main characters in this movie, just like those in all of Burton's other films, suffer from alienation. It is worth noting that the aliens themselves are not the alienated ones here. The single character who stands out as suffering from a genuine sense of alienation is Richie Norris, played by Lukas Haas. His character is similar to that of Vincent in the short film of the same name, Lydia in *Beetlejuice* and Edward Scissorhands. He is the young loner who is seen as odd by those about him and he is also the character who saves the day, along with a little accidental help from his grandmother, whose is well on the way to losing her marbles.

Though at first glance the film seems to have no personal link with Burton, this relationship between Richie and his grandmother is one aspect which does relate to the director. This on-screen relationship echoes the closeness he shared with his own grandmother, whom Burton lived with whilst growing up in Burbank. This link is made all the more clear due to the fact that Richie is an alienated individual, who reflects the feelings of isolation Burton felt as a boy when he wasn't understood or accepted by his parents.

It is of note that Richie and his grandmother are two of the only characters who don't get vaporised. They are also two of the only characters who are not ridiculed other than by Richie's parents. Together with the President's daughter, Taffy Dale (played by Natalie Portman) they are treated more kindly by Burton, and this is undoubtedly due to the fact that they are alienated characters whose experiences reflect those of his childhood. This is the case with Taffy because she clearly has nothing in common with her parents, just as Burton didn't have anything in common with his, and she finds herself restricted within her own home as the White House tourist tours prevent her from going where she wants.

When it comes to Burtonesque touches two can be seen in the alien spacecraft, when the President of the United States addresses the Martians after their hostile response to the initial meeting with humans. Firstly, the printout of the President's words comes out of a computer console. More specifically, it comes from part of the console which resembles a face. The same kind of technological representation of biological forms can be seen in *Edward Scissorhands* where Edward's creator has a cookie making machine, many of the parts of which were designed to look like biological forms, such as people.

Ultimate Quote
'Jack [Black] really energised the project. He's perfect to go up against the Martians' – Tim Burton[8]

Secondly, there is the further use of dark humour. The President's address is good natured and encourages peace between the two species. However, when the Martian leader reads the printout he bursts into laughter, something the audience finds amusing because they instantly understand how the aliens view their human counterparts. We also soon see, with the issuing of a formal apology from the little Martians and their following extremely deadly address to Congress, that they are toying with the human race, treating the whole affair as one, big prank.

Also adding to the Tim Burton feeling of this movie is the fact that the people who save the day are all on the outskirts of social acceptability or are alienated. There are two hooky playing boys who save the President's life. There is the alienated Richie Norris and his grandmother, who has been sidelined in an old people's home, the two of them discovering a way to kill the Martians completely by accident. And there's also Byron, an ex-boxer now in an unrewarding career as a 'meeter and greeter' in a Vegas casino who saves Tom Jones and co. from a horde of Martian invaders.

Other Burtonesque touches include the gangway that unravels from the Martian spacecraft when it first lands on earth, which looks like a huge tongue. There is also the image of a dove of peace being turned into a microwave meal in one zap, a very blatant display of Burton's dark humour. Dogs are again a recurring emblem, firstly in regards to Nathalie Lake's Chihuahua and secondly in relation to the President's dog, which is fried by the alien who gets into the White House in disguise. However, it is the stunning visuals that really stamp the film with Burton's unique fingerprint – especially because of the pronounced use of colour and the well-paced action.

The film's colourful appearance and brightness work hand-in-hand with its humour, complementing it while also adding to the garish, B-movie style. They give it a vivid look which compliments its trading card inspiration. This bright and colourful nature seems rather apt coming after the black and white *Ed Wood* and the visual darkness of *The Nightmare Before Christmas* and *Batman Returns*. It also reflects the cartoonist nature of the aliens and the violence they commit.

Adding to the atmosphere of the film is its vibrant energy, something which bares a resemblance to that in *Beetlejuice*, the mad-cap, zany Martians being similar in behaviour to Betelgeuse himself as well as to the Joker in *Batman*. They have no regard for life, treating humans as toys to be played with for the sake of humour and experiment. Their system of morals seems to be non-existent, something which, as with Betelgeuse and the Joker, gives them a certain kind of dangerous freedom. They are not restricted by moral boundaries or any sense of fair play. Due to this the Martians have no qualms about using their lasers at every given opportunity, seeing human life not as sacred, but as expendable in the name of fun.

Mars Attacks! sees Burton using intertitles for the first time in his movies, the only other time being *Charlie and the Chocolate Factory*. They are essential in the case of *Mars Attacks!* as the narrative moves from one location to another on a regular basis, just as it does in many classic invasion films and disaster movies. It is also necessary because to follow the narrative the audience require a

> **Ultimate Fact**
>
> The Chihuahua who accompanies Sarah Jessica Parker's character, TV presenter Nathalie Lake, is actually Lisa Marie's dog and she found it in the street while in Japan.

clear timeframe in which the events of the Martian invasion actually happen. Without these intertitles we wouldn't be able to understand when the events depicted occur with any degree of certainty, which would detract from our enjoyment of the film.

The movie has clear resonances with 1950s alien invasion films such as *The War of the Worlds* (Haskin, 1953), *Target Earth* (Rose, 1954), and *Earth Vs. the Flying Saucers* (Sears, 1956). The trading cards featuring the Martians were released in the 1960s, as was *Dr. Strangelove*, with which *Mars Attacks!* shares a number of similarities. There is also 1970s popular culture in evidence, the aliens watching 'The Dukes of Hazzard' in their command ship and the Bee Gees' song 'Staying Alive' playing in a trailer as two people have sex with a couple of Martian perverts steaming up a window as they watch. This mixing of cultural symbols from varying decades is accentuated by the CG special effects, which are clearly from the 1990s. The movie successfully displays a postmodern blend of cultural eras and references to other cultural creations which aren't based on anything real.

Mars Attacks! also displays a postmodern blend of the arts, Tom Jones not only appearing in the film, but performing his 1965 hit 'It's Not Unusual' (something which adds to the era blending in the movie). Another addition to its postmodern credentials is the chaotic nature of its narrative, which happily parodies 1950s B-movie sci-fi and 1970s disaster movies such as *The Towering Inferno* (Guillermin, 1974) and *Earthquake* (Robson, 1974). These films involved a number of different plotlines unfolding as the disaster developed. They also employed various locations in which these plotlines took place. Both of these aspects are reflected in *Mars Attacks!*, which, like said disaster movies, successfully ties most of these narrative elements together at the end.

It is worth pointing out that one of the 1970s pop-culture references mentioned above further underlines the sense of humour found in this film. The use of the Bee Gees' song 'Staying Alive' is obviously meant to be ironic as at this point in the story very few people are actually staying alive, most being frazzled by laser fire.

The final, brain-spattering demise of the Martians due to the music of Country singer Slim Whitman seals the film's 1950s sci-fi heritage. This reflects the endings of *Target Earth* and *Earth Vs the Flying Saucers*, both of which used sound waves to kill the alien invaders. *Mars Attacks!* also shares other common ground with *Earth Vs the Flying Saucers* in particular. This common ground includes the destruction of the Washington Monument and the scenes in front of the destroyed White House at the end of the movie. The end of

Burton's flying saucer extravaganza also arguably echoes the death of the invaders in *The War of the Worlds*, though on that occasion it is the common cold which thwarts the alien hopes of world domination.

This ending is part of the film's humour, it is darkly comic, reflecting much of the humour evident in the film, it reflects 1950s science fiction flicks, and allows for more computer effects as the Martians' heads explode in their helmets, adding a few extra dashes of green to the colourful visuals.

The war room scenes in the movie are reminiscent of those seen in the classic Peter Sellers film *Dr. Strangelove or: How I Learned to Stop Worrying and Love the Bomb* (Kubrick, 1964). In *Mars Attacks!* the slight air of madness and ill-founded self-assurance that 'everything is going to be fine' create an air of hysterical tension and bring to mind the mad professor character played by Sellers in the film.

The war room isn't the only thing that Burton's movie of mayhem has in common with *Dr. Strangelove*. In both films there is an actor appearing in more than one role. In *Mars Attacks!* Jack Nicholson plays dual roles, whereas in *Strangelove* Peter Sellers played no less than three characters. However, this was not an intentional link, Nicholson asking Burton if he could play the dual roles after reading the script rather than the other way round.

Another link with *Dr. Strangelove* is the presence of a jingoistic, 'nuke 'em' general. In *Mars Attacks!* this role is effectively played by Rod Steiger and in *Strangelove* it was played by George C. Scott, both of their characters desperate to use force in making the enemy succumb, regardless of whether or not this is a good approach

The use of nuclear weapons is also subject to the film's humour sensibilities, just as it is in *Dr. Strangelove*. Such weapons are usually viewed with utmost seriousness, but in *Mars Attacks!* this is not the case at all, as we see when a Martian device sucks in the nuclear explosion and then the leader of the invaders inhales it like helium, his voice going up in pitch in a great moment of humour. This highlights the fact that nothing is sacred in this movie, that everything is open to mockery and parody.

So many science fiction films take themselves extremely seriously, and it is great to see one that is completely the opposite. Of course, there have been other tongue-in-cheek and humorous sci-fi's, such as *The Fifth Element* (Besson, 1997), *Starship Troopers* (Verhoeven, 1997), *Galaxy Quest* (Parisot, 1999) and *Evolution* (Reitman, 2001), but none have pushed the boat out as far as *Mars Attacks!* does. For Burton and script writer Jonathan Gems nothing is sacred and nothing warrants serious treatment.

Gems and Burton worked closely on rewrites of the script, though Burton didn't ask for any credit for this. Because of his help, Gems dedicated his novelisation of the film to its director, and he has said of the script writing that 'a lot of the process was me writing and Tim drawing. He would say everything in terms of pictures.'[9]

This visual core to Burton's directing style (and indeed to communicating in general) is perfectly matched to the films he chooses to work on and *Mars Attacks!* is no exception, the Martians needing a director with strong visual qualities to bring their garish, B-movie world to life. Any director deciding to take on such a bizarre narrative requires a highly inventive mind (involving as it does a bunch of madcap aliens creating havoc with joyful glee) and, fortunately for anyone who has enjoyed this film, once again we see that imagination is something Burton possesses – and in great quantities.

Endnotes

1. Salisbury, M. (ed.) – *Burton on Burton* – *Revised Edition*, p.145 (Faber and Faber, 2000, UK)

2. Salisbury, M. (ed.) – *Burton on Burton* – *Revised Edition*, p.153 (Faber and Faber, 2000, UK)

3. Ebert, R. – Mars Attacks! (http://rogerebert.suntimes.com/apps/pbcs.dll/
   article?AID=/19961213/REVIEWS/612)

4. Fraga, K. (ed.) – *Tim Burton Interviews*, p.43 (University Press of Mississippi, 2005, US)

5. Fraga, K. (ed.) – *Tim Burton Interviews*, p.123 (University Press of Mississippi, 2005, US)

6. McMahan, A. – *The Films of Tim Burton: Animating Live Action in Contemporary Hollywood*,
   p.107 (Continuum Books, 2005, US)

7. Fraga, K. (ed.) – *Tim Burton Interviews*, pp.121-122 (University Press of Mississippi, 2005, US)

8. Fraga, K. (ed.) – *Tim Burton Interviews*, p.112 (University Press of Mississippi, 2005, US)

9. Salisbury, M. (ed.) – *Burton on Burton* – *Revised Edition*, p.148 (Faber and Faber, 2000, UK)

References

Blackwelder, R. – 'Mars Attacks!' (http://splicedwire.com/96reviews/mars)

Coates, T. – 'Mars Attacks!' (www.bbc.co.uk/films/2001/06/21/mars_attacks_1996_review)

Laforest, K.N. – 'Mars Attacks!' (www.montrealfilmjournal.com/review.asp?R=R0000356)

Unknown – Mars Attacks! (www.scifimoviepage.com/mars)

Unknown – www.bluntinstrument.org.uk/elfman/comment/mars/trackbytrack)

www.imdb.com

10. Sleepy Hollow

*'Now the Hessian wakes.
He's on the rampage, cutting off
heads where he finds them'*
– Baltus Van Tassel

Not one to stick to a particular genre, *Sleepy Hollow* is Tim Burton's foray into horror. It takes that extra step from *Beetlejuice*, which was a supernatural horror-comedy. Its darkness is heightened by Danny Elfman's haunting score, which adds weight and atmosphere to the on-screen visuals and narrative, filled with mist, darkness, and rolling, severed heads.

Sleepy Hollow was based on a short story by Washington Irving entitled 'The Legend of Sleepy Hollow' which was first published in 1820. Disney made a version of the tale called *The Adventures of Ichabod and Mr Toad* (Algar & Geronimi). This was a cartoon released in 1949 and combined Irving's story with elements of *The Wind in the Willows* by Kenneth Grahame, the film version of which was released the same year and also directed by Geronimi. There was also a 1980 made-for-TV film of the tale starring Jeff Goldblum (Schellerup). In relation to the inspiration for his version, Burton has stated, 'it was a story I'd known from childhood and the Disney cartoon.'[1]

The story was adapted by screenwriter Andrew Kevin Walker, whose other credits include the David Fincher films *Seven* (1995), in which the character played by Gwyneth Paltrow has her head severed, and *Fight Club* (1999). The screenplay was then worked on extensively by British playwright Tom Stoppard, whose other works include *Rosencrantz and Guildenstern are Dead.* Johnny Depp has said of his rewrite, 'Stoppard did a fabulous job,'[2] and this is borne out by a great script which is done justice by a group of excellent character actors appearing in the film.

The script for *Sleepy Hollow* arrived after Burton had been working on a proposed new *Superman* film with actor Nicolas Cage set to star as the superhero. However, the project fell through and wouldn't find its way to the big screen until 2006, though the lead actor had changed by that time. After the disappointment Burton felt at the collapse of the *Superman* project he used the making of *Sleepy Hollow* as a cathartic vent for his feelings.[3]

Sleepy Hollow was released in 1999 and cost just under $80 million to make. Burton decided to shoot it in England, as he had with *Batman* and would also do with *Charlie and the Chocolate Factory*. One reason for this was because he had already worked with the craftsmen and this created a bond of trust, one which meant he didn't have to explain every little detail.

> **Ultimate Fact**
>
> The town of Sleepy Hollow was constructed around a small pond on the Hambleden Estate in Buckinghamshire, England.

This is very telling in that it highlights Burton's preference for working with the same people on more than one occasion, something we have already seen in relation to cast members as well as crew. It also highlights his dislike of too much verbal communication because, when talking about recasting the same craftsmen on this film, he stated, 'it's great because you don't have to verbalise.'[4]

Tim Burton's film deviates from Irving's original story in two main ways. Firstly, the narrative itself is altered. In the original it is never clear whether the headless horseman who is central to the story actually exists or if he is simply a fiction made up by a group of men in a tavern. In Burton's movie there is no doubt about the Hessian's existence beyond the grave and the story is turned not so much into a who-done-it, but into a supernatural tale of neck slicing and one man's attempt to investigate these murders.

This brings us to the other major change between the story and the film, which is the appearance of the criminal investigator, Constable Ichabod Crane, who was a schoolteacher in Irving's original work. Irving created him as a rather ugly, gangly man with a long nose, arms, and legs. Though Johnny Depp, who plays the New York constable, wanted to wear makeup in order to resemble the character from Irving's short story, Burton didn't want him to. What Burton wanted was to keep Ichabod's eccentricities, along with his awkwardness, something which was partially created by his long limbs in the original tale.

> **Ultimate Quote**
>
> 'With a Tim Burton movie you're invited into Tim Burton world. That's a great gift for any technician – for an audience, for that matter. But it is still a collaborative effort' – Johnny Depp[5]

This was Johnny Depp's third appearance in a Burton live-action movie and he plays Crane with a degree of the same quirkiness seen in both *Ed Wood* and *Charlie and the Chocolate Factory*, as well as in Terry Gilliam's 1998 film *Fear and Loathing in Las Vegas* when he played infamous writer

Hunter S. Thompson.

Sleepy Hollow's producer, Scott Rudin, has stated that, 'basically Johnny Depp is playing Tim Burton in all of his movies.'[6] In *Edward Scissorhands* we saw Burton as an awkward teenager unable to communicate. In *Ed Wood* Burton's real-life relationship with Vincent Price was reflected on screen by Wood's relationship with Lugosi, and there was also the obvious connection of Wood being a film director. As far as *Sleepy Hollow* is concerned, Depp has said that Ichabod Crane reflects Burton's battle with the Hollywood studio system and even the world. Burton responded to this by saying, 'it's probably true in a simple sort of way.'[7] Some of this battling with the studio system occurred in relation to the aforementioned collapse of the *Superman* project.

Depp used three main influences for the way he chose to play the character. The first of these was the way in which Basil Rathbone played Sherlock Holmes in the classic 1940s films based on the novels of Arthur Conan Doyle, Depp taking his inspiration from 'the sort of drive' connected to that performance. There is actually a connection between Rathbone and *Sleepy Hollow* in that he was the narrator for the Disney version.

The second influence on Depp's characterisation of Ichabod was Roddy McDowall, who Johnny has described as 'a great friend', and who starred as Cornelius in the original *Planet of the Apes* (Schaffner, 1968). Finally, and possibly the most important influence, was Angela Lansbury's performance in the 1978 film *Death on the Nile* (Guillermin), which was an adaptation of an Agatha Christie work. She starred as Salome Otterbourne with Peter Ustinov in the lead as the Belgian detective Hercule Poirot. What Depp was interested in was 'the energy and sort of righteousness she had,' and this is what he wanted to apply to the character of Ichabod Crane.[8]

All of these influences can be seen in Crane. Firstly, there is his drive to solve the riddle of the headless horseman's killings and the affected nature of his character – he has an effeminate air to the way he carries himself. And finally, he has a touch of righteousness in relation to his use of science and his negative view of superstition.

> **Ultimate Fact**
>
> For Johnny Depp's birthday Tim Burton gave him a signed photograph of Angela Lansbury with the words 'from one sleuth to another' written on it.[9]

Depp received much praise for his performance, as he has done with other roles he has played in Burton's films. Critic Roger Ebert described his acting as 'superb' and went on to describe Depp as 'an actor able to disappear into characters.'[10] This comment on Depp's acting ability has been reiterated by Burton himself, stating, 'I love actors who like to transform and he's a major transformer.'[11]

The way Depp plays the character, with the required air of eccentricity and awkwardness, makes Ichabod Crane stand out from the rest of the townspeople in Sleepy Hollow. This works well as Crane is from New York and this difference is a defining point. The city is the origin of new fangled ideas and inventions. The country is where people remain set in their ways and still believe tales of hocus-pocus.

Crane believes in 'sense and reason, cause and consequence' and is happy to discover the murders are ultimately conducted by 'someone of flesh and blood,' as he'd always hoped. Therefore his scientific ways and reasoned means of deduction can still be applied to the murders, and are used to deduce who is responsible for the bloody deaths.

Crane uses a number of gadgets in order to investigate the crimes and this is an element common to quite a few other films that Burton has made. In *Edward Scissorhands* Edward's creator employed gadgets and machinery to make things like cookies and even Edward himself. In both the *Batman* films the caped crusader often uses them and we also see the Joker using things like an electrified hand buzzer and the Penguin employing a copter-brolly. In *Charlie and the Chocolate Factory* Willy Wonka uses a dazzling array of machinery in order to create his sweets. There are even examples of gadgets in Burton's stop-motion animation *The Nightmare Before Christmas*, in which we see them being employed to make toys in Christmas Town and by inventor Dr Finkelstein in Halloween Town.

The backstory for Ichabod Crane is shown to the audience with the use of flashbacks in the form of terrible nightmares. This past explains his wish to use science and his shunning of superstition, which we learn consigned his mother to a bloody end at the hands of a zealous Christian who punished her for her pagan ways by putting her in an iron maiden, where she was pierced by the metal spikes inside its door as her eyes peered out of a small slit. She was played by Lisa Marie in her third role in a Burton movie.

These flashbacks give us a horrific sense of what Crane witnessed as a child. They also tell us that he is an orphan, something which he has in common with Bruce Wayne and the young boy who ends up helping him investigate the murders in the town of Sleepy Hollow. There is also a link with *Charlie and the Chocolate Factory* in that flashbacks are used to create Willy Wonka's backstory in relation to a parental matter, specifically the estrangement between him and his father.

Due to witnessing his mother's gruesome demise, Crane, like Batman, Edward Scissorhands, Catwoman, the Penguin, and Willy Wonka, is mentally disfigured. It is also of note that, apart from in the case of Catwoman, these disfigurements are all linked to the character's parents, something which echoes Burton's own problems of communication and understanding in regards to his own parents.

Sleepy Hollow is a small town in wooded countryside and Ichabod Crane is sent to investigate the decapitation of several of the townspeople in the year 1799. There his devotion to scientific methods and science itself is to be put to the test. His nerves are also tested as he initially clings to the idea that there is no such thing as a headless horseman prowling the locale. He doesn't believe in ghosts and ghouls, at least, not until it's blatantly clear that there's no other explanation for the creepy head severings.

His character is placed in juxtaposition with that of the headless horseman. Ichabod Crane thinks a lot, he uses his head to try and solve the murders, to bring the narrative to a conclusion, whereas the horseman clearly has no head at all, but is the defining force of the narrative. Thus the thinker, the man who uses his mind, overcomes the mindless at the end of the film.

Christopher Walken stars as the Hessian, the murderous individual who becomes the headless rider of doom. He also starred in *Batman Returns* as Max Shreck, a businessman with a distinct lack of moral fibre. As usual, Walken is very effective at portraying a vicious character and looks fantastically evil as the Hessian with his teeth filed into sharp points.

Christopher Lee has a small part at the start of the film as the Burgomaster and also appears in *Charlie and the Chocolate Factory* and provides a character voice in *Corpse Bride*.

His appearance creates a link to old horror films, which Burton draws on for some of his inspiration. Lee is famous for having played Dracula and Burton said having him at the film's start set 'the movie off on the right tone' because of his horror movie links, specifically to the Hammer horrors.[12]

This leads on to the fact that Burton was interested in retaining the sense of atmosphere the piece had, an atmosphere which reminded him and Depp of the monster movies they'd grown up watching. In relation to this Burton has commented, 'what I got out of the original was a sense of atmosphere, of romantic horror and fable legend, the image of the horseman and the great names of the characters,' going on to say, 'those were the things that we felt we wanted to keep true to and that we could expand on.'[13]

A sense of atmosphere is created with great depth and was noted by critics, who gave this element of the film a glowing response. Comments included, 'the overall visual scope of this movie is awe-inspiring,'[14] and, 'it is as unique and visually captivating as anything you are ever likely to see.'[15]

Hammer horror films were the biggest influence on the looks and atmospherics of the film, Burton saying, 'a lot of the Hammer horror films are the kind of films where the images sort of burn in your consciousness.'[16] Another filmic influence was Mario Bava's 1960 horror film *Black Sunday*, which was also called *La Maschera Del Demonio* and had an otherworldly quality which Burton liked and hoped to evoke to a degree in *Sleepy Hollow*.

Adding to the film's horror heritage is the fact that the Hessian cannot cross holy ground, and this use of the holy against beasts of the night and the undead is often seen in such movies.

Because of the stunning visuals art director Rick Heinrichs

and set decorator Pete Young won an Academy Award for Art Direction. Heinrichs, in his Oscar acceptance speech, said, 'I share this award with an artist whose unique brilliance I got a glimpse of twenty years ago... Tim Burton, whose vision of *Sleepy Hollow*

> **Ultimate Quote**
>
> 'This is among other things an absolutely lovely film, with production design, art direction and cinematography that create a distinctive place for the imagination' – Roger Ebert[17]

was the inspiration we all keyed off of.'[18] In relation to the movie's look, he stated that what they were trying to achieve with the town of Sleepy Hollow was a kind of 'colonial expressionism' and with the surrounding countryside they wanted a 'kind of natural expressionism.'[19] The latter can be seen as expressionist in that it is a twisted, exaggerated form of the natural world, one in which angst and torment can easily be imagined. This ties into the expressionist nature of many of Burton's other films.

The mist and woodland of Sleepy Hollow give the location a mysterious quality, one which adds greatly to the overall atmosphere of the film. They are ideal haunting grounds for the Hessian, perfectly matched to the brutal murders that take place there. They also create a sense of a fairy tale, of a place removed from reality, hidden away in the mists.

The town and its surroundings are places where the unusual can and will happen, where the idea of normality is completely different from that in the city and of the present day. The strange and supernatural is accepted as true and Ichabod's scientific methods are viewed with scepticism, a role reversal when compared with the world today.

The use of witches in the story places it firmly in the supernatural. It also links this film to *The Nightmare Before*

Christmas and *Big Fish*, in which we also see witches. The Western Woods Crone and Lady Mary Van Tassel are twin sisters who use witchcraft, and the Crone's cave dwelling adds to the fantasy feel of the film. Both are played brilliantly by Miranda Richardson.

Following this fairy tale theme we can see that Ichabod is the prince, though not a traditional brave and fearless prince. Katrina Van Tassel, played by Christina Ricci, is the princess, though in a twist of the normal tale she also uses witchcraft and is mistaken as a wrongdoer by Crane. The Hessian horseman is the misunderstood monster to a degree. Initially the beheadings are thought to be all his doing, but in truth he is only a pawn in the evil, greed-fuelled machinations of the real villain of the piece, Lady Mary Van Tassel. She is revealed as such at the end when it is discovered that she controls the horseman, directing it to kill who she desires by manipulating his skull.

The use of such things as owl hoots and scarecrows adds to the spooky aesthetic of the movie. Elements like these are often present in ghost stories, especially ones heard, seen, or read in our youth. Therefore this film has the power to stir memories and feelings of fear and trepidation linked to the ghoulish material we've come into contact with during our lives. It can touch a place within us, a dark place where haunting sounds echo. Novelist Washington Irving, screenwriters Yagher and Walker, and Tim Burton all key into an aspect of the audience's psyche which makes the impact of the movie greater.

Another aspect which increases the film's impact is the use of physical effects rather than computer generated ones. This gives the locations and events taking place in them more of a presence, and is a common element of Burton's work,

Mars Attacks! being the only film to deviate from this belief in trying to create something with physicality. As Burton has said, 'as amazing as digital technology is, you can still feel it on the screen while you're watching the movie, there's a certain thinness.'[21] CG effects can remove you

> **Ultimate Fact**
>
> As Ichabod and his young assistant approach the Crone's cave Crane pushes the boy in front of him. This was an improvised addition by Depp, who felt the action befitted Crane's character.[20]

from the enjoyment and atmosphere of films because you're thinking 'wow, how great are those computer effects' rather than thinking about the narrative itself.

An interesting point in regards to this tale, and one which adds to the horror, is the killing of a small boy by the headless horseman despite the child trying to hide beneath the floorboards of his home. This is not common in even the most gruesome of horror flicks. Young children are usually spared, seen almost as untouchable, something which is common to the majority of films and not just those in this genre. However, the sacredness of childhood holds no sway for the prowling Hessian. In this sense *Sleepy Hollow* acts as a minor reflection of Burton's previous film *Mars Attacks!*, in which nothing was held as sacred.

The tonal quality of the film has been altered to help in creating greater atmospherics. The colour has been muted to create additional greyness and a lack of vitality in the locations where the narrative takes place, something which is the opposite of *Mars Attacks!*, which was a riot of colour. This lack of vitality reflects that of the horseman's victims and is befitting of a horror film, many of which glory in the use of darkness.

Due to all of the above we can see this film is a clear example of Burton communicating visually with the audience. The dark and misty woods with their old, twisted trees, the muted colours, the fallen leaves, the ramshackle town and its muddy streets, all come together to create a powerful use of imagery, so powerful that we can almost smell the musty scents of autumn issuing from the screen.

> **Ultimate Quote**
>
> 'I've always wanted to make a movie where one of the characters didn't have a head' – Tim Burton[22]

An emphasis on the visual approach is apparent in all of Burton's films, though he changes tack from one movie to another, shifting from the use of darker colours to bright, garish ones in *Mars Attacks!* and using a more vibrant palette in *Big Fish* and inside Willy Wonka's chocolate factory. Each movie communicates feelings to the audience through its visual qualities, like Gotham City's greyness and deep shadows representing not only the down-trodden nature of the residents, but also the darkness apparent in Batman's psyche.

Sleepy Hollow communicates a haunting sense of foreboding, of danger lurking behind every gnarly tree. It uses imagery we are familiar with from previous horrors and creates an atmosphere which is a kind of gothic dream landscape. It adds greatly to the story, such is its strength. We can see how fearful the surroundings can be, imagine evil in the woods beyond the fringes of the town and how this would make Sleepy Hollow's inhabitants feel. We can also understand how superstitions might arise in such a locale. All of this means an empathic bond is created between the audience and the townspeople to a degree because we understand their terror at the notion of a headless horseman hunting them down one by one, prowling the darker hours in order to collect their severed heads.

The humour evident in the film reflects the toned down nature of the colour. It is sedate when compared to other Burton movies and is predominantly linked to the character of Ichabod Crane, specifically his mild bungling and the fact that his city ways seem preposterous when transposed to the countryside. This bungling nature highlights the point that he is no hero. He is simply a flawed individual who manages to undo the spell of the horseman with luck and the help of others.

Crane is scared of spiders and this phobia is part of the humour relating to his character. His affected manner creates humorous moments in otherwise tense situations, such as when the headless horseman kills magistrate Samuel Philipse (Richard Griffiths) in the fields and the victim's head rolls into Ichabod's lap. The expression on his face and his mannerisms make this moment amusing yet gory, an interesting mix which can also be seen in such horror films as Peter Jackson's *Braindead* (1992) and Rodriguez's *From Dusk Till Dawn* (1996).

As well as the use of dark humour, we also see other Burton trademarks, the most prominent is the use of a graveyard, something also seen

> ### Ultimate Quote
> 'We jumped at every opportunity for me to be a complete ham and kind of glutton for twisted humour' – Johnny Depp[23]

in *Frankenweenie*, *Beetlejuice*, *Batman Returns*, *The Nightmare Before Christmas*, *Ed Wood*, *Big Fish*, *Planet of the Apes* and *Corpse Bride*. This is a staple location for Burton, one which has a classic horror atmosphere, something added to when Crane has to exhume five of the horseman's victims from four graves.

As a child, Burton and his friends would play in a nearby

graveyard in Burbank. The imagery and atmosphere of that place have obviously remained with him and would have been strengthened by the large dose of horror films which he watched as a boy. Further to this graveyard use is the appearance of scarecrows and pumpkins, which are also used in *The Nightmare Before Christmas*.

The windmill during the Hessian chase scenes also links this film to Burton's Disney short *Frankenweenie*. In that film there was a smaller version of the windmill on a miniature golf course. That building also burnt down and the one depicted in *Sleepy Hollow* pays tribute to this great short by the director. The inclusion of the windmill also pays homage to a similar scene in James Whale's 1931 film *Frankenstein* (as did the windmill in *Frankenweenie*).

Burton also uses snow in this film, but only right at the end when the narrative returns to New York. Snow is also used in *Edward Scissorhands*, *Batman Returns*, *The Nightmare Before Christmas*, *Charlie and the Chocolate Factory* and *Corpse Bride*, and is one Burton's most regular trademarks after the use of graveyards.

Another common Burton touch is the use of a young person in a key role. This can be seen with Lydia in *Beetlejuice*, Edward, Kim and Jim in *Edward Scissorhands*, the three trick-or-treat children in *The Nightmare Before Christmas*, Richie Norris, Taffy Dale and the Williams boys in *Mars Attacks!*, Birn in *Planet of the Apes*, Charlie and the other children in *Charlie and the Chocolate Factory*, and Victor and his two brides in *Corpse Bride*. In *Sleepy Hollow* we find this young person in the form of a boy called Masbath, played by Marc Pickering. Thanks to the headless horseman he is an orphan and therefore shares common ground with Ichabod Crane. Because of this he asks Crane if he can assist with the investigations. He is key in Crane's ponderings on the subject as he provides local information and moral support to the eccentric crime fighter. Masbath is also vital in the final scenes of confrontation with Lady Mary Van Tassel and the horseman. Crane is only able to get his hands on the Hessian's skull thanks to the boy hitting Lady Mary over the head with a large piece of wood.

> **Ultimate Fact**
>
> Johnny Depp got in trouble in the first grade for drawing pictures of Frankenstein and Dracula in class, an activity stemming from his love of horror films.[24]

Also relating to the finale is a book entitled *A Compendium of Spells, Charms and Devices of the Spirit World* which Katrina gives to Crane, though he is not particularly thrilled at receiving such an unscientific work. When she gives it to him she tells him, 'Keep it close to your heart, it is sure protection against harm.' These words prove to be providential when a bullet fired at the constable's chest by Lady Mary is stopped by the book. Not only does this imply that Katrina may have the power of foresight, but it also symbolic of how the supernatural, as well as the reasoned and scientific, has helped Crane to survive and solve the riddle of the headless horseman.

Starring alongside those already mentioned are Steven Waddington who had a main role in *The Last of the Mohicans* (Mann, 1992), Casper Van Dien from *Starship Troopers* (Verhoeven, 1997), Richard Griffiths from the cult British comedy *Withnail & I* (Robinson, 1987), and Michael Gambon who can also be seen playing Albus Dumbledore in two of the Harry Potter films. There is also the reappearance of Jeffrey Jones, who can be seen in *Beetlejuice* and *Ed Wood*. Another cast member of special note it Michael Gough. He had starred as Dr. Charles Decker in the classic 1961 film

Konga (Lemont) and Burton said it was 'just such a pleasure' to work with him.[25] Gough, along with Christopher Lee and Johnny Depp, would go on to supply a character's voice for Burton's stop-motion film *Corpse Bride*.

Burton also loved using Christina Ricci as Katrina Van Tassel, stating, 'Christina is like a silent movie actress... She brings this great ambiguous quality... I like it because it's a real mysterious quality.'[26] This mystery works well as the audience never quite knows her motives until the end of the film and because of this she is somewhat of an unknown quantity, who could have something to do with the murders.

All of these cast members show off Colleen Atwood's brilliant costumes and play their roles with a perfect air of conspiracy while also looking upon Crane as a rather odd and inept constable. They give the town its heart of yokels who are both superstitious and introverted to a degree, highlighted by the fact that they keep secrets from the outsider who has arrived in their midst.

This leads on to the theme of illusion and deception which are apparent within the story. Central to this is Crane's spinning device depicting a cage on one side and a bird on the other. When the device is spun the bird appears to be caged, an optical illusion being created. It is symbolic of the illusion maintained throughout a great deal of the narrative that the Hessian is acting of his own free will, exacting revenge for reasons that Crane must uncover. It also symbolises the deception of the townspeople, who keep the constable in the dark about certain facts relating to the case. In Sleepy Hollow things are definitely not as they seem.

What can be deduced from all this is that this is an engaging film with a tense and gripping narrative and visuals which create a great sense of atmosphere suited to the story.

Burton's influence is clear in both his artistic touch and the traits common to his main characters. He has made a film with a strong presence, tentacles of mist winding about our minds as we enter the landscape of *Sleepy Hollow* with him, becoming wide eyed and lost in the woods as we wait for the horseman to strike again.

Endnotes

1. Spelling, I. – "Sleepy Hollow": Heads up for Tim Burton
   (http://members.tripod.com/VanTassell/article/ho111999ii)

2. Grady, P. – Johnny Handsome: From Jump Street to Sleepy Hollow, Johnny Depp has Proven he's More Than a Pretty Face (www.reel.com/reel.asp?node=features/ interviews/ depp)

3. Salisbury, M. (ed.) – *Burton on Burton – Revised Edition*, p.179 (Faber and Faber, 2000, UK)

4. Salisbury, M. (ed.) – *Burton on Burton – Revised Edition*, p.176 (Faber and Faber, 2000, UK)

5. Grady, P. – Johnny Handsome: From Jump Street to Sleepy Hollow, Johnny Depp has Proven he's More Than a Pretty Face (www.reel.com/reel.asp?node=features/ interviews/depp)

6. Salisbury, M. (ed.) – *Burton on Burton – Revised Edition*, p.178 (Faber and Faber, 2000, UK)

7. Salisbury, M. (ed.) – *Burton on Burton – Revised Edition*, p.179 (Faber and Faber, 2000, UK)

8. Grady, P. – Johnny Handsome: From Jump Street to Sleepy Hollow, Johnny Depp has Proven he's More Than a Pretty Face (www.reel.com/reel.asp?node=features/ interviews/depp)

9. Fraga, K. (ed.) – *Tim Burton Interviews*, p.133 (University Press of Mississippi, 2005, US)

10. Ebert, R. – Sleepy Hollow (http://rogerebert.suntimes.com/apps/pbcs.dll/ article?AID=/19991119/REVIEWS/911)

11. Unknown – Burton Talks Sleepy Hollow
    (www.amazon.co.uk/exec/obidos/tg/feature/-/316193/026-3830763-8027648)

12. Spelling, I. – "Sleepy Hollow": Heads up for Tim Burton
    (http://members.tripod.com/VanTassell/article/ho111999ii)

13. Cranky Critic – Cranky Critic Star Talk with Tim Burton

(www.crankycritic.com/qa/timburton)

14. Unknown – Sleepy Hollow

(http://efilmcritic.com/review.php?movie=2777&reviewer=128)

15. Sandell, A. – Sleepy Hollow (www.juicycerebellum.com/199927)

16. Cranky Critic – Cranky Critic Star Talk with Tim Burton

(www.crankycritic.com/qa/timburton)

17. Ebert, R. – Sleepy Hollow (http://rogerebert.suntimes.com/apps/pbcs.dll/

article?AID=/19991119/REVIEWS/911)

18. Heinrichs, R. – Official Oscar Site

(http://members.tripod.com/VanTassell/article/oscar)

19. Salisbury, M. (ed.) – *Burton on Burton – Revised Edition*, pp.169-170 (Faber and Faber, 2000, UK)

20. Cranky Critic – Cranky Critic Star Talk with Johnny Depp

(www.crankycritic.com/qa/johnnydepp)

21. Fraga, K. (ed.) – Tim Burton Interviews, p.141 (University Press of Mississippi, 2005, US)

22. Turan, K. – Sleepy Hollow

(www.calendarlive.com/movies/reviews/cl-movie000406-129,0,7199568)

23. Cranky Critic – Cranky Critic Star Talk with Johnny Depp

(www.crankycritic.com/qa/johnnydepp)

24. Cranky Critic – Cranky Critic Star Talk with Johnny Depp

(www.crankycritic.com/qa/johnnydepp)

25. Spelling, I. – "Sleepy Hollow": Heads up for Tim Burton

(http://members.tripod.com/VanTassell/article/ho111999ii)

26. Cranky Critic – Cranky Critic Star Talk with Tim Burton

(www.crankycritic.com/qa/timburton)

References

Bradshaw, P. – 'Sleepy Hollow' (*The Guardian*, 7 January 2000, UK)

11. Planet of the Apes

Just follow your sequence and come home.
Understand? Home'
— Captain Leo Davidson

Released in 2001, *Planet of the Apes* had a record-breaking opening weekend at the box office in the US, taking nearly $70 million, something which reflected the fact Franklin J. Schaffner's 1968 film of the same name also broke box office records and was 20th Century Fox's highest grossing and most profitable film of that year. However, the film's budgets differed greatly, Schaffner having only $5.8 million to spend while Burton having closer to $100 million.

The most important thing to say about *Planet of the Apes* is that is not a remake of the 1968 film, which starred Charlton Heston as George Taylor. Tim Burton has described this as a 're-imaging', and it is one which takes its lead as much from Pierre Boulle's original novel, entitled *La Planete des Singes* (Julliard 1963), as from the first movie. The book's main themes were race and class division, something which is apparent in Burton's film, though in a less conspicuous way than in the 60s version. The subtlety of the content in Burton's film is more apt for a time when stories with more blatant meanings have worn thin and people are searching for more in the way of entertainment. Thus Burton entrenches the film's depth in an entertaining narrative, not allowing it to dominate or become too overwhelming.

A more blatant approach worked in the original film because of the issues of that time. The Civil Rights movement was in full swing, the US was at war in Vietnam, involved in an arms race with the Soviet Union, and its population was becoming increasingly divided. Burton's film is about misperception, as are a number of his other movies, in this case the apes misperceiving the humans.

One thing that Burton was fully aware of when making this film was the whole mythology surrounding the subject matter. This was created by the initial film, four sequels made between 1970 and 1974, a television series which had some of its fourteen hour-long episodes turned into TV movies, and an animated series called *Return to the Planet of the Apes*. All of this material created a solid background, but the first three films created a real circularity to the story, one which explained how apes had come to dominate humans on Earth.

> ### Ultimate Fact
> The 1968 film had the largest budget for makeup in Hollywood history at that time, exceeding $1 million and making up over one sixth of the entire film budget.

Burton appreciated that this circularity created an interesting and engaging narrative in totality, and so analysed the body of *Planet of the Apes* material, stating, 'I was thinking about it…in terms of the overall, weird, big picture mythology.'[1] This led to his movie containing a degree of circularity which stretched beyond the on-screen narrative and explained the origins of the apes and humans on the planet in question, giving the audience the 'big picture' without having to show it on screen.

One very noticeable element which sets this film in stark contrast to the original is the ape makeup. It is much more realistic in the newer movie, which isn't surprising considering advances in special effects techniques, though John Chambers did win a special Academy Award for the makeup in 1968. The faces of Burton's apes carry more in the way of expressions and have a reality which aids in characterisation, especially with the characters General Thade and Ari. The former is played by Tim Roth, who starred in Tarantino's *Reservoir Dogs* (1992) and *Pulp Fiction* (1994). The second is played by Helena Bonham Carter in the first of three live-action roles she has had in Tim Burton films, her voice also being used for the title character in *Corpse Bride*.

> **Ultimate Fact**
>
> Before making *Planet of the Apes* Tim Burton was terrified of simians and after filming nothing had changed.[2]

Her performance received a great deal of critical praise, reviewers giving her such compliments as, 'Helena Bonham Carter brings an astounding depth of character to the human-sympathiser Ari.'[3] It was also during production of *Planet of the Apes* that Helena and Burton first met, and they would later become a couple who remain together to this day.

Using the apes' appearance to increase characterisation was intentional. Makeup designer Rick Baker has stated that he 'wanted each creature to be uniquely different.'[4] Baker is a six-time Academy Award winner, one of his Oscars having been won for his work on Burton's *Ed Wood*. He was the obvious choice to work on this movie because he has an expert on apes, having worked on *Greystoke: The Legend of Tarzan, King of the Apes* (Hudson, 1984), *Gorillas in the Mist:*

> ### Ultimate Quote
>
> 'I wanted to do this film based on the title and Tim Burton... I'm a makeup geek and an ape-geek so this is the ultimate film for me' – Rick Baker[5]

The Story of Dian Fossey (Apted, 1988) and *Mighty Joe Young* (Underwood, 1998). He also appeared on screen in *Planet of the Apes* as an old ape.

The makeup took up to four hours to apply to the actors and was primarily a mix of rubber, hair, and glue. The false teeth made it hard to speak and the costumes took some getting used to, but once the actors became acclimatised to their new, hairy personas they found the makeup and costumes helped them a great deal in being able to become convincing apes.

Also of help was the fact they were effectively wearing masks, something which Burton believes gives actors a certain freedom, also witnessed with the characters of Betelgeuse, Batman, the Joker, and even Edward Scissorhands to a degree. 'When you cover up you can let something else weird leak through,' said the director,[6] which was supported by Bonham Carter, who stated, 'I loved the idea that I could be free of my face and inhabit somebody else's.'[7]

The makeup was so good that when Mark Wahlberg, who plays astronaut Captain Leo Davidson, was asked if he ever forgot there were humans underneath, he replied, 'I did with Tim [Roth] and Michael [Clarke Duncan], especially because they were extremely violent.'[8]

In the original film chimpanzees were portrayed as peace-loving. However, real chimps can be highly aggressive and violent, something which Wahlberg found out for himself when he hugged Bonham Carter and was attacked by the chimps the cast were working with. She underlines the true nature of this species, saying, 'they're so loveable and affectionate one moment, but if you don't do what they want they practically rip your arms out of their sockets.'[9]

Because the apes are so like humans in many ways this not only creates a duality in regards to their characters, but it also makes sudden outbursts of anger and violence all the more shocking. This violent and somewhat unpredictable nature is reflected in Tim Roth's portrayal of Thade, one which critics have praised. He is totally convincing as an ape, particularly in his aggression and the desire to mark out his territory at any given opportunity, something which is common with the dominant male in a group of apes.

Thade's behavioural traits are perhaps so believable because the members of the cast playing apes had to attend 'ape school'. During their classes they were taught the ways in which apes move and their characteristics when it comes to such things as the importance of smell and grooming. These classes were given by Terry Notary, a movement coordinator who had previously been a performer with Cirque du Soleil. He said, 'we needed to loosen up the actors to approximate real ape body language... In essence, we had to teach the actors how to find their own sense of being primal, to tap into their own inner ape.'[10]

Because of the ape school the movement of the apes, like the makeup, is far more realistic than in the 1968 film. They have a stooped look and are able to both leap and climb like normal apes, something which wasn't seen in the original. This leaping was aided by wires, like the action seen in *Crouching Tiger, Hidden Dragon* (Lee, 2000). Both this and the makeup allow for a greater suspension of disbelief.

Thade's character displays a degree of insanity. It marks Thade out as the 'bad guy' whilst also creating a sense of unpredictability to his character over and above that of him being a chimpanzee. We, as the audience, don't know what to expect from his behaviour from one moment to the next, though it is usually underpinned by anger as he seems to have a lot of rage pent up within him.

When asked about the violent content of the film being greater than in his other work Burton said, 'there is a possibility that I'm somehow trying to exorcise and relieve more aggression.' He went on to say, 'in the movies you try to work through things to some degree.'[11]

Roughly at the same time that Burton was involved with this project he lost both of his parents within a relatively short period of time and his relationship with Lisa Marie came to an end. These large events in his personal life must have had some effect on the director's approach to the film. The violence may have been a form of cathartic release for the emotional turmoil Burton must have been going through and reflects the same sort of catharsis he found in making *Sleepy Hollow* after the collapse of the *Superman* project.

> **Ultimate Quote**
>
> 'I like science fiction very much, but it is Tim Burton that has the special appeal for me' – Tim Roth[12]

Though there are emotional connections made with ape characters such as Thade, there are few made with the humans in this film. Their characters seem more shallow, without much background or anything to make us care what happens to them. This means there is little emotive content in regards to these humans. We are not concerned with their characters, only with how they are going to survive the overwhelming ape onslaught.

This is because these humans fall into the shadows of the magnificent apes, like Batman in the shadows of the bright and vibrant Joker. As with that relationship, the one between the apes and humans is a necessity because of their characters and their social positions. The apes are naturally more noteworthy, not only because of their great makeup, costumes and their often enthralling behaviour, but also because they are the more civilised and the humans are no better than barbarians who are not supposed to speak unless spoken to. This means the humans are quieter, while at the same time their roles as slaves means they are rather subdued. It is only natural that in relation to the apes the humans should seem somewhat colourless. This was also the case in regards to the Maitlands and Betelgeuse, the former seeming quite bland when compared to the madcap bio-exorcist. But this creates a powerful juxtaposition of master and slave in the case of *Planet of the Apes*, a juxtaposition which accentuates the characteristics of both groups. It also has one other interesting effect; the audience identifies with the apes, especially in the case of Ari. This means Burton's film is one of only a handful that allows us to identify with non-humans, others including his very own *Edward Scissorhands* and *The Nightmare Before Christmas*.

Linked to this identification with non-humans is a trademark of the director which is rarely acknowledged. *Planet of the Apes* contains one of the clearest examples of Burton showing 'abnormal' sexuality and attraction. Ari is clearly attracted to Davidson; ape to human. Because we identify so strongly with her this attraction is made all the more prominent. It is also the case that the notion of an amorous attraction between these two characters exists in Boulle's original novel.[13]

This display of 'unusual' sexuality is seen to varying degrees in eleven of the twelve films individually discussed in this book and is therefore a very prominent trademark of the director. In *Beetlejuice* we saw a bio-exorcist trying to make out with the dead Barbara Maitland and being satisfied by undead call girls. In *Batman* there is a relationship between a man who dresses as a bat and a woman with a bat fetish. In *Edward Scissorhands* there is a love between a non-human man with scissors for hands and a human girl. *Batman Returns* contains a relationship between two mentally disfigured individuals who need to dress up in costumes and roam Gotham City. *The Nightmare Before Christmas* shows us an attraction between Jack Skellington and Sally, who, like Edward Scissorhands, is a created non-human. In *Ed Wood* the main character likes to dress in women's clothing and in *Mars Attacks!* there is a relationship between a severed head and a dog-woman. *Sleepy Hollow* gives us a love between a mentally disfigured crime investigator and a witch. *Big Fish* is more subtle in its relationship between a woman and a man-fish, while *Corpse Bride's* off-kilter approach to sexuality is clear in the movie's title.

All of these examples make it clear that Burton likes to play with views of sexuality and to portray it beyond the bounds of normality. On the whole this theme is rather subtle, but here, in *Planet of the Apes*, there is no way to avoid its presence. Part of the reason for this is that the relationship between Ari and Davidson has more potency than that between Daena and Davidson, Daena being his human love interest who does very little other than to pout at him.

> ## Ultimate Quote
>
> 'The coolest thing about the experience was meeting Tim the person, getting to know a fantastic human being... I rushed to work every day just to hang out with Tim. I never had so much fun, felt so comfortable on a set and around somebody' – Mark Wahlberg[14]

Because Ari's characterisation is amongst the strongest in the movie, we identify with the ape's attraction to the astronaut and it takes precedence. This is also partly due to the attraction being so unusual and possibly also because we can see the potential of Davidson responding, something helped by the very effective makeup which gives Ari a distinct air of femininity.

Ari suffers from alienation, which is typical of Burton's lead characters and is also evident in relation to Davidson, which makes her attraction to him even more emotive as they share this characteristic. Ari is a human sympathiser and because of this she is at odds with the majority of other apes, even being mocked by an ape child who calls her 'human-lover'. This echoes similar comments which were made to people who sympathised with the Jews in World War II, and this underlines this film's covert meanings. This one relates to the maltreatment of others purely due to ignorance and misguidance, the ape child's father having told him it is acceptable to mistreat humans.

This link to anti-Semitism during the war is also made by the children taunting the captured humans as they are taken into Ape City. This reflects the scene in which a child mocks the Jews crammed into the carriages of a train bound for Auschwitz in Spielberg's hard-hitting film *Schindler's List* (1993).

Davidson's alienation is more intense then Ari's and stems from his arrival on the new planet, where he finds himself a complete stranger in a completely strange land. However, he does find allies in the other humans, all of which are in a position of alienation on this topsy-turvy planet.

Davidson appears to end up acting like a sort of messiah for these human inhabitants, saving them from the servitude they have suffered while also saving the entire planet from the tyranny of Thade. However, the truth is that Ari gets the small band of fleeing humans out of Ape City and it is the arrival of the chimpanzee called Pericles who brings peace at the end of the film. Therefore it is impossible to argue that Davidson is actually the hero, for he doesn't save the day, but is a man intent on getting home to Earth, only deciding to fight the apes when there is no other option open to him. This lack of a hero fits with Burton's other films as he doesn't portray heroes, just people in often extraordinary circumstances, humans and non-humans doing their best in the situations they find themselves in and often with the help of others.

Further reflecting other Burton movies is the position of Ape City, which is situated high up on a rocky tor. This is akin to the Maitlands' house in *Beetlejuice*, Batman's mansion, the gothic home of Edward Scissorhands, the home of Dr Finkelstein in *The Nightmare Before Christmas*, the Martians' ships in *Mars Attacks!*, the Bloom's home in *Big Fish* and Willy Wonka's chocolate factory in that they all are placed above the surrounding areas. Many of these places also

> **Ultimate Fact**
>
> Roddy McDowall and Kim Hunter, who played the lead chimps in the 1968 film, researched their roles by observing chimpanzees at Los Angeles Zoo.

have a brooding darkness, something seen in the look of Ape City.

The tone of the film, helped by the jagged appearance of the city, is suitably dark for a film by Tim Burton. This can be seen when two gorillas show Thade where Davidson's space craft crash landed in the forest. The area has a similar feel to the twisted woodland in *Sleepy Hollow*, including the presence of mist. We also see Thade attack his two fellow apes in a frenzy which he seems to enjoy, an air of satisfaction seen in his face when the soldiers are dead.

This leads on to one of the themes of the movie. Because the apes so closely resemble us and our society, albeit at a lesser stage of technological advancement, their violent behaviour hiding just beneath the surface makes us think of ourselves. The apes possess what is like a raw humanity with few social boundaries holding them back and Burton has said, 'without saying anything it shows you about the underside of humanity.'[15] The film doesn't explicitly tell the audience anything, but allows us to see the themes, to understand them for ourselves without them being forced upon us.

> **Ultimate Fact**
> Bill Broyles and Adam Rifkin wrote the first revisionist *Planet of the Apes* script in 1988.[16]

Another theme which isn't forced upon the audience is concerned with evolution verses creationism. However, *Planet of the Apes* doesn't support one viewpoint or the other, but actually combines the two with only one ingredient missing; God. Life on the planet was accidentally created by the space station crashing onto it, not through any divine plan. It then evolved to the state Davidson finds it in.

The premise that the space station seeded ape and human life on the planet is related to a time travelling element in the electromagnetic storm which brings Davidson to the planet. This origin of life is hinted at by the design of the slave brand, which is a symbolic representation of the space station. These origins are then confirmed later in the film.

As well as being about human nature and containing a combined view of evolution and creation, the film is also about ignorance and misperception. This is one of Burton's common themes and is connected to the idea of a misperceived monster, such as Sparky the dog in *Frankenweenie*. Here we find that it is not the monsters that are being misperceived, but the humans. Therefore the usual depiction is turned on its head, this being reminiscent of how Burton turned the usual haunted house story on its head in *Beetlejuice*. In this way we can see from what is normally the monster's point of view, but in this film is a human point of view. We can understand how easy it is to misunderstand other's motives and actions. We also see how ignorance of the ways of other races and species can affect how they are treated, and this treatment can be utterly abhorrent.

So, in this way, *Planet of the Apes* encourages a greater degree of understanding in regards to those who are different from us, both humans and other creatures. It is a film which allows us to see how easy it is to misperceive, and therefore encourages us to be more thoughtful in matters relating to difference, not allowing ignorance to guide our actions as it guides the actions of the majority of apes in the movie.

> **Ultimate Quote**
>
> 'We didn't want to do a remake because the original is a classic, but beyond being a classic, it's a "classic of its time"' – Tim Burton[17]

Despite huge differences between the 1968 movie and Burton's offering, a few nods to the original can be found in the newer film. These include the use of lines from the first film which have been given a suitable twist. For example, when the apes first capture Davidson Colonel Attar states, 'take your stinking hand off me, you damn dirty human.' The same line was used by Charlton Heston's character in the original when he was recaptured after an unsuccessful escape attempt, though the word 'ape' was used instead of 'human'.

Heston actually makes a cameo appearance in the Burton film as Thade's father, Zaius, and this is another nod of acknowledgement to the original, not only because it is Heston, but because of the character's name and his words,

> **Ultimate Fact**
>
> Tim Burton has categorically denied rumours that more than one ending was shot for the film, stating, 'we shot just one ending about two-thirds of the way through production, end of story.'[18]

including 'I warn you, their [the human's] ingenuity goes hand in hand with their cruelty. No creature is as devious and violent.' These words echo those spoken by the orang-utan Dr Zaius in 1968 and are rather ironic considering Heston is the president of America's National Rifle Association. Also, immediately following the above statement Zauis (as played by Heston) states, 'damn them, damn them all to hell' just before dying, a line said by Heston's character, Taylor, right at the end of the original movie.

Further nods to the original can be seen with the inclusion of a human called Nova, who became Taylor's 'mate' in the 1968 film. There is also the use of a Forbidden Zone, though the reasons for it being a no-go area have been drastically altered. These references make it obvious that Burton appreciates the original film, but also serve to underline the fact that this isn't a remake.

These references to Schaffner's film create a degree of humour, but the main source of the humour is the human slave trader Limbo, played by Paul Giamatti. Like Ichabod Crane in *Sleepy Hollow*, he is the primary conduit of humorous dialogue and expressions. Limbo effectively provides a bit of comic relief in what are often serious and tense situations.

A further link to the 1968 version is the use of Lake Powell as the location for the encampment of the ape army. This is because a different section of the lake was used in the previous film. The final confrontation between the humans and apes was filmed at the Trona Pinnacles, which are located in the California Desert Conservation Area and consist of unique, geological spires of rock.

The set for Ape City was constructed on a sound stage at Sony and displays Burton's usual flare for visual drama. In fact, the entire film has received high praise for this typically Burtonesque ability to create memorable on-screen impact.

Unusually for a Burton film there is only one notable cast member who had previously appeared in his work, and this is Lisa Marie, who plays Nova in the last of her four roles in Tim Burton films, something which coincided with the break up of their relationship. However, there is the first appearance of Helena Bonham Carter, who would go on to have roles in every other Burton movie to date. Also appearing in the first of four subsequent Burton roles is Deep Roy, who plays a young gorilla and Thade's niece, and would go on to star in *Big Fish*, as the Oompa-Loompas in *Charlie and the Chocolate Factory*, and provide the voice for General Bonesapart in *Corpse Bride*.

The crew does display a number of regular Burtonites, not least Danny Elfman, whose score underpins the on-screen action with its often tribalistic connotations created by drums and woodwind instruments. Also working with Burton again is editor Chris Lebenzon and, as has already been mentioned, makeup designer Rick Baker. There is also the continued collaboration with production designer Rick Heinrichs, who won an Oscar for his work on Burton's previous film, *Sleepy Hollow*.

As well as Heinrichs, Burton also made use of the great talent of costume designer Colleen Atwood again, these two members of the production combining to ensure Burton's vision of the ape planet came to the big screen, their usual flare and creativity helping to make *Planet of the Apes* as visually striking as the director's other movies.

Unlike Burton's other work, this film contains one serious plot hole which there is no getting away from, and this is the film's ending. There's only one possible way that Earth could be run by apes on Davidson's return, and that's if Pericles the chimp went there before arriving on the Planet of the Apes, presuming also that he travelled back to a time when humans were still extremely primitive, stayed a while to teach other apes until they reached his level of intelligence, and had enough fuel and knowledge to re-launch and find his way back to the electromagnetic storm (if it was still there). However, even if all these events could have taken place Thade could not have existed on Earth. Firstly, he has no means of getting there or even knowing where 'there' is. Secondly, he is descended from the chimp called Semos, who crashed on the other planet and not on Earth.

In relation to this ending there is also no way the ape's social, cultural and technological evolution would have gone down exactly the same road as ours. This is especially the case when considering the different bodies apes have in comparison to humans, something ironically highlighted in this film much more than in the 1968 version through the ape's movements. This being the case, the apes wouldn't have developed cars and other vehicles, and even buildings, in the same way as humans. This difference is shown in Pierre Boulle's novel, the apes using extra-large vehicles to make allowances for their different physique. However, one thing is clear; the writers, Konner and Rosenthal, took their inspiration from Boulle's work rather than the first film, even if they ultimately failed to make the ending work, an ending that the original screenwriter, Bill Broyles, didn't create. In fact, he stated at the time, 'I don't understand it, I have no idea what it means.'[19]

Something that this ending does do effectively is set up the possibility of a sequel. When asked about the chance of agreeing to direct a follow-up Burton said, 'I'd rather jump out the window.'[20] This is similar to his reaction when asked about directing a sequel to *Batman*, which of course, he did actually go on to do. He also answered in the negative when asked about doing sequels to *The Nightmare Before Christmas* and *Charlie and the Chocolate Factory*. When Wahlberg was asked about an *Apes* sequel he stated, 'If Tim wants to, I'd love to – it really depends on him.'[21]

> ## Ultimate Quote
> 'When you say *Planet of the Apes* and Tim Burton in the same breath, that idea is instantly explosive, like lightning on the screen' – Producer Richard D. Zanuck[22]

Despite the ending this is still a very entertaining film, both in a visual and narrative sense. It also contains much symbolism and depth, should you wish to look for it, and bears the unmistakable stamp of Burton's directorial approach.

Endnotes

1. Unknown – "Planet of the Apes": Tim Burton Interview

    (http://mymovies.net/interviews/text_feature.asp?featureid=FTRE/340/

    1312200114064763&filmid=340&sec=trailers)

2. Fischer, P. – Tim Burton Goes Ape (www.iofilm.co.uk/feats/interviews/t/tim_burton)

3. Coates, T. – Planet of the Apes (2001)

   (www.bbc.co.uk/films/2001/08/03/planet_of_the_apes_2001_review)

4. Unknown – Planet of the Apes

   (www.contactmusic.com/new/home.nsf/webpages/apes2)

5. Unknown – Planet of the Apes

   (www.contactmusic.com/new/home.nsf/webpages/apes2)

6. Sragow, M. – 'The Ape Man' (*The Guardian*, 3rd August 2001, U.K.)

7. Hladik, T. (int.) – Director Tim Burton and Cast have a Big Adventure Reinventing Planet
   of the Apes (www.scifi.com/sfw/issue223/interview)

8. Hladik, T. (int.) – Director Tim Burton and Cast have a Big Adventure Reinventing Planet
   of the Apes (www.scifi.com/sfw/issue223/interview)

9. Unknown – Helena Goes Ape

   (www.tiscali.co.uk/entertainment/film/interviews/helena_bonham_carter)

10. Unknown – Planet of the Apes

   (www.contactmusic.com/new/home.nsf/webpages/apes2)

11. Hladik, T. (int.) – Director Tim Burton and Cast have a Big Adventure Reinventing Planet
   of the Apes (www.scifi.com/sfw/issue223/interview)

12. Hladik, T. (int.) – Director Tim Burton and Cast have a Big Adventure Reinventing Planet
   of the Apes (www.scifi.com/sfw/issue223/interview)

13. Sragow, M. – The Ape Man (*The Guardian*, 3rd August 2001, U.K.)

14. Hladik, T. (int.) – Director Tim Burton and Cast have a Big Adventure Reinventing Planet
   of the Apes (www.scifi.com/sfw/issue223/interview)

15. Unknown – "Planet of the Apes": Tim Burton Interview

   (http://mymovies.net/interviews/text_feature.asp?featureid=FTRE/340/
   1312200114064763&filmid=340&sec=trailers)

16. Sragow, M. – 'The Ape Man' (*The Guardian*, 3rd August 2001, U.K.)

17. Sragow, M. – 'The Ape Man' (*The Guardian*, 3rd August 2001, U.K.)

18. Fischer, P. – Tim Burton Goes Ape

   (www.iofilm.co.uk/feats/interviews/t/tim_burton)

19. Medsker, D. (int.) – Interview with Bill Broyles

   (www.bullz-eye.com/mguide/interviews/2006/bill_broyles)

20. Unknown – Tim Burton on Planet of the Apes

(http://film.guardian.co.uk/interview/interviewpages/0,,537982,00)

21. Hladik, T. (int.) – Director Tim Burton and Cast have a Big Adventure Reinventing Planet of the Apes (www.scifi.com/sfw/issue223/interview)

22. Unknown – Planet of the Apes

(www.contactmusic.com/new/home.nsf/webpages/apes2)

References

Cavagna, C. – 'Planet of the Apes' (www.aboutfilm.com/movies/p/planetoftheapes)

Clinton, P. – 'Monkey See, Monkey Run from "Apes"'

(http://archives.cnn.com/2001/SHOWBIZ/movies/07/06/review

Ebert, R. – 'Planet of the Apes'

(http://rogerebert.suntimes.com/apps/pbcs.d11/article?AID20010727/

REVIEWS/107270305/1023)

Honeycutt, K. – Planet of the Apes

(www.hollywoodreporter.com/thr/article_display.jsp?vnu_content_id=969926)

Jackson, M. & McDermott, A. – Tim Burton Biography (www.timburtoncollective.com)

12. Big Fish

'A man tells his stories so many times that
he becomes his stories, they live on after him,
and in that way he becomes immortal'
— Will Bloom

The screenplay for *Big Fish* was written by John August and based on the novel *Big Fish: A Novel of Mythic Proportions* by Daniel Wallace. However, the novel is not as fantastical as the film, is much more sedate and less adventurous. There are also huge differences relating to the characters, locations and events that take place, the book acting more as inspiration than a blueprint for the movie.

Released in 2003, once again this film is highly personal to Burton, more than ever due to its content. Its defining relationship is that between a father and his son. They have been somewhat estranged, but the father's imminent death brings them together. The same estrangement was apparent between Burton and his father, who was a baseball player who retired from the game due to injury.

Burton himself has pointed out this fact, admitting, 'I wasn't close to my father,'[1] and this film gave him the opportunity to work through emotions connected with this relationship. The catharsis afforded by Burton's work on *Big Fish* was especially heightened because his father died not long before he received the script,[2] and two months before the release of the film he became a father himself, when Helena Bonham Carter gave birth to their first child, Billy.

In relation to his father's death and their often strained relationship prior to his passing away, Burton said that making the movie was 'an amazing way' to explore his feelings and to enable some sort of release.[3] As Burton said, 'I try to treat all [my films] personally, but this one ranks up there.'[4]

An interesting fact relating to this father-son aspect is that Burton said the film gave him the chance of exploring his feelings visually. This is noteworthy because Burton – as we have already mentioned – has always preferred using visual modes of expression to verbal communication, as has been seen in relation to his use of artwork in attempting to find an identity when in his youth. It soon becomes clear that he uses the visual to explore elements of his own life, using his more personal movies to work through emotions which might otherwise have called for therapy.

> **Ultimate Fact**
>
> Steven Spielberg was interested in directing the movie at one point, but chose to make *Catch Me if You Can* instead.

As *Big Fish* granted Burton such a valuable opportunity to explore his relationship with his father, it is hardly surprising that he agreed to direct. Another element which probably influenced his decision was the fact that his previous movie had been *Planet of the Apes* and he wanted to return to the more intimate type of film which he excels at, others including *Edward Scissorhands* and *Ed Wood*.

Big Fish is not only one of the most personal films Burton has directed, it's also one of the most emotive. It encourages us to jump into the water and take a swim upstream. It is a good natured story about the stages of life we all go through. The opening scene brings this fact home with its depiction of the seasons and the changing silhouette of a boy moving into manhood.

This is a film with true depth, and in that depth you'll find the big fish swimming through clear waters filled with memories. These memories are presented as fantastical stories told by the lead character, Edward Bloom, who, unusually for one of Burton's 'good guys', is an extrovert. The younger Edward is played by Ewan McGregor and the older Edward is played by Albert Finney.

Both actors have received praise for their roles. Comments about Finney's impressive performance include 'Albert Finney is sublime as the aging storyteller,'[5] and 'Albert Finney in a touching, towering performance'[6] – especially high praise considering the majority of Finney's performance is limited to the character's deathbed. As for McGregor, his reviews were also glowing, one critic commenting appreciatively that, 'In *Big Fish* he delivers an entertaining and wonderful performance.'[7]

The important thing about these two actors was that the audience really could believe that they were Edward Bloom at different points in his life. Burton saw pictures of Finney from the 1963 film *Tom Jones* (Richardson) and could see the similarity with McGregor. It was also the case that an old copy of *People* magazine was found which contained a 'Separated at Birth' feature showing the two actors, something that Burton used to support his argument when suggesting the actors to the studio.[9] The choice of Finney

> **Ultimate Quote**
>
> 'Tim is terrific... He's also such an enthusiastic director. It makes you feel good when someone responds to what you are doing' – Albert Finney[8]

and McGregor has proven to be the correct one on screen, partly due to their great acting and partly because it is so easy to imagine McGregor turning into Finney.

This said, some have criticised the 'gee whiz acting' which is apparent in relation to Ewan McGregor's depiction of Edward. However, the acting is supposed to be this way. Any doubt that this is the case can be dispelled by Burton's own words when he states that McGregor is 'one of the few actors that can do this sort of heightened reality humour, give it some emotional qualities, and still make it believable all at the same time.'[10]

The style of acting, along with a certain artificiality of the sets created in part by heightened colours, is entirely intentional and adds to the fantastical and humorous elements of the film. These two elements contribute to a general feeling of wonderment, while also being reminiscent of a kind of 1950s innocence, something that goes hand in hand with the fact that the stories are about growing up and discovering the wider world. Without these elements the tales told by Albert Finney's Edward would become lifeless and dull to a degree, and so Burton's decision to use these devices works in perfect harmony with the story sequences.

> **Ultimate Quote**
>
> 'There's a beautiful ease about him [Burton]. There is absolutely no stress about him from the time he says "action" to the time he says "cut"' – Ewan McGregor[11]

Another vital element concerning the casting relates to Sandra in her youth and at a later stage of life. The latter is depicted by Jessica Lange and the former by Alison Lohman. These actors were the perfect choice because, as with Finney and McGregor, the link between the different life stages of Sandra's character is a believable one, the two actresses perfectly matched.

The Edward of the present day is a man near death, so near that his wife, Sandra, played to perfection by Jessica Lange, calls their son back home to Alabama to see his father before he dies. The son is called Will, played by Billy Cudrup, and he is a journalist who is more interested in facts rather than the perceived fictions his father reels off at every opportunity, even at Will's wedding to his French wife, Josephine.

On returning home after a long period of both physical and emotional distance between himself and his father, Will tries to discover the truth behind the stories his dad always tells. We are then drawn into a world of unlikely and fantastic stories which are effectively flashbacks to various, chronological points throughout Edward's life. During these flashbacks we find an interesting link to *Edward Scissorhands* in that Edward Bloom was a travelling salesman selling a device called 'Handi-Matic', which is a hand with various implements on its fingers, something reminiscent of Edward's 'scissor fingers' in the aforementioned film.

Between the tales of Edward Bloom's past we see scenes of the present, of death coming closer and Edward in his bed waiting for the inevitable. Death is one of the most important themes of this movie. It is made central when, in one of the first stories, the young Edward visits an old, swamp-bound house where the local witch lives. The children who have accompanied him dare him to go, and this he does, showing a bravery and confidence which will continue to be clearly evident in the following tales from his life.

The witch has a glass eye and in it people are afforded visions of how they will die. Edward sees his death in the eye and because he knows how he will depart this world his confidence and self-assurance are increased. He has no need to be afraid of such things as giants and trees which try to ensnare him because he knows his fate doesn't rest in their hands or branches.

The seeing of his death in the witch's eye is linked with the idea of destiny. Edward is sure his destiny lies beyond his home town, and soon he is sure his destiny lies in the arms of the woman with whom he has fallen in love. This belief in his destiny causes Edward to forge ahead despite various obstacles and trials, like some adventurer after a treasure or some hero of old. Because of this Edward makes the most of his life.

> **Ultimate Fact**
>
> John August wrote the screenplay for *Big Fish*, but his first major screenplay was for the critically acclaimed 1999 film *Go*, directed by Doug Liman.

The witch with the glass eye is played by Helena Bonham Carter in one of two roles she has in the movie. Bonham Carter's second character, Jenny, lives in a house that in its run-down state looks akin to the strange afterlife corridors in *Beetlejuice* and the Maitland's house when the title character is trying to wed Lydia – and this is largely due to the darkness and the slanted doors and windows.

Again as with *Beetlejuice*, and all of Burton's feature films bar *Ed Wood*, Danny Elfman provides the score. During the present day scenes there is a sombre and sentimental tone to the music, adding to the emotion of the near-death situation and the interactions of the family members.

During the stories of Edward's past the music takes on Elfman's more fantastical tones, is filled with a pervading sense of wonder which helps to carry the audience along with the narrative, adding to our own excitement. The score is also effectual in heightening those moments in the film that are meant to be sinister, as when a giant arrives in Ashton, the town where Edward lives. This sinister mood created by the music leads us to suspect the giant is bad, just as the townspeople do. However, as with many of Burton's films, this is a case of monster misperception. This giant isn't cruel or horrifying in any way, simply misunderstood.

During the initial confrontation between Edward and the giant called Karl, played perfectly by Matthew McGrory, we are granted further evidence of the dark humour that is typical of Burton's films. Edward tries to persuade the giant to eat him, something which is funny in itself. He even states that he'd eat his legs if needs be because they've got some 'good eating on them.' This, in the context of the meeting and our expectations of at least a little bone crunching, is humorous.

One of the most important stories in the context of the film's overall meaning is when Edward first visits the town of Spectre. It has a somewhat surreal feeling and exists beyond the ordinary world. There are streets, but they're covered in grass and all the residents go bare foot. They also keep grinning at each other inanely, as if they're all keeping a secret from Edward.

When he first enters the town there is a person playing a banjo on a front porch, reminiscent of a similar scene from the quite disturbing film *Deliverance* (Boorman, 1972). Amusingly, this character is played by Billy Redden, whose only other film part was as the banjo playing boy in *Deliverance*. In that film the scenery was beautiful, but the area had a dark secret which followed Burt Reynolds and his friends along the river and finally revealed itself when the locals attacked them. In Spectre the dark secret is soon revealed. No one leaves. Once you arrive in Spectre you're expected to stay – forever! However, Edward does leave, shocking the inhabitants and making it clear that this segment of the plot is related to life in general and is about not stagnating, about continuing to seek out new experiences.

In a sense Spectre is very similar to the environment where the Maitlands live in *Beetlejuice* and the suburbia where Peggy Boggs and friends live in *Edward Scissorhands*. Both of these places are rather bland and passionless, with most inhabitants set in their ways until something happens to stir them into activity. In the case of Spectre, Edward acts as the catalyst for stirring up activity, just as the Maitland's death and the discovery of Edward Scissorhands are the catalysts in the aforementioned films. Edward leaving Spectre not only surprises the locals, but is also causes Norther Winslow, the town's poet laureate and a previous visitor who has settled there, to finally continue on his own journey. Winslow is played by the consistently brilliant Steve Buscemi, who brings a fantastic sense of the quirky and inadequate to this amusing character.

Spectre is like a retirement home of sorts, a place where we are due to find rest at the end of our journey, not during it. And this is a key point in relation to the movie. It is about life being a journey, being an adventure to be savoured. It is also about the fact that life isn't simply about going from A to B, it is about enjoying and making the most of the journey between the two points of birth and death.

Soon after the first visit to Spectre in the movie Danny DeVito makes a memorable appearance as a circus owning werewolf after having already waddled through a performance as the Penguin in *Batman Returns*. His attorney and sidekick in *Big Fish* is played by Deep Roy, who would later appear as the Oompa-Loompas in *Charlie and the Chocolate Factory*.

It is during this 'circus story' that the youthful Edward discovers the love of his life: Sandra. The emotive content of the film is underpinned by the relationship between these two characters. This is seen in brief in the present day scenes prior to the circus story. Then we see Edward discovering that love at first sight causes time to stand still and then speed up. He is then prepared to endure all sorts of trials and tribulations as he works for DeVito's character, Amos Calloway, at the circus and receives one fact a month about the girl of his dreams.

The circus tale itself wasn't in the novel that the film is based on, but was used by John August to bring together a number of smaller stories which occur in the book at various stages throughout Edward's life.[12] It proves to be highly effective in this task, and also contains a number of typically Burtonesque elements of humour. One such element is related to another misunderstood monster.

Amos is actually a werewolf, and though he at first appears to be the typical, tooth baring, salivating creature of legend, it soon becomes apparent that this is not the reality. Edward throws a stick for the full-moon beast and, like a domestic dog, he happily chases after it. This simple scene therefore reflects two of Burton's typical touches, the first being dark humour and the second being a beast which is misperceived.

Edward eventually meets Sandra and wins her heart despite the fact she is initially engaged to another man. This entire backstory of his love and their initial meetings shows us the strong bond created between the pair, one given even more strength when Edward leaves to go and fight in World War II. As critics have noted, 'this amorous subplot is

> ### Ultimate Fact
> Tim Burton held auditions with real circus entertainers in order to find suitable performances for the film. As soon as he saw the act in which a cat leaps down onto a pillow he thought, 'Wow, that was the best act I saw all day,' and decided to use it in the movie.[13]

magical and visceral from the moment Edward discovers that time really does stand still for love at first sight.'[14]

This story of their love adds a great deal of emotional power to the portrayal of their relationship on screen. This is made clear when Sandra finds Edward fully clothed in the bath during a scene from the present. She climbs in with him and the feelings shared by the couple are visceral, making the audience feel deeply sorry for the couple as Edward's death looms ever closer and they share a tender moment together.

> **Ultimate Quote**
>
> 'I didn't know any of the other actors before, but I think it's getting on very well. It felt almost like a family within the first few days' – Albert Finney[15]

At the heart of *Big Fish* is a fairy tale sensibility, not only in the fantastical nature of Edward's stories, but also in the lessons this narrative can teach us about our own lives. Fairy tales carry messages and touch on what it is to be human, and this is exactly what *Big Fish* does. Burton has said that 'in fairy tales…the symbolism is not so much intellectual as emotional,'[16] and this is certainly the case with *Big Fish*.

This fairy tale element is also seen in the use of a white house on a hill for the home of Edward and Sandra. It echoes the Maitland's home in *Beetlejuice*, even to the extent of having a small turret. This is the symbolic castle, one where both the prince and princess have found a home. It also stands in stark contrast to the dark hilltop homes of both Bruce Wayne and Edward Scissorhands, and also to the stark hilltop factory of Willy Wonka in *Charlie and the Chocolate Factory*.

Despite the fantastical nature of the stories they are grounded by the locations in Alabama used for the film. John August has said that the movie 'needs a reality that you wouldn't get on some Hollywood sound stage.'[17] This is because the stories are already so fanciful that to film them on an artificial set would be to remove them from any sense of reality. This underlying reality is vital because many of the stories are based on real events in Edward's life, so the locations need to be real to underpin this fact, one made clear when the characters from the tales are present at Edward's funeral at the end of the film.

Another grounding in reality is created by the deathbed environment of the present day, one which stands in a stark contrast to the bright vibrancy of the tales of Edward's past. This juxtaposition, the use of dark and light both literally and in the situations portrayed, echoes those used in *Beetlejuice* and *Edward Scissorhands*, and is equally as effective. It serves to bring home the harsh reality that Edward is nearing the end of his life, adds to it a sense of extreme sadness. At the same time the stories stand out more because of their brightness and general happiness.

Part of this juxtaposition is concerned with movement. In the present day scenes movement is restricted. Edward's life has come to a virtual standstill due to the fact that he is confined to his bed. In the stories he is still active, his life is always changing and he is experiencing new things. This highlights the most important theme of this film, which is about making the most of life while you have the chance.

Everyone tells stories from their past experiences and everyone embellishes them, though perhaps not as much as Edward. The point is that you need to have had the experiences to be able to relate them to others, without them you'd remain silent on your death bed. So this film is one about living life to the full, having stories to tell because you've made the most of your life.

Josephine is clearly taken by Edward and enjoys hearing

his stories. She doesn't feel the need to challenge his tales, is content to allow Edward to tell them and entertain her. Will, on the other hand, is trying to make demands of his father, to impose his own views on Edward, to make his dad 'fit' with the usual way people are supposed to relate their lives. Will treats the truth as guaranteed objective fact when many argue that it is actually subjective. However, at the end of the film Will realises that he shouldn't be so judgemental, that he should allow his father to express his past in the way he wishes, and due to this he joins in with the storytelling to weave his father's final moments into another fantastical tale.

The final scene, during which Will finally realises the truth about his father, and accepts that he has always known the reality, however complex, concerning who his father 'really' is, is emotionally charged. This is especially so after Jenny's admission that she is a mere fantasy, and by extension so are all of Edward's stories, whereas Edward's home life, his wife and son, are what was real to him. This adds to the impact of the final scene between father and son, as the son has realised how important he is to his father and, in turn, how important his father is to him. In this realisation he can see his dad as a man who loves him, a man who passes the gift of storytelling on to his son.

> **Ultimate Fact**
>
> Before agreeing to take the role of the older Edward Bloom, Albert Finney had lunch with Tim Burton to get to know him as he only works with directors he likes.

This last point is especially significant. In getting Will to tell the final tale, Edward is passing on the mantle from one life to the next. It creates a continuation of Edward through the life of his son, just like every child is in part the continuation of their parents. Therefore this end is symbolic of the movement from one generation to the next, the torch of life kept burning brightly into the future, as all our stories interlink to create a wondrous tapestry of experience.

Ultimately, Edward *is* a storyteller. He's not trying to be something that he's not, he is being true to his character and true to aspects of his past. It is Will who has to understand he has been seeing the true side of his father, and that is all he's ever seen. To try and enforce Edward not to tell stories is effectively like trying to get him not to be himself, which is paradoxically exactly what Will doesn't want.

> **Ultimate Fact**
> Ironically, Matthew McGrory, who plays Karl the giant, is afraid of heights.

Big Fish is about the joy of life. Edward's tales are versions of the truth of his life, ones which concentrate on the joy of being alive, on the vibrant nature of life and all its possibilities. It is about how you feel indestructible when young, as if you can take on the whole world, but when you're old you're reduced to stories about those times. The juxtaposition of these two ends of the spectrum, the first when death seems so far away and the second when death is patiently hovering at the end of the bed, makes the film all the more beautiful, powerful, and poetic.

The movie is also about a thirst for life and experience. As Edward states, 'The truth is I've been thirsty all my life.' The fact that we've seen Edward's vibrant youth, the adventure of growing up and of becoming an adult, makes the end of the movie all the more moving, not only because we identify with the characters, but because we are reminded of our own mortality. Thus *Big Fish* makes us thoughtful about our lives, makes us want to live more thoroughly, more completely so that when we are lying on our deathbeds we will have lots of stories to tell our children.

Another theme, though less obvious, is that we all touch other's lives and they touch ours. This is applicable to us all. Those we meet become part of our life experience, and we become part of theirs. This fact makes us mindful of what kind of mark we leave when meeting and interacting with others.

This film brings the magic and mystery back to the cinema and to what it means to be alive. It is filled with a sense of wonder, one which is gloriously infectious as the audience watch the strange events unfold and see Will realise the reality behind his father's tales; that they do not cover up the truth, they enliven it and bring to it a sense of the amazing, of the feelings of youth, of falling in love, of having new experiences, meeting new people, each of whom is special in some way.

> **Ultimate Quote**
>
> 'From the beginning of the film I thought that I was somehow in safe, good hands with Tim' – Albert Finney[18]

We are ultimately all fish and grow according to our experiences. Edward is a big fish because he has made the most of his life, continued to experience and grow. The film therefore confronts us with a number of questions. Do we want to keep growing? Do we want to become big fish ourselves by living our lives to the full? Do we want our stories to live on long after we've gone?

It's through what you do that you live on beyond this life. This is the meaning of the final voiceover when Will says that his father lives on through his stories, ones which were created by what he did with his life. And I guess what this film is asking us at the last is what stories are we creating in life's grand adventure?

Endnotes

1. Unknown – 'Tim Burton'

> (http://entertainment.timesonline.co.uk/article/0,,14931-1695710_3,00)

2. Russell, J. – 'Tim Burton: Big Fish'

> (www.bbc.co.uk/films/2004/01/21/tim_burton_big_fish_interview)

3. Russell, J. – 'Tim Burton: Big Fish'

> (www.bbc.co.uk/films/2004/01/21/tim_burton_big_fish_interview)

4. Simon, B. – 'A Whimsical Reconciliation' (www.ent-today.com/covers/cover121903)

5. Toscano, T. – 'Big Fish' (2003) (Talking Pictures, US)

6. Travers, P. – 'Big Fish' (*Rolling Stone*, 20th November 2003)

7. Utichi, J. – Review – Big Fish (www.filmfocus.co.uk/review.asp?ReviewID=14)

8. Harmon, R. – 'Glitz Doesn't Faze Finney' (*Montgomery Advertiser*, 26th January 2003, US)

9. Topel, F. – 'Tim Burton Reels in Big Fish' (http://filmforce.ign.com/articles/442/442609)

10. Russell, J. – 'Tim Burton: Big Fish'

> (www.bbc.co.uk/films/2004/01/21/tim_burton_big_fish_interview)

11. Simon, B. – 'A Whimsical Reconciliation' (www.ent-today.com/covers/cover121903)

12. Harmon, R. – 'A Vision Comes to Life' (*Montgomery Advertiser*, 14th January 2003, US)

13. Topel, F. – 'Tim Burton Reels in Big Fish' (http://filmforce.ign.com/articles/442/442609)

14. Blackwelder, R. – 'Hook, Line & Sinker' (www.splicedwire.com/03reviews/bigfish)

15. Harmon, R. – 'Glitz Doesn't Faze Finney' (*Montgomery Advertiser*, 26th January 2003, US)

16. Fraga, K. (ed.) – *Tim Burton Interviews*, p.51 (University Press of Mississippi, 2005, US)

17. Harmon, R. – 'A Vision Comes to Life' (*Montgomery Advertiser*, 14th January 2003, US)

18. Simon, B. – 'A Whimsical Reconciliation' (www.ent-today.com/covers/cover121903)

References

Wallace, D. Big Fish: A Novel of Mythic Proportions (Pocket Books 2003, UK)

13. Charlie and the Chocolate Factory

'I wouldn't give up my family for anything,
not for all the chocolate in the world'
— Charlie Bucket

Charlie and the Chocolate Factory was based on a story of the same name written in 1964 by Roald Dahl. Released in 2005, it was the second film Tim Burton had directed which was a remake of a previous work, the first having been *Planet of the Apes*. The first film version of Dahl's book was Mel Stuart's 1971 film *Willy Wonka and the Chocolate Factory*, which wasn't particularly successful at the box office at the time, but has gained considerably in popularity over the years.

This was the second film treatment of a Dahl book that Burton had been involved with. He also co-produced *James and the Giant Peach* (1996), which was directed by his friend Henry Selick, and, like two of Burton's own films, is a feature-length stop motion animation.

The story of *Charlie and the Chocolate Factory* has a very strong moral and emotional core. The moral backbone concerns ideas of good behaviour in children. Charlie Bucket is the model child who is both loving and obedient and comes from a warm and caring family. This is in contrast to the other children in the story. Though their parents are undoubtedly loving, their love is flawed. For example, the love of Veruca

Salt's parents causes them to spoil her rotten.

Emotional weight is given to the narrative because of audience empathy with Charlie, created by images of Charlie's family and their poverty-stricken existence. We feel sorry for him and wish Charlie the best, hoping that his family will come upon easier times. This means we become emotionally attached to him and also to a good outcome for the Buckets.

As with *Batman Returns*, this movie begins with the Warner Brothers logo in snowfall to the sounds of Danny Elfman's score, giving us three Burton trademarks within the first few seconds of the movie.

It is this film that most clearly illustrates why Burton likes to use snow in so many of his creations. The

> **Ultimate Quote**
>
> 'What I love about the book is Dahl's writing. That's why I wanted to do it' – Tim Burton[1]

magical, almost mystical quality of snowfall is accentuated by the wonderment most of us felt when we were children and saw snow falling and covering the world we knew, creating a new, pure landscape removed from everyday reality. In *Charlie and the Chocolate Factory* the image of snow is used very effectively to increase the fairy tale feel and the magic of the movie.

The chocolate factory itself, which is first introduced during the snowfall in the title sequence, was created by talented production designer Alex McDowell who had already worked with Johnny Depp on *Fear and Loathing in Las Vegas* (Gilliam, 1998), and Helena Bonham Carter on *Fight Club* (Fincher, 1999). The film's vast sets took over nearly all of Pinewood Studios in London and included a 270 foot river containing 200,000 gallons of fake chocolate.

Wonka's factory is a Burtonesque trademark and is akin

to the Maitlands' house in *Beetlejuice,* Bruce Wayne's mansion in the *Batman* films, Edward Scissorhands' mansion looming above suburbia in the film of the same name, and the Blooms' house in *Big Fish.* It is the symbolic fairy tale castle upon a hill. It looms over the town about it, just like the dark mansion in Scissorhands. Its stark appearance is set in direct contrast with Charlie's family home, a run-down cottage which has seen much better days and in which not only he and his parents live, but also all four of his grandparents. This house is not only dilapidated, it is also wonky, much like Jenny's house in *Big Fish* and the afterworld corridors in Beetlejuice. The cottage is also both expressionist and reminiscent of a dwelling from a fairy tale, the kind of place you'd expect to find three bears or seven dwarves living in. Another important element in regards to both the cottage and its inhabitants is that Burton has created them as the original book describes, staying true to Dahl's words.

When the five winners of golden tickets first go to the factory entrance with the family members who have been chosen to accompany them we see a mechanical welcoming show. This show is happy, bright, and colourful, but ends in flames. This implies that though everything at the factory seems bright and cheery, there is a hidden darkness. Though this sequence isn't in Dahl's book it is a very effective prelude to the vibrant yet sinister nature of the chocolate factory.

This mixture of both light and dark elements is seen in every room visited during the factory tour. They each appear to be fantastic, wonderful places, but this feeling is soon juxtaposed with a darker undertone when each of the four dislikeable children meets their doom. In Burton's film this can be seen to reflect the darker side of Willy Wonka's personality. He is suspicious thanks to people previously stealing his recipes, tormented because of his father's abandonment,

> **Ultimate Fact**
>
> Roald Dahl was so angered by 1971 film version of his story that he refused to sign over sequel rights to the next book, *Charlie and the Great Glass Elevator.*

and socially maladjusted, as can be seen in his inability to relate to those on his tour. This mix of light and dark also implies that even when things are good, if you are bad then you cannot (or will not) appreciate the goodness in them.

All five children who win golden tickets display different traits, as do their relations. Augustus Gloop shows greed and is sucked up a huge, chocolate vacuum cleaner. Violet Beauregard shows an over-competitive nature, encouraged by her mother. She also displays arrogance and over-confidence until she eventually expands into an overblown blueberry. Veruca Salt is arrogant and extremely spoilt, her parents helping to create such an obnoxious child, and this nature causes her downfall in the nut sorting room in the factory. Mike Teavee is destructive, forceful and rude, and eventually meets his doom by being shrunk when transmitted by televisual means.

Finally there is Charlie Bucket. He shares a special bond with one of his grandparents in particular. This is Grandpa Joe, who tells Charlie stories about Wonka and the time when he worked for him in the chocolate factory. The strength of their relationship is highlighted when on Charlie's birthday

Grandpa Joe is prepared to part with his secret treasure, a single coin, which is a small fortune to the Buckets. He does this in order to try and make Charlie's wish of finding a golden ticket come true, his primary concern being his grandson's happiness.

> ### Ultimate Fact
>
> In 2005 Warner Bros. set a film industry record with three films grossing over $200 million each in the USA alone. These were *Charlie and the Chocolate Factory*, *Batman Begins* (Nolan) and *Harry Potter and the Goblet of Fire* (Newell).

Charlie displays a sweetness and general goodness which makes him stand out from the other children. This is clearly intentional as he is the child which all audience members can see deserves to win the competition. When the other children are dispatched there is no pity for them because we can equally see that they deserve their fates.

Of special note are the songs sung when each of the four unpleasant children meet their end. These are actually based on ones that Roald Dahl wrote in the original book, though the choice of musical style and harmonics was down to Burton and Elfman. Because each song has an individual sound they can be easily identified as belonging to the relevant children's departing moments. The first, Augustus Gloop's, shows a Bombay influence and the second has a 1970s funk feel, occurring after Violet has become a human blueberry. The third song occurs after Veruca Salt's departure and is influenced by 60s psychedelia.

The fourth and final song which is sung after Mike Teavee has been shrunk is worth particular mention. It is influenced by The Beatles and Queen's 'Bohemian Rhapsody'. In the same scenes which take place in the transmitting room we see the use of music from Stanley Kubrick's *2001: A Space*

Odyssey (1968) when the bar of chocolate is transmitted. This is humorously linked to the pictures on the TV screen where the bar materialises, which are from that highly acclaimed film, the bar taking the place of the black monolith as the apes jump around its base, confused and disoriented by its presence. Also apparent in these scenes is a reference to Alfred Hitchcock's film classic *Psycho* (1960).

The above elements display a direct pop-culture referencing not usually present in Burton's films. This is a post-modern aspect of this movie, one which possibly reflects the fact that this film is aimed at both children and adults as these pop-culture references are not likely to be recognised by children, but can be enjoyed by the adults accompanying them.

The chocolate factory can be seen as a reflection of Willy Wonka's mind. It is closed off, reflecting Wonka's introverted nature. Inside it is bright and colourful, though also somewhat mysterious, like the character's eccentricity coupled with his aloofness. There is also a darker side to the factory and in Wonka this can be seen in his relationship with his father and the mental anguish it has caused him. Further to this, the factory is a sprawling place filled with strange rooms, which is akin to Wonka's strange mind.

Like Edward Scissorhands, Willy Wonka (also played by Johnny Depp) is said to live alone in the expansive factory, though we discover this isn't actually the case when we are introduced to the Oompa-Loompas. Also like Edward, in Burton's version of this story Wonka is distanced from his

> **Ultimate Fact**
>
> Burton and Depp worked on *Charlie and the Chocolate Factory* and *Corpse Bride* at the same time in London, spending the day on the first film and then going to work on the second in the evenings.

father, though not through death. This element also creates a link with Bruce Wayne in *Batman*. He lost his parents when only a boy, and this is the same point at which Wonka is abandoned by his father. This father-son estrangement also links this film with *Big Fish*, in which the defining relationship is that of a father and his estranged son.

Such an estrangement is reflected in Burton's own life. He and his father had a strained, sporadic relationship, which perhaps explains why the backstory of Wonka and his father was added into this film (it did not feature in either the original book or the earlier film version). Wonka's personal distance from his father is intimated by his inability to say the word 'parents' when first meeting his visitors. It is also shown when he has a momentary flashback. During this brief instant of what appears to be mild madness he says a number of words which all apply to fatherhood. His disturbed expression and words clearly show that there is something wrong in regards to his relationship with his father.

Visual flashbacks are later used to illustrate this strained relationship. We learn that Wonka's father was a dentist who frowned upon the eating of chocolate and who is very effectively played by Christopher Lee, who many will equate with the role of Saruman in the amazing *Lord of the Rings* trilogy (Jackson) and who also had a small role as Burgomaster in *Sleepy Hollow*.

This backstory gives Wonka additional depth and creates a stronger bond between him and Charlie when the boy helps to reunite him with his father.

Flashbacks are also used to show Wonka's worldwide reputation as a maker of chocolate with a particular story about an Indian prince asking for a palace to be built out of the confectionary. They also give us the backstory of where the Oompa-Loompas came from, an episode in which Depp adds to the excellent oddity of his performance when speaking in sign language to the leader of the little people.

Another personal bond between director and narrative beyond that of the father-son estrangement is created through Charlie's relationship with his grandparents when he was young. As a child, Burton moved out of his family home and went to live with his grandmother, the two of them sharing a much closer bond than he did with his parents. This kind of closeness is seen in the Bucket family between Charlie and his grandparents, although he also has a loving relationship with his parents.

The Bucket family's situation is one in which wealth does not feature. Mr Bucket has been made redundant and the family are clearly struggling. However, the family members get on well and clearly share a strong bond of love, something which contrasts with Willy Wonka's lack of family and estrangement from his father.

This difference accentuates both the warmth of the Bucket family and the coldness of Wonka's lonely existence in the vast factory. In this sense the film's message is highlighted early on. This message is concerned with the importance of having a family, but not just any family, one which is warm and loving. It urges us to make the most of our families when we have the chance for, like Wonka, we never know when they will be gone.

Another comparison clearly evident is that between the outside world and the interior of the factory. The former has the same colour muted look that is evident in *Sleepy Hollow*, with nothing being particularly bright. However, the latter is bright and cheery, its colourfulness reflecting that seen in *Mars Attacks!*. The difference between the two creates a strong sense of the surreal and magical when it comes to the factory's interior, something which is clearly intentional and which aids the narrative in making Wonka's domain a fantastical place removed from the everyday reality.

The transition from the 'real' world to the fantastical interior of the factory is much like that of the 1939 classic *The Wizard of Oz* (Fleming). That movie begins in black and white, but when Dorothy finds herself in Oz with Toto the colour is riotous in a very similar way to Burton's film once we enter Wonka's factory. This link is rather apt as *The Wizard of Oz* was also a modern fairy tale, and one which reflects Burton's penchant for darkness with the existence of the wicked witch of the west and her nasty minions.

Linked to this transition from the outer world to the inner one is the opening of doors, an act which is prevalent in *Charlie and the Chocolate Factory*. This especially occurs inside the factory itself, each of the spectacular rooms being hidden behind doors of various kinds. Burton has said, 'I like the opening of doors,'[3] and this is because they can lead to new experiences and new sights, and are symbolic of moving on, of passing from the past into the future. They also have a certain mystery in that you don't know what's on the other side until they're open.

> **Ultimate Fact**
>
> When it comes to confectionary, Tim Burton has stated that he prefers 'dark, bitter chocolate.'[4]

There is a great deal of humour evident in the movie which derives from the book, the script, and the great performances. The nut sorting room filled with squirrels is amusing and was in the original book, though it was omitted from the 1971 film and replaced with a room where geese laid golden eggs. There are real squirrels in the room which were especially trained for the movie and these are mixed with puppets and computer generated versions. These little nut munchers actually freaked Burton out and he described them as being 'like rats on speed, so quick and so strange.'[5]

Another element of the film's humour can be seen in regards to an Oompa-Loompa who has eaten hair toffee and is now a walking carpet, the latter element added in the script. Depp's performance as Willy Wonka tops all the book and script elements off perfectly, his expressions and statements often highly amusing. Examples include when Violet's mother gives him the eye and he quickly gets everyone to board the river boat with an expression of mild dread on his face and when Mr Salt asks him if uses the Havermax 4000 to do the nut sorting, to which Wonka chuckles and says, 'No, you're really weird' in his strange voice, a great moment.

Wonka displays a trait common to all of Burton's main characters, and this is alienation, something which Charlie also displays on a social level beyond the warmth of his family. Wonka is alone in a family and social sense while also being very different from ordinary people due to his strange behaviour and aloofness. He is also introverted, like Bruce Wayne and Edward Scissorhands, hiding away in his factory with only the Oompa-Loompas for company.

Wonka is in some ways like Tim Burton and this reflection of the director in one of his main characters can be seen in numerous other movies he has made, such as with Vincent in the short of the same name and Lydia in *Beetlejuice*. Wonka is introverted and communicates visually to a great extent through his expressions and the rooms of his factory, which are an expression of his creative imagination. He has trouble communicating verbally with the guests, especially early on when they first arrive at the factory and begin their tour.

Finally, the link between Burton and Wonka is underscored by the strained father-son relationship experienced by both of them and their undeniable creativity.

The role of Willy Wonka was Johnny Depp's fourth in a Burton film, and that's not counting the provision of a character's voice in *Corpse Bride*. He was the first choice for the role and Burton said 'it was the first time the studio brought his name up before I did.'[6] Depp follows in the footsteps of Gene Wilder, who played Wonka in Stuart's version of Dahl's book. Though Depp hasn't got the same mildly insane sparkle in his eyes that Wilder had, he certainly fits the role with his odd portrayal.

On the whole critics were positive about Depp's casting and acting. Peter Travers of *Rolling Stone* described Depp's take on Wonka as 'deliciously demented,'[8] and it is certainly the case that his portrayal of the king of chocolate is touched with a great deal more self-absorbed madness than Wilder's. Peter Bradshaw of *The Guardian* stated, 'Johnny Depp is terrific casting as Wonka,'[9] and BBC reviewer Stella Paramichael commented, 'straight away it's clear that Wonka is a few fondants short of a whole box.'[10]

> **Ultimate Quote**
>
> 'One of the things Tim and I share is a kind of fascination with people, with human beings... Most people are really nuts and that's fascinating to watch, you know?' – Johnny Depp[7]

Some have compared the way he plays the role with the pop star Michael Jackson, though there was no intentional link. Burton and Depp discussed how Wonka should act and the final result is based on children's TV presenters Depp grew up watching, all of whom displayed weirdness and craziness to varying degrees. This is mixed with a take on game-show hosts, which includes the 'all-important, positive smile,' as Depp himself put it.[11] As for the Jackson link, Burton puts that to bed very simply by stating, 'there's a big difference: Michael Jackson likes children, Willy Wonka *can't stand them.*'[12]

Other actors appearing for further outings in Burton films include Helena Bonham Carter and Deep Roy, who appeared in *Big Fish* as one of the circus troupe. In *Charlie and the Chocolate Factory* Bonham Carter plays Charlie's loving mother and Deep Roy has a multiple role as all of the Oompa-Loompas. There is also the reappearance of Missi Pyle playing Violet Beauregard's mother after having played Mildred, one of the townspeople of Spectre in *Big Fish*.

There are a number of other performances of special note. Noah Taylor is great alongside Helena Bonham Carter as Charlie's poverty stricken father, and all four grandparents are played excellently, especially in the case of Grandpa Joe, played by Irish actor David Kelly. Christopher Lee displays his usual brilliance as the daunting and domineering father of Wonka and the parents accompanying the children are also well suited to their roles, James Fox being of particular note as the rich and snooty Mr Salt.

The children's acting has been roundly praised. Freddie Highmore, starring as Charlie, had already working alongside Depp in *Finding Neverland* (Forster, 2004) and has described his much older co-star as 'fantastic,' going on to add, 'he's better than chocolate. He's a really special person and he treats everyone as equal, and I think that's a really good thing.'[13] This admiration is two-way, Depp saying of Highmore that his acting abilities are 'endless' and 'he's super talented.'[14]

This film when compared with the original version is much more of a fairy tale. Elfman's score aids greatly in this, creating additional emotion and suspense. This latter point is important because even though we know Charlie finds a golden ticket we still feel tense and have our eyes glued to the screen to see what will happen when he opens the chocolate bars. This shows not only the power of Dahl's story, but also the script (by *Big Fish* screenwriter John August), the music and Burton's intimate and visually compelling directing.

> **Ultimate Fact**
>
> Freddie Highmore was on holiday at the Grand Canyon when he received the news that he'd got the part of Charlie and his first reaction was, 'Yes! I'm going to get to work with Johnny again.'[15]

Freddie Highmore has said he believes Burton's film is better than Stuart's for one principle reason; that 'Charlie's kept more pure and he doesn't drink a bubbly solution and laugh to the roof.'[16] The scenes he refers to in the original film do not exist in the book and put Charlie in the same bracket as the other children, ignoring Wonka's instructions and misbehaving. This was a major flaw in the 1971 movie as Charlie and Grandpa Joe should have been shown the exit because of this transgression, something which has been highlighted in an amusing parody of the movie in an episode of the cult cartoon series 'Family Guy' called 'Wasted Talent.'

Burton's version of the book had the full support of Roald Dahl's widow, Felicity, who has said she believes this is what her late husband would have wanted to see on screen. Burton and Felicity also worked together when they produced *James and the Giant Peach*.[17]

When Burton's movie is compared with Dahl's book we find it follows the tale much more closely than the 1971 version, which deviates a great deal from the original story through such things as additional songs and scenes. As Tim Burton said, 'our goal…was to try and be a little more true to the spirit of the book.'[18] We can see this to be the case with elements such as the Oompa-Loompas' backstory being followed almost to the letter, the Chocolate Room appearing just as described, and the other rooms resembling their book descriptions pretty closely. It is also evident in the behaviour of most of the characters and especially in the case of Charlie.

However, there are some major differences. In the book Willy Wonka is happy to see the children and is able to say the word 'parents', as he was in the first film. Gene Wilder's depiction of Wonka is also much closer to Dahl's original vision, being energetic, friendly, quirky, and having blue, sparkling eyes. This said, both films contain Oompa-Loompas which are greatly removed from the description in the book, which states that they have rosy-white skin, golden-brown hair, and wear deerskins and leaves.[19]

Possibly the biggest difference between Burton's movie and the book comes at the end of the film. This is connected to Wonka's backstory, which, as has already been stated, doesn't exist in Dahl's story. The book ends with Charlie, Grandpa Joe, and Wonka putting the rest of the Bucket family into the glass elevator after it has crashed through the roof of the cottage and taking them back to live in the factory. In the film this doesn't occur immediately and what we see instead is the necessary conclusion of Wonka's backstory when he is reunited with his father by Charlie, who had refused to go and live in the factory because Wonka wasn't including his family in the invitation.

Though Burton's ending isn't as concise and does feel a little rambling, it does suit his personal approach to his films in that it gives closure to the father-son relationship that creates an emotional bond between the director and the narrative. This end also seems to reflect his time spent at Disney with the emphasis put on the importance of family in the movie's sugary sweet closing scenes and final words of the narrator.

This narrator, an Oompa-Loompa, links the film to both the short film *Vincent* and *Big Fish*, which both employ narration to differing degrees. It is this narrator that creates a small example of postmodern circularity in that he speaks at the start and end of the story, which is similar to the elderly Kim speaking at the beginning and end of *Edward Scissorhands*.

As for going on to film the sequel, *Charlie and the Great Glass Elevator*, Burton has said, 'No, and you can count on that from me,'[20] although we must remember that he did say the same thing about doing a *Batman* follow-up. Whether or not he goes on to do another film about the adventures of Charlie Bucket, what we have in *Charlie and the Chocolate Factory* is a fantastical fairy tale, one complete with a happy ending, and with a moral message, unlike many of Hollywood's offerings for younger audiences.

With this film Tim Burton not only scored another big hit at the box office, but he created a classic piece of heart-warming entertainment, as did screenwriter John August, production designer Alex McDowell, Danny Elfman, the rest of the film's crew, and the superb cast who helped draw us into a wonderful story that shows us happiness isn't found in things, it's found in people.

Endnotes

1. Head, S. (int.) – Interview: Tim Burton (http:filmforce.ign.com/articles/632/632453)

2. Utichi, J. – 'Burton's London as Charlie Premieres'
    (www.filmfocus.co.uk/newsdetail.asp?NewsID=347)

3. Smith, G. (int.) – 'Tim Burton Interviewed by Gavin Smith'
    (http://minadream.com/timburton/EdWoodInterview)

4. Turan, K. – 'Charlie and the Chocolate Factory'
    (www.calendarlive.com/movies/turan.cl-et-charlie15jul15,0,150671.story)

5. Unknown – 'Tim Burton'
    (http://entertainment.timesonline.co.uk/article/0,,14931-1695710_3,00)

6. Utichi, J. – 'Burton's London as Charlie Premieres'
    (www.filmfocus.co.uk/newsdetail.asp?NewsID=347)

7. Lee, P. (int.) – 'Tim Burton and Johnny Depp Whip up a Weird Confection in Charlie and
    the Chocolate Factory' (www.scifi.com/sfw/issue430/interview)

8. Travers, P. – 'Charlie and the Chocolate Factory' (www.rollingstone.com)

9. Bradshaw, P. – 'Charlie and the Chocolate Factory' (*The Guardian*, 29th July 2005, UK)

10. Papamichael, S. – 'Charlie and the Chocolate Factory'
    (www.bbc.co.uk/films/2005/07/18/charlie_and_the_chocolate_factory_2005_review)

11. Lee, P. (int.) – 'Tim Burton and Johnny Depp Whip up a Weird Confection in Charlie and
    the Chocolate Factory' (www.scifi.com/sfw/issue430/interview)

12. Head, S. (int.) – Interview: Tim Burton (http:filmforce.ign.com/articles/632/632453)

13. Lee, P. (int.) – 'Tim Burton and Johnny Depp Whip up a Weird Confection in Charlie and
    the Chocolate Factory' (www.scifi.com/sfw/issue430/interview)

14. Lee, P. (int.) – 'Tim Burton and Johnny Depp Whip up a Weird Confection in Charlie and
    the Chocolate Factory' (www.scifi.com/sfw/issue430/interview)

15. Lee, P. (int.) – 'Tim Burton and Johnny Depp Whip up a Weird Confection in Charlie and
    the Chocolate Factory' (www.scifi.com/sfw/issue430/interview)

16. Lee, P. (int.) – 'Tim Burton and Johnny Depp Whip up a Weird Confection in Charlie and
    the Chocolate Factory' (www.scifi.com/sfw/issue430/interview)

17. Unknown – 'Tim Burton'
    (http://entertainment.timesonline.co.uk/article/0,,14931-1695710_3,00)

18. Head, S. (int.) – Interview: Tim Burton (http:filmforce.ign.com/articles/632/632453)

19. Dahl, R. – *Charlie and the Chocolate Factory*, pp.101-102 (Puffin Books, 2001, UK)

20. Head, S. (int.) – Interview: Tim Burton (http:filmforce.ign.com/articles/632/632453)

References

Keller, L. – Charlie and the Chocolate Factory

> (www.urbancinefile.com.au/home/view.asp?a=10709&s=Reviews)

Toto, C. – Dark 'Chocolate' (*The Washington Times*, 15th July 2005, U.S.A.)

Turan, K. – 'Charlie and the Chocolate Factory'

> (www.calendarlive.com/movies/turan.cl-et-charlie15jul15,0,150671.story)

Vonder Haar, P. – 'Charlie and the Chocolate Factory'

> (www.filmthreat.com/index/php?section=reviews&Id=7723)

Weinberg, S. – Charlie and the Chocolate Factory

> (www.efilmcritic.com/review.php?movie=12582&reviewer=128)

www2.warnerbros.com/main/company_info

14. Corpse Bride

'With this candle, I will light your way in darkness.
With this ring, I ask you to be mine'
– Victor Van Dort

Released in 2005 by Warner Brothers and inspired by a 19th century Russian folktale, *Corpse Bride* was the second feature length stop-motion movie that Tim Burton had been involved with and came twelve years after the release of the first; *The Nightmare Before Christmas*. It is the only film he's ever co-directed, the man chosen to ride shotgun being Mike Johnson, who had been an assistant animator on *Nightmare* and an animator on *James and the Giant Peach* (Selick, 1996). When talking about the origins of the film he said, 'the original folktale is beautiful and concise, but it's only three paragraphs long. It's about self-sacrifice and we still keep to that.' Johnson's role was handling the day-to-day work and when asked about directing puppets he responded by saying, 'it's directing animators, so there's some parallels with live action because animators are performers.'[1]

Burton oversaw the entire project while also having the final say. This influence is obvious when it comes to the superb production values of the film, ones which echo Burton's artistic background and the original sketches he drew in relation to the story, something he started working on many years before filming actually began. When it did finally start it took two years to complete using digital cameras instead of normal film. The benefits of this change were immediate; the animators were able to check each shot and then move on or delete as appropriate straight away. Because of this digital technology the quality of the picture is improved and Pixar were even convinced that it was computer generated.

As mentioned in Chapter Seven: *The Nightmare Before Christmas*, the stop-motion effects created by Ray Harryhausen have been a great influence on Burton. When interviewed about this in relation to *Corpse Bride*, he said he thinks his love of animation comes from seeing Harryhausen's work where 'his monsters had more personality than most of the actors in the movies.'[2]

Burton's use of such animation can be seen in the Disney short entitled *Vincent* and is put to good use for effects in *Beetlejuice*. He even considered using this format for *Mars Attacks!*, but computer generated effects were eventually used mainly because of the substantial reduction in production time and costs. Some of the puppets used for *Corpse Bride* cost around $30,000 each. If you also consider that there were fourteen models of the title character made and twelve each of the other two main characters, not to mention the use of over one hundred sets, you then get a small idea of the work and money that went into producing this wonderful film.

As with most of Burton's pictures the

Ultimate Fact

Tim Burton, Johnny Depp and Helena Bonham Carter visited Ray Harryhausen at his London home and then the king of stop-motion visited the set of *Corpse Bride*, production grinding to a halt and Mike Johnson describing the visit as 'definitely the highlight for me and most of the crew.'[3]

titles sequence is used to introduce us to the tone of the film. Here we see the muted colours of the world of the living, something we also saw Burton utilise in *Sleepy Hollow*. Both in that film and in this it reflects the horror content in part, though in *Corpse Bride* this is not particularly dark in tone, having more of a Roald Dahl sensibility, this being very apt considering Burton's previous release, Dahl's *Charlie and the Chocolate Factory*. The two movies were actually made at the same time in London, which is why Burton needed a co-director and was an experience that composer Danny Elfman described as 'intense,' going on to say, 'fortunately they were different styles.'[4]

> **Ultimate Fact**
> On average an animator is able to shoot around seventy frames of action per day. At twenty-four frames a second, that equals less than three seconds a day.

This was Elfman's twelfth time scoring for Burton and the third time that he had written songs and put his own voice to the lyrics. His favourite piece is the song performed by the lively bag o'bones called Bonejangles. It is entitled 'Remains The Day' and is Elfman's pick of the bunch not because it is him singing, but because of the bony instrumental break when skeletons dance and play parts of each other's bodies, Elfman stating, 'it brought me back to my love of Max Fliesher cartoons.'[5] Fliesher had created Betty Boop, and a character from that cartoon provided the inspiration for Oogie Boogie in *Nightmare*.

As well as the animation and songs, the script also helps to make this such a great movie. It was written by John August, who had already worked with Burton on *Big Fish*, Caroline Thompson, who'd penned *Edward Scissorhands* and *The Nightmare Before Christmas*, and Pamela Pettler. There was also the involvement of production designer Alex McDowell, who was another member of the team who was working on both *Corpse Bride* and *Charlie and the Chocolate Factory* at the same time, his talent helping to make both films memorable for their look as much as for their content.

When asked about directing two films at the same time Burton has stated, 'I'd never do it again.' He said it was exhausting, but that working on *Corpse Bride* in the evenings and nights gave him something else to focus on, meaning he went back to *Charlie and the Chocolate Factory* with a fresh outlook.[6] Along with Burton, Danny Elfman and Alex McDowell, there were also three cast members who were working on both movies at the same time. These were Christopher Lee, Helena Bonham Carter and Johnny Depp.

Ultimate Fact

Johnny Depp was due to sing a song for inclusion in the film, but it was cut just before he was supposed to go into the studio to record it.[7]

Returning to the muted colours and existence of the real world which we first see in the titles sequence, we soon discover that this is juxtaposed with a decidedly more vibrant and colourful Land of the Dead, something which turns usual depictions on their heads. The land of the living is loosely based on the Victorian era, its houses tightly crammed along the streets and the society tightly crammed into norms of behaviour straightjacketed by a firm class system. The afterlife is bright and vivacious, everyone mixing together and joining in with the fun. We can see that the implication is that in the real world the characters are dead, like zombies following their social codes without question, but in the Land of the Dead the inhabitants are actually more alive in a sense, free of the social boundaries they are subject to in life.

The afterlife is commonly portrayed as a dark and subdued place, certainly not a place of songs and happiness. Therefore Burton toys with usual conventions to create a more interesting narrative. This capsizing of conventions also applies when the dead rise to the world of the living. This is initially as it might be in other films; the living are frightened out of their wits and the dead seem to be threatening and malicious. However, this is soon overturned when the dead turn out to be people's beloved relatives and are reunited with the living with hugs and kisses. Not only does this show a different side to zombie invasions, it also shows children that the dead and death itself are not necessarily things to be feared.

The topic of death is of special note because it's one which is often avoided when it comes to kids. Burton ignores this unspoken rule and goes for broke in a film devoted to death, murder, devious plans, sacrifice and love both in life and beyond the grave. Instead of hiding the subject of death from children he brings it out into the open so as to dispel its taboo qualities. Therefore, unlike other adults, he doesn't talk down to children, but confronts them with one of life's realities (something he also does in *The Nightmare Before Christmas* with the idea that some things in life don't work out).

The subject of death has been seen in nine of the films discussed in this book, but not often as a main theme. For example, Martians invade and joyfully kill humans in *Mars Attacks!* and there is also plenty of blood-letting in *Planet of the Apes*. One other film where it was thematic was *Big Fish*. In *Corpse Bride* the dichotomy of life and death is made even more central than in that movie. In fact, it's important to point out that the film is actually as much about life as it is death. The zombie-like existence of the living is shown to be unnecessary when juxtaposed with the liberty found in the afterlife, a liberty which we could experience while still alive if we were prepared to rid ourselves of class divisions and enjoy life while we have the chance.

When Burton was asked about the subject of death in the film he talked about how our society looks on it as a dark subject, but societies like that in Mexico see it in a more positive light. He has also said that his fascination with the undead stems from growing up in Burbank, which was essentially a place filled with living zombies.[8] Helena Bonham Carter has commented that the film is 'about death, but it's an immensely hopeful outlook.'[9] This hopefulness is created by the idea that we may be reunited with those we love and care for when we pass on, that they are waiting for us and such feelings can last beyond the grave.

As well as the muted tone of the 'real' world, the titles also introduce us to Victor Van Dort, the lead character who shares his first name with the boy in *Frankenweenie*. The link between these two characters goes further than mere names as both are connected with undead sidekicks of sorts. In Burton's Disney short the lead's reanimated companion was a dog called Sparky. In this movie it is the character referenced by the title, the *Corpse Bride*, whose name is Emily and whose voice is provided by Helena Bonham Carter in her fourth role in one of his films, though he has said that he'd originally wanted her for the role of Victoria. Bonham Carter had to audition for her part

> **Ultimate Quote**
>
> 'They [kids] love the dark side and wicked side of things. All the ancient fairy tales have been scary and dark. There's nothing new in that' – Helena Bonham Carter[10]

like anyone else and says of appearing in Burton's work, 'of course I have to be right for something otherwise it would be appalling.'[11]

Victor is given his voice by Johnny Depp in his fifth Burton role and the puppet bares a resemblance to the star even though it was made a year before he became part of the project. Despite Depp being involved in less than half of Burton's films the actor has become synonymous with the director's work, mainly because the characters he has portrayed have been so memorable and well acted. In *Corpse Bride* Depp's shy and awkward stuttering matches Victor's character perfectly, which is given a clear delicate and creative nature at the outset when he is shown sketching a butterfly and then setting his subject free, having kept it safely inside a glass jar.

> **Ultimate Quote**
>
> 'I definitely like working with the same person twice – and three times and four times – particularly if they're Tim' – Helena Bonham Carter[12]

The fact that Depp does such a great job of giving Victor a suitable verbal persona is no mean feat when we discover that he basically conjured up this characterisation in around fifteen minutes while he and Burton were making their way from the set of *Charlie and the Chocolate Factory* to the recording studio. As he has said, 'you could imagine my surprise when, as I was very, very focused on Wonka, Tim arrives on set and says, "Hey, you know, maybe tonight we'll go and record some of *Corpse Bride*."'[13] In relation to this quick change from one character to another and Depp's ability to find a sense of who Victor was in such a short space of time, Burton stated, 'great thing is he likes to work spontaneously...and really in that one session he got it.'[14]

Victor is being railroaded into a marriage of convenience,

social convenience in the case of his *nouveaux riches* parents and financial convenience in the case of his live bride, Victoria Everglot. Because of his bumbling characterisation Victor loosely resembles Ichabod Crane, therefore creating another link with *Sleepy Hollow*. Like all the main characters in Burton's films, Victor is not a hero. In the finale his life is saved by the intervention of Emily's body, much like the intervention of Katrina Van Tassel's book in saving Ichabod Crane in *Sleepy Hollow*. Then the villain of the tale, Lord Barkis Bittern, finds his doom by accident, not by intent, rather like the Joker in *Batman*.

> **Ultimate Quote**
>
> 'I love him [Depp] because he's basically like a character actor in a leading man's body... He's always looking for a new challenge' – Tim Burton[15]

Lord Barkis, played by Richard E. Grant, has a great sense of malevolent evil, the kind you'd expect from a villain in what is essentially a children's fairy tale. The same kind of obvious evilness is evident in such characters as Cruella De Vil in *101 Dalmatians* (Herek, 1996), and the Wicked Witch of the West in *The Wizard of Oz* (Fleming, 1939). This, far from reducing suspense, helps to heighten it when coupled with the fact that other characters don't seem to notice and we wonder how Victor will manage to put an end to the Lord's macabre and greed-motivated machinations. Thus, knowing who the villain is increases enjoyment of the narrative.

Even the minor characters in this film are a treat to behold. Pastor Galswells, played by Christopher Lee in his third Burton role, is gloriously menacing and authoritarian, his voice adding a great deal of weight to both of these characteristics and his on-screen presence. The regular Burtonite Deep Roy provides the voice of General Bonesapart, one of numerous dead characters in the afterworld who enjoy jazz-styled song and dance routines. Most of the servants we see display the simple, but very effective touch of having their backs bent after years of servitude, this adding to the overall tone of the class system evident in the 'real' world. The butler to the Everglot household, called Mayhew, is perfect as the upper-crust servant with his exaggerated nose permanently upturned as he regards everyone with an air of superiority.

An element of exaggeration is evident throughout the film, which is described by one critic as 'another of Burton's evocations of German Expressionism.'[16] It is apparent in most of Burton's films and underscores the expressionist elements which are again evident in this work, including the angst of all three main characters; Victor, Victoria, and Emily, the Corpse Bride.

Both Victor and Victoria are alienated by their enforced betrothal. They find themselves trapped and with little hope of getting out of the situation created by their parents. Difficult parents can be seen in all of Burton's films other than *Ed Wood*. In *Corpse Bride* it is both parents of both characters who try to force their will on their children. However, rather fortuitously, the young couple fall for each other during a scene which is glorious in its sensuous simplicity. This scene involves Victor playing a tune on a piano in the grand entranceway of the

> **Ultimate Quote**
>
> 'What I love about stop-motion animation is that it's so tactile. There's something wonderful about being able to physically touch and move the characters and to see their world actually exist' – Tim Burton[17]

Everglots' home, a tune which becomes his theme throughout the rest of the film. Victoria hears and sees him playing and the beauty of this creative act forges a connection between them. This is reminiscent of a similarly beautiful scene in the French film *Betty Blue* (Beineix, 1986) in which two characters communicate their feelings through the piano.

This scene demonstrates Burton using creativity and creative acts to bring people together – a device that can be seen in his other works. In *Beetlejuice* it is the simplicity of decorating a house for the Maitlands. In *Edward Scissorhands* the title character's creative skills not only brought him to the attention of the suburbanites, but also allowed him to express his feelings and created a special bond between Edward and Kim. *Ed Wood* showed the creativity of film writing and directing, one which was a driving force despite the bad reception the director's films received and which brought an oddball group of people together.

> **Ultimate Fact**
>
> Bar Albert Finney and Joanna Lumley, who provided the voices for Mr and Mrs Everglot, the actors did not work together, but had stand-ins reading other parts.

As far as *Charlie and the Chocolate Factory* is concerned, we see the confectionary creativity of Willy Wonka, one that brings him and Charlie close in their shared love of chocolate.

Playing on a piano also brings Victor and Emily back together after her disappointment at finding him with Victoria. The simplicity and beauty of music again unites him with a woman, though this one has a habit of falling apart. In this way Emily is similar to Sally in *The Nightmare Before Christmas*. Both can come apart, though for different reasons. This displays the idea that we all consist of different parts in a very overt way.

As with *The Nightmare Before Christmas* Burton uses an

announcer as part of the narrative structure. In *Nightmare* this role was conducted by Halloween Town's mayor and in *Corpse Bride* there is a town crier who announces Victor's misfortunes to the world.

Also creating a link with *Nightmare* is Scraps, the skeletal dog. He is reminiscent of Zero, the ghost dog, while also continuing the common use of dogs in Burton's films. Other elements seen in both *Corpse Bride* and *The Nightmare Before Christmas* include a full moon, a wood, coffins and a graveyard, this latter location appearing for the ninth time out of twelve films. All of these reflect the aesthetics of Burton's live action movies, especially in the construction of a dreamlike world with a sense of both the magical and the mysterious. The coffins in particular are used to great effect to increase the deathly theme of the underworld.

However, there is one noticeable difference between this movie and *The Nightmare Before Christmas*. The musical content is much reduced, down from ten songs to six. These songs feel much more integrated into the narrative, less obvious and shorter in general. Also, befitting the atmosphere of the land of the living, all the songs taking place in the 'real' world are sedate in comparison with the

> **Ultimate Quote**
>
> 'I've always been an admirer of Danny [Elfman] and his music – I just think he has genius – but he's a real modest man' – Helena Bonham Carter[18]

good old knees up which takes place when Victor first finds himself in the underworld.

Adding further to the Burton heritage of this film is Elder Gutknecht's home, which sits high above the surrounding landscape, reflecting the position of living quarters seen in all Burton's films other than *Ed Wood*. The Martians in *Mars*

Attacks! are the most extreme example of this as they live high above the Earth. It is also noteworthy that Michael Gough provides the voice for Gutknecht and played Notary James Hardenbrook in *Sleepy Hollow*, both characters which are connected with books and learning.

The humour is suitably dark for a Burton film and much of it revolves around the theme of death, as it did in *Beetlejuice* and *Sleepy Hollow*. The scenes in the Land of the Dead are injected with a good dose of humour, much of which is displayed by the bunch of lively denizens. These include the aforementioned Bonesapart, who has been driven through with a sword which still remains in place. There is also a character with a cannon ball hole through his torso and a man with a knife stuck in his head. However, probably the funniest of all is the head waiter, who is just that; a severed head, something which creates another connection with *Sleepy Hollow*.

The character of Emily also supplies humour because she is coupled with a maggot that lives inside her brain and makes wise cracks in his Peter Lorre-like voice (Lorre having starred in such films as *Casablanca* [Curtiz, 1942]) and the 1930s series of Mr Moto movies). This Emily/Maggot pairing shows Burton's enjoyment of juxtaposing humour with horror, something which is seen especially in *The Nightmare Before Christmas* and *Sleepy Hollow*. Here we find that, despite the fact that Maggot is living inside Emily's brain, the situation and his words are amusing even though this would normally be a rather gruesome scenario.

One of Bonham Carter's favourite scenes is when Maggot, whose voice is provided by Enn Reitel, pops Emily's eye out. When speaking about the little wriggly creature using her character's brain as a bedchamber she said, 'I think we all have maggots, you know? They don't necessarily pop out, but…mine certainly chats away.'[19] In essence she is suggesting that we all have voices inside our heads, – which are more often depicted as a little angel and a little devil in cartoons. In this case Maggot represents both entwined into one.

Taken in this context, Maggot and Emily can also be seen to represent a duality, which is also evident in Burton characters such as Bruce Wayne/Batman and Selina Kyle/Catwoman. A much more obvious example of duality within *Corpse Bride* is related to a character in The Land of the Dead who has been sliced right down the middle. Both of these examples display Burton's assertion that we all have different sides to our personalities, something evident in the simple fact that we have public and private personas.

> **Ultimate Quote**
>
> 'It's a terribly romantic notion that we're going to meet the people that we miss and the people that have gone before us' – Helena Bonham Carter[20]

Corpse Bride is ultimately a love story underpinned by sacrifice. Emily essentially sacrificed her life for love and Victor is prepared to give his life for her, despite his true love being Victoria. Unlike *The Nightmare Before Christmas* and a number of Burton's other films, this one does have a happy ending as Victor and Victoria are brought together and Emily's murderer pays for his crime with his own demise (something which isn't done in a revengeful manner as Lard Barkis dies accidentally).

Critics greeted this film with enthusiasm and their expectations, created by *Nightmare*, were more than matched by this piece of delightful entertainment. 'The animation is astounding, and the story and characters are just as compelling,' said one reviewer,[21] another stating, 'this film shows that Tim Burton doesn't just have a way with live actors, but with stop-motion ones as well.'[22] Both echo the sentiments of many in regards to this amazing and touching film about love, life, and death without fear.

Endnotes

1. Epstein, D.R. (int.) – Mike Johnson (Co-Director)

    (www.ugo.com/channels/filmtv/features/corpsebride/johnson)

2. Murray, R. (int.) – 'Filmmaker Tim Burton Discusses His "Corpse Bride"'

    (http://movies.about.com/od/thecorpsebride/a/corpsetb092005_2)

3. Epstein, D.R. (int.) – Mike Johnson (Co-Director)

    (www.ugo.com/channels/filmtv/features/corpsebride/johnson)

4. Aames, E. (int.) – 'Danny Elfman on "The Corpse Bride"'

    (www.cinecon.com/news.php?id=0509192)

5. Wilson, S. (int.) – 'Corpse Bride' – Interviews From the Toronto Film Festival

    (http://horror.about.com/od/movierelated/a/int_corpse)

6. Unknown – Tim Burton

    (http://entertainment.timesonline.co.uk/aticle/0,,14931-1695710_3,00)

7. Wilson, S. (int.) – 'Corpse Bride' – Interviews From the Toronto Film Festival

    (http://horror.about.com/od/movierelated/a/int_corpse)

8. Murray, R. (int.) – 'Filmmaker Tim Burton Discusses His "Corpse Bride"'

    (http://movies.about.com/od/thecorpsebride/a/corpsetb092005_2)

9. Fischer, P. (int.) – Bonham Carter Plays Dead

    (www.filmmonthly.com/Profiles/Articles/HelenaBonhamCarterCorpseBride)

10. Aames, E. – 'Helena Bonham Carter on "The Corpse Bride"'

    (www.cinecon.com/news.php?id=0509152

11. Unknown – 'Bonham Carter Auditions For All Roles'

    (www.contactmusic.com/new/xmlfeed.nsf/mndwebpages/bonham%20carter%20auditions%20for%20all%20roles)

12. Fischer, P. (int.) – 'Bonham Carter Plays Dead'

    (www.filmmonthly.com/Profiles/Articles/HelenaBonhamCarterCorpseBride)

13. Wilson, S.L. (int.) – Corpse Bride – Interview With Johnny Depp
        (www.horror.com/php/article-945-1)

14. Murray, R. (int.) – 'Filmmaker Tim Burton Discusses His "Corpse Bride"'
        (http://movies.about.com/od/thecorpsebride/a/corpsetb092005_2)

15. Statton, D. (int.) – 'Tim Burton's Corpse Bride Interview'
        (www.abc.net.au/atthemovies/txt/s1500904)

16. Chaw, W. – 'Tim Burton's Corpse Bride'
        (http://filmfreakcentral.net/screenreviews/corpsebride)

17. Bowen, K. – 'Tim Burton's Corpse Bride'
        (www.hollywood.com/movies/reviews/id/2445072)

18. Fischer, P. (int.) – 'Bonham Carter Plays Dead'
        (www.filmmonthly.com/Profiles/Articles/HelenaBonhamCarterCorpseBride)

19. Wilson, S. (int.) – "Corpse Bride" – Interviews From the Toronto Film Festival
        (http://horror.about.com/od/movierelated/a/int_corpse)

20. Fischer, P. (int.) – 'Bonham Carter Plays Dead'
        (www.filmmonthly.com/Profiles/Articles/HelenaBonhamCarterCorpseBride)

21. Puig, C. – 'Corpse: Death is Beautiful'
        (www.usatoday.com/life/movies/reviews/2005-09-15-corpse-bride_x)

22. Tait, S. – In an interview for this book.

References

Barbagello, R. (int.) 'From Concept Art to Finished Puppets: An Interview with Graham G.
        Maiden' (www.animationartconcervation.com/corpse_bride)
Unknown – 'Corpse Bride – Set Visit'
        (www.mymovies.net/interviews/text_feature.asp?featureid=FTRE/3551/
        0709200515151998&filmid=3551&sec=interviews)

15. The Fairy tale Goes On...

*'Movies work on levels so deep down in your
brain that it doesn't help to calculate
the sources and influences. Just let it happen creatively'*
— Tim Burton[1]

We've looked at Tim Burton's past and now it's time to look ahead and find out what the future has in store for him. There have been numerous rumours concerning possible projects, about which Burton has said 'it's strange because I've read on the internet all these projects I'm meant to be doing... I feel like I have a psychotic or evil twin doing things on my behalf and I don't know about it.'[2]

Speculation has included the possibilities of sequels to *Beetlejuice*, *Edward Scissorhands* and *The Nightmare Before Christmas*, but Burton debunked all of these in an interview conducted in February 2006. It was also in this interview that he expressed an interest in producing a movie based on an Edgar Allen Poe story at some point in the future,[3] which shouldn't come as a surprise considering his love of the horrors starring Vincent Price which were also based on Poe's work.

The only project that Burton is currently involved with is a film called *Believe It or Not*. The film is named after a newspaper column written by its title character, the explorer and writer Robert Ripley. In this column Ripley reported on his search for the weird and wonderful the world has to offer. During this search he began to appreciate the odd humans he came across, started to see them as more than mere subjects to be written about. Apparently, Jim Carrey has been signed for the lead by Paramount, whose co-president, Brad Weston, has stated, 'it's a great fit for both Jim and Tim, because it is a visual action-adventure setting, but a character with emotion, humanity and comedic sensibilities, all qualities Jim is best at.'[4]

Chinese actress Gong Li has been linked to the project, one website claiming that she has 'been invited by director Tim Burton to lead the Hollywood movie...according to Paramount Pictures.'[5] Li has already appeared in a number of Hollywood movies including *Memoirs of a Geisha* (Marshall, 2005).

> **Ultimate Quote**
>
> 'There's something about the printed word, whether it's gossip or not, somehow it has a reality to it which is sometimes a little bit frightening' – Tim Burton[6]

Believe It or Not is due to start filming in London in 2006 and will be Burton's second biopic. *Ed Wood* was the first and its writers Scott Alexander and Larry Karaszewski are also responsible for the new film's script – both films being only loosely based on the subject's lives. It is due for release late in 2007 and will therefore be Burton's first film for two years.

As for projects beyond *Believe It or Not*, we can be pretty certain that Burton will go on to direct for many years to come, and most likely with his regular collaborators at his side. As Burton favourite Johnny Depp has said, 'for me, if you get to a place where you're satisfied, you're happy with your success, you're dead. It's over. You're not hungry anymore. You won't try anything.'[7] As we have seen in his roles from the disfigured Edward Scissorhands to providing the English accented voice for Victor in *Corpse Bride*, Depp has stayed eager for new challenges. We have also seen his great respect for Burton, and their friendship which has lasted sixteen years to date. It's more a question of 'when' they will work together again rather than 'if'.

The same is true of Danny Elfman, who has been associated with Burton's work since the director's first foray into feature length films, *Pee-Wee's Big Adventure*, and has scored every film bar *Ed Wood*. Of their working relationship, Elfman has said, 'he gives me complete freedom, but then, once I've done something, we're going to work tightly together to form it into its final version.'[8] The success of this formula is clear and it is one we can only hope will continue long into the future.

In addition to these two obvious Burtonites, there are numerous crew members who he has worked with on more than one occasion, such as designer Rick Heinrichs. These people are also likely to find themselves by Burton's side in future productions as he's said, 'it's really nice to work with people who understand and really love the artistry of building sets, it's great.'[9]

> **Ultimate Quote**
>
> 'Aside from the fact he's one of the great visionary filmmakers of all time, he's a dream for an actor... He inspires you to go out there and do whatever you feel like doing' – Johnny Depp[10]

Another indicator of Burton continuing to work in Hollywood was given indirectly by Helena Bonham Carter. She said, 'I look at his little notepad and he just jots around – and sketches incessantly.'[11] This simple fact is important for two reasons. Firstly, it shows that Burton's imagination is still as fertile as ever, that his creative fire is far from extinguished. Secondly, it's a hopeful sign for the future as it means he is still arriving at new ideas.

His imagination and his notepad played huge parts in the conception of *Edward Scissorhands* and *The Nightmare Before Christmas* and his other films found their visual basis in the same way. We can only hope that his drawings and note-taking will again inspire such wonderful fairy tales

Burton was asked by film critic Mark Kermode if he intends to publish any more books of his artwork or possibly some of his photography. He responded by commenting on how great it was to be able to be creative in such ways without being chained to an animation table, referring to his time as an animator at Disney. He even went on to say, 'I just use it as a great form of thinking and enjoyment, and so long as I don't have to draw foxes I'm fine,' which directly relates to his time working on *The Fox and The Hound* (Berman & Rich, 1981). As far as publication was concerned, Burton wasn't prepared to commit himself, saying of his work, 'if it's not too bad I guess some of it will get published.'[13]

> **Ultimate Quote**
>
> 'The movies...they tap into your dreams and your subconscious...are truly a form of therapy and work on your subconscious in the way fairy tales were meant to' – Tim Burton[12]

One important thing to note from his comments is the fact that Burton says he uses his art and photography as a 'great form of thinking.' This fits perfectly with what we have come to know about the director; that he is predominantly a visual communicator, something clearly seen in his films and many of their lead characters.

Burton's visual style has become his auteur trademark, along with the characteristics commonly found in his lead characters, such as alienation and social awkwardness. He finds these feelings of being an outsider reflected in two of the people closest to him, who have also starred in a good many of his films.

In relation to Johnny Depp he has said, 'he is sort of looked upon as this handsome leading man, but I don't think in his heart he feels that way.' When it comes to his partner of five years, Helena Bonham Carter, Burton has stated, 'if you read the London papers she's one of the worst dressed people in the history of Britain or some posh aristocrat… She is completely misperceived.'[14] These statements underline why Burton is so close to Depp and Bonham Carter, finding elements of himself reflected in them. It is also an indicator that this shared alienation and misperception will keep him working with Depp and together with Bonham Carter for many years to come.

> **Ultimate Quote**
> 'For me I see myself as just a very, very lucky boy who has been drafted to come along for the ride'
> – Johnny Depp[15]

The name 'Tim Burton' has become a brand name, but one associated with a director within the Hollywood studio system creating personal films in his own personal way. These films have reached out and touched millions of people worldwide thanks to their production values, strong visuals and audience identification with characters and themes. Many have been fairy tales at heart with an expressionist slant and have shown evidence of Burton's personal touch. Put quite simply, the movies have the power to create a touch of magic.

Endnotes

1. Elliot, D. – 'Tim Burton: The Man Behind *Batman*'

　　(www.timburtoncollective.com/articles/bat5)

2. Kermode, M. (int.) – 'Tim Burton Interviewed by Mark Kermode' (II)

　　(http://film.guardian.co.uk/Guardian_NFT/interview/0,4479,120877,00)

3. Unknown – 'Tim Burton' (http://en.wikipedia.org/wiki/Tim_Burton)

4. Weinberg, S. – 'Burton & Carrey to do Ripley… Believe It or Not'

　　(www.rottentomatoes.com/news/comments/?entryid=266534)

5. Lin, H. – 'Gong Li, Not Zhang Ziyi, to Lead Hollywood Movie "Believe It or Not"'

　　(http://news.xinhuanet.com/english/2006-04/17/content_4434376)

6. Kermode, M. (int.) – 'Tim Burton Interviewed by Mark Kermode' (II)

　　(http://film.guardian.co.uk/Guardian_NFT/interview/0,4479,120877,00)

7. Grady, P. – 'Johnny Handsome: From Jump Street to Sleepy Hollow, Johnny Depp has

　　Proven he's More Than a Pretty Face'

　　(www.reel.com/reel.asp?node=features/interviews/depp)

8. Aames, E. (int.) – 'Danny Elfman on *The Corpse Bride*'

　　(www.cinecon.com/news.php?id=0509192)

9. Kermode, M. (int.) – 'Tim Burton Interviewed by Mark Kermode' (II)

　　(http://film.guardian.co.uk/Guardian_NFT/interview/0,4479,120877,00)

10. Cranky Critic – 'Cranky Critic Star Talk with Johnny Depp'

　　(www.crankycritic.com/qa/johnnydepp)

11. Fischer, P. (int.) – 'Bonham Carter Plays Dead'

　　(www.filmmonthly.com/Profiles/Articles/HelenaBonhamCarterCorpseBride)

12. Salisbury, M. (ed.) – *Burton on Burton – Revised Edition*, p.124 (Faber and Faber, 2000, UK)

13. Kermode, M. (int.) – 'Tim Burton Interviewed by Mark Kermode' (II)

　　(http://film.guardian.co.uk/Guardian_NFT/interview/0,4479,120877,00)

14. Murray, R. (int.) – 'Filmmaker Tim Burton Discusses His *Corpse Bride*'

　　(http://movies.about.com/od/thecorpsebride/a/corpsetb092005_2)

15. Unknown – 'Johnny Depp Talks Corpse Bride!' (www.movieweb.com/news/65/9265)

Appendix One
Tim Burton: Main Credits

Directing Credits

1. *Believe It or Not* (2007)
2. *Corpse Bride* (2005)
3. *Charlie and the Chocolate Factory* (2005)
4. *Big Fish* (2003)
5. *Planet of the Apes* (2001)
6. *The World of Stainboy* (2000)
7. *Sleepy Hollow* (1999)
8. *Mars Attacks!* (1996)
9. *Ed Wood* (1994)
10. *Batman Returns* (1992)
11. *Edward Scissorhands* (1990)
12. *Batman* (1989)
13. *Beetlejuice* (1988)
14. "Alfred Hitchcock Presents" – The Jar (1986) TV Episode
15. *Pee-wee's Big Adventure* (1985)
16. *Frankenweenie* (1984)
17. "Faerie Tale Theatre" – Aladdin and His Wonderful Lamp (1984) TV Episode
18. *Hansel and Gretel* (1982/II) (TV)
19. *Luau* (1982)
20. *Vincent* (1982)

21. *Stalk of the Celery* (1979)

22. *The Island of Doctor Agor* (1971)

Producing Credits

1. *9* (2007) (producer)

2. *Corpse Bride* (2005) (producer)

3. *The World of Stainboy* (2000) (producer)

4. *Lost in Oz* (2000) (TV) (executive producer)

5. *Mars Attacks!* (1996) (producer)

6. *James and the Giant Peach* (1996) (producer)

7. *Batman Forever* (1995) (producer)

8. *Ed Wood* (1994) (producer)

9. *Cabin Boy* (1994) (producer)

10. *The Nightmare Before Christmas* (1993) (producer)

11. *Batman Returns* (1992) (producer)

12. "Family Dog" (1992) TV Series (executive producer)

13. *Edward Scissorhands* (1990) (producer)

14. "Beetlejuice" (1989) TV Series (executive producer)

15. *Luau* (1982) (producer)

16. *Stalk of the Celery* (1979) (producer)

Writing Credits

1. *The World of Stainboy* (2000)

2. *Lost in Oz* (2000) (TV) (story) (pilot)

3. *The Nightmare Before Christmas* (1993) (story and characters)

4. *Edward Scissorhands* (1990) (story)

5. "Beetlejuice" (1989) TV Series (creator)

6. *Beetlejuice* (1988) (story) (uncredited)

7. *Frankenweenie* (1984) (idea)

8. *Hansel and Gretel* (1982/II) (TV) (idea)

9. *Luau* (1982)

10. *Vincent* (1982)

11. *Stalk of the Celery* (1979)
12. *The Island of Doctor Agor* (1971)

Miscellaneous Crew

1. *Shadows of the Bat: The Cinematic Saga of the Dark Knight - Dark Side of the Knight* (2005) (V) (archive source)
2. *Charlie and the Chocolate Factory* (2005/II) (VG) (extra special thanks)
3. "Family Dog" (1992) TV Series (character designer) (uncredited) (design consultant)
4. "Beetlejuice" (1989) TV Series (developed by)
5. "Amazing Stories" (1985) TV Series (character designer) (episode "Family Dog")
6. *Tron* (1982) (animator) (uncredited)
7. *The Fox and the Hound* (1981) (animator) (uncredited)
8. *Stalk of the Celery* (1979) (animator)

Acting Credits

1. *Singles* (1992)....Brian
2. *Luau* (1982)... The Supreme Being/Mortie
3. *The Muppet Movie* (1979) (voice) (uncredited)...Additional Muppet Performer

Art Department

1. *The Black Cauldron* (1985) (conceptual artist) (uncredited)
2. *Frankenweenie* (1984) (storyboard artist) (uncredited)

Appendix Two
Films: Main Cast and Crew

Beetlejuice

Directed by Tim Burton

Writing credits
Tim Burton...story (uncredited)
Michael McDowell...also story
Warren Skaaren
Larry Wilson...story

Main Cast
Alec Baldwin...Adam
Geena Davis...Barbara
Annie McEnroe...Jane Butterfield
Maurice Page...Ernie
Hugo Stanger...Old Bill
Michael Keaton...Beetlegeuse
Rachel Mittelman...Little Jane
Catherine O'Hara...Delia
Jeffrey Jones...Charles
Winona Ryder...Lydia

Glenn Shadix...Otho
Patrice Martinez...Receptionist
Cindy Daly...3 Fingered Typist
Douglas Turner...Char Man
Carmen Filpi...Messenger
Simmy Bow...Janitor
Sylvia Sidney...Juno

Produced by
Michael Bender...producer
Richard Hashimoto...producer
June Petersen...assistant producer
Larry Wilson...producer
Eric Angelson...associate producer (uncredited)

Original Music by
Fitzroy Alexander (song "Sweetheart from Venezuela")
William A. Attaway (song "Day-O")
Irving Burgie (song "Day-O")
Frédéric Chopin (song "Marcha Funebre, Sonata Piano No 2")
Danny Elfman
Robert Gordon (song "Sweetheart from Venezuela")
Areza Riandra (song "I Dream")
Stephen Somvel (song "Jump in the Line [Shake, Shake Senora]")
Norman Span (song "Man Smart, Woman Smarter")
Richard Wagner (song "Lohengrin")
Franz von Suppé (song "The Light Cavalry")

Cinematography by Thomas E. Ackerman

Film Editing by Jane Kurson

Casting by

Janet Hirshenson

Jane Jenkins

Production Design by Bo Welch

Art Direction by Tom Duffield

Set Decoration by Catherine Mann

Makeup

Steve LaPorte...makeup artist

Ve Neill...makeup artist

Robert Short...effects makeup artist

Yolanda Toussieng...hair stylist

Dale Brady...special makeup effects artist (uncredited)

Thomas Floutz...special makeup effects artist: crew (uncredited)

William Forsche...Barbara/Adam transformation assistant
(uncredited)

Matt Rose...special makeup effects artist (uncredited)

Special Effects by

Joe Day...special effects

Edward J. Franklin...special effects crew

Chuck Gaspar...special effects supervisor

Elmer Hui...special effects

William Lee...special effects

Thomas Mertz...special effects

Jeffrey A. Wischnack...special effects

Yancy Calzada...special effects department

Joerg Fiederer...special effects crew

Visual Effects by

David Beasley...model shop supervisor
James Belohovek...miniature production
Beverly Bernacki...optical effects
Doug Beswick...visual effects: sandworm sequence
William S. Conner...optical effects (as William Conner)
Thomas Conti...miniature production
Jammie Friday...animation production
Spencer Gill...optical effects
Rick Heinrichs...visual effects consultant
Rick Kess...miniature production
Peter Kuran...visual effects
Tim Lawrence...visual effects: Barbara/Adam transportation
Jo Martin...optical effects
James D. McGeachy...construction supervisor
Alan Munro...visual effects supervisor
Mark Myer...animation production
Sarah Pasanen...optical effects
Ted Rae...visual effects: snake sequence
Jacqueline Zietlow...visual effects coordinator
Jim Aupperle...stop-motion camera (uncredited)
Les Bernstien...visual effects (uncredited)
David Stump...visual effects cameraman (uncredited)

Batman

Directed by Tim Burton

Writing credits

Bob Kane...Batman characters
Sam Hamm...story

Sam Hamm...screenplay
Warren Skaaren...screenplay

Main Cast
Michael Keaton...Batman/Bruce Wayne
Jack Nicholson...Joker/Jack Napier
Kim Basinger...Vicki Vale
Robert Wuhl...Alexander Knox
Pat Hingle...Commissioner Gordon
Billy Dee Williams...Harvey Dent
Michael Gough...Alfred
Jack Palance...Grissom
Jerry Hall...Alicia
Tracey Walter...Bob the Goon
Lee Wallace...The Mayor
William Hootkins...Lt. Eckhardt
Richard Strange...Goon
Carl Chase...Goon
Mac McDonald...Goon
George Lane Cooper...Goon

Produced by
Peter Guber...producer
Barbara Kalish...associate producer
Chris Kenny...co-producer
Benjamin Melniker...executive producer
Jon Peters...producer
Michael E. Uslan...executive producer

Original Music by
Danny Elfman...score
Prince...songs

Cinematography by Roger Pratt (director of photography)

Film Editing by Ray Lovejoy

Casting by Marion Dougherty

Production Design by Anton Furst

Art Direction by
Terry Ackland-Snow
Nigel Phelps

Set Decoration by Peter Young

Costume Design by
Linda Henrikson (Ms.Basinger's costumes by)
Bob Ringwood
Tony Dunsterville (uncredited)

Edward Scissorhands

Directed by Tim Burton

Writing credits
Tim Burton (story) & Caroline Thompson (story)
Caroline Thompson (screenplay)

Main Cast
Johnny Depp...Edward Scissorhands
Winona Ryder...Kim
Dianne Wiest...Peg

Anthony Michael Hall...Jim
Kathy Baker...Joyce
Robert Oliveri...Kevin
Conchata Ferrell...Helen
Caroline Aaron...Marge
Dick Anthony Williams...Officer Allen
O-Lan Jones...Esmeralda
Vincent Price...The Inventor
Alan Arkin...Bill
Susan Blommaert...Tinka
Linda Perri...Cissy
Biff Yeager...George
Marti Greenberg...Suzanne
Bryan Larkin...Max

Produced by
Tim Burton...producer
Denise Di Novi...producer
Richard Hashimoto...executive producer
Caroline Thompson...associate producer

Original Music by Danny Elfman

Non-Original Music by
Les Reed (song "Delilah")
Les Reed (song "It's Not Unusual")

Cinematography by Stefan Czapsky (director of photography)

Film Editing by
Colleen Halsey
Richard Halsey

Casting by Victoria Thomas

Production Design by Bo Welch

Art Direction by Tom Duffield

Set Decoration by Cheryl Carasik

Costume Design by Colleen Atwood

Batman Returns

Directed by Tim Burton

Writing credits
Bob Kane (Batman characters)
Daniel Waters (story) and Sam Hamm (story)
Daniel Waters (screenplay)

Main Cast
Michael Keaton...Batman/Bruce Wayne
Danny DeVito...Penguin/Oswald Cobblepot
Michelle Pfeiffer...Catwoman/Selina Kyle
Christopher Walken...Max Shreck
Michael Gough...Alfred Pennyworth
Michael Murphy...The Mayor
Cristi Conaway...Ice Princess
Andrew Bryniarski...Charles 'Chip' Shreck
Pat Hingle...Commissioner James T. Gordon
Vincent Schiavelli...Organ Grinder
Jan Hooks...Jen

Steve Witting..Josh
Paul Reubens...Penguin's Father
Diane Salinger...Penguin's Mother

Produced by
Ian Bryce...associate producer
Tim Burton...producer
Denise Di Novi...producer
Larry J. Franco...co-producer (as Larry Franco)
Peter Guber...executive producer
Benjamin Melniker...executive producer
Jon Peters...executive producer
Michael E. Uslan...executive producer

Original Music by
Danny Elfman
Steven Severin (song "Face to Face")
Siouxsie Sioux (song "Face to Face")

Non-Original Music by
Rick James (song "Super Freak")
Alonzo Miller (song "Super Freak")

Cinematography by Stefan Czapsky (director of photography)

Film Editing by
Bob Badami
Chris Lebenzon

Casting by Marion Dougherty

Production Design by Bo Welch

Art Direction by Rick Heinrichs

Set Decoration by Cheryl Carasik

Costume Design by
Bob Ringwood
Mary E. Vogt

Special Effects by
Jan Aaris...special effects
Bill Basso...art department: Stan Winston Studio
David Beneke...art department: Stan Winston Studio
Larry Bolster...mechanical department: Stan Winston Studio
Douglas Calli...special effects technician
Kenneth C. Clark...special effects
Mitchell J. Coughlin...art department: Stan Winston Studio
Richard Davison...art department: Stan Winston Studio
Jon Dawe...mechanical department: Stan Winston Studio
Marilyn Dozer-Chaney...art department: Stan Winston Studio
Mike Edmonson...special effects foreman
Andy Evans...special effects
Greg Figiel...art department: Stan Winston Studio
Scott Forbes...special effects
Nathalie Fratti-Rapoport...art department: Stan Winston Studio
Rick Galinson...mechanical department: Stan Winston Studio
Chuck Gaspar...special effects supervisor
Dan Gaspar...special effects
Dave Grasso...art department: Stan Winston Studio
Beth Hathaway...art department: Stan Winston Studio
Rich Haugen...mechanical department: Stan Winston Studio
Rob Hinderstein...art department: Stan Winston Studio
Elmer Hui...special effects

Adam Jones...art department: Stan Winston Studio
Mark Jurinko...art department: Stan Winston Studio
Richard J. Landon...mechanical department: Stan Winston Studio
Mark Lohff...production coordinator: Stan Winston Studio
Greg Manion...mechanical department: Stan Winston Studio
Tara Meaney-Crocitto...production coordinator: Stan Winston Studio
Paul Mejias...art department: Stan Winston Studio
Brian Namanny...mechanical department: Stan Winston Studio
Karl Nygren...special effects
Jeff Periera...art department: Stan Winston Studio
Robert Ramsdell...mechanical department: Stan Winston Studio
Joe Reader...art department: Stan Winston Studio
Mike Reedy...mechanical effects supervisor: second unit
Steve Riley...special effects technician
Bruce Robles...special effects
Alan Scott...mechanical department: Stan Winston Studio
Shannon Shea...art department: Stan Winston Studio
Patrick Shearn...mechanical department: Stan Winston Studio
Kirk Skodis...animatronic puppeteer
Alfred Sousa...mechanical department: Stan Winston Studio
Christopher Swift...art department: Stan Winston Studio
Michiko Tagawa...art department: Stan Winston Studio
Mike Trcic...art department: Stan Winston Studio
Mike Weaver...special effects

Visual Effects by
Tim Angulo...director of photography: Chandler Group
Don Baker...effects supervisor: Chandler Group
Craig Barron...visual effects supervisor: Matte World
James Belkin...director of photography: 4-Ward Productions
Jennifer C. Bell...production coordinator: 4-Ward Productions
Brent Boates...art director: Boss Film Studios

Brent Boates...visual effects co-supervisor: Boss Film Studios
Holly Borradaile...associate producer: 4-Ward Productions
Stephen Brien...model and miniature set supervisor:
4-Ward Productions
John Bruno...visual effects supervisor: Boss Film Studios
Vin Burnham...visual and technical costume effects supervisor
Wade Childress...camera operator: Matte World
Keith Claridge...stage manager: Chandler Group
Kevin Clark...optical line-up: Boss Film Studios
Michael Cooper...optical supervisor: Boss Film Studios
Philip Crescenzo...technical supervisor: Boss Film Studios
Joshua Cushner...motion control operator: Chandler Group
Robin L. D'Arcy...line producer: 4-Ward Productions
Krystyna Demkowicz...executive in charge of production:
Matte World
Barry Dempsey...animator: PDI
Patrick Denver...miniature set fabricator and operator:
4-Ward Productions
Les Dittert...optical supervisor: PDI
George C. Dodge...director of photography: 4-Ward Productions
Drummand S. Edmand...camera assistant: Matte World
Christopher Evans...matte artist: Matte World
Michael L. Fink...visual effects supervisor

The Nightmare Before Christmas

Directed by Henry Selick

Writing credits
Tim Burton (story and characters)
Michael McDowell (adaptation)

Caroline Thompson (screenplay)

Main Cast

Danny Elfman...Jack Skellington (singing)/Barrel/Clown with the Tear away Face (voice)

Chris Sarandon...Jack Skellington (voice)

Catherine O'Hara...Sally/Shock (voice)

William Hickey...Dr. Finkelstein (voice)

Glenn Shadix...Mayor (voice)

Paul Reubens...Lock (voice)

Ken Page...Oogie Boogie (voice)

Edward Ivory...Santa (voice)

Susan McBride...Big Witch, W.W.D. (voice)

Debi Durst...Corpse Kid, Corpse Mom, Small Witch (voice)

Greg Proops...Harlequin Demon, Devil, Sax Player (voice)

Kerry Katz...Man Under the Stairs, Vampire, Corpse Dad (voice)

Randy Crenshaw...Mr. Hyde, Behemoth, Vampire (voice)

Sherwood Ball...Mummy, Vampire (voice)

Carmen Twillie...Undersea Gal, Man Under the Stairs (voice)

Glenn Walters...Wolfman (voice)

Produced by

Tim Burton...producer

Denise Di Novi...producer

Danny Elfman...associate producer

Kathleen Gavin...co-producer

Jill Jacobs...associate producer

Diane Minter Lewis...associate producer

Philip Lofaro...associate producer

Jeffrey Katzenberg...co-producer (uncredited)

Original Music by Danny Elfman

Cinematography by Pete Kozachik (director of photography)

Film Editing by Stan Webb

Casting by
Mary Gail Artz
Barbara Cohen

Art Direction by
Deane Taylor
Barry E. Jackson (uncredited)

Production Management
Sara Duran...post-production supervisor
Philip Lofaro...production manager

Art Department
Allison Abbate...artistic coordinator
Susan Alegria...set production assistant
Kelly Asbury...assistant art director
Bill Boes...assistant art director
Phil Brotherton...set builder
Mike Cachuela...storyboard artist
Hortensia Casagran...paint supervisor
Jennifer Clinard...scenic artist
Kendal Cronkhite...assistant art director
Fon Davis...set builder
Norm DeCarlo...sculptor
Randy Dutra...sculptor
Greg Dykstra...sculptor
Shane Francis...assistant artistic coordinator
Joel Friesch...set dresser

Rick Heinrichs...visual consultant
Lee Bo Henry...set construction supervisor
Loren Hillman-Morgan...scenic artist
Peggy Hrastar...scenic artist
Jorgen Klubien...storyboard artist
Shelley Daniels Lekven...sculptor
Todd Lookinland...set builder
Steve Moore...storyboard artist
Ben Nichols...set builder
Gregg Olsson...dressing supervisor
Gregg Olsson...set designer
Linda Overbey...scenic artist
Allessandro Palladini...set builder
Bob Pauley...storyboard artist
Jill Ruzicka...production coordinator: art department
Gretchen Scharfenberg...set dresser

Visual Effects by
Loretta A. Asbury...cel model painter
Jim Aupperle...camera operator
Gordon Baker...effects animator
Jon Berg...moldmaker
Bill Boes...model maker
Nick Bogle...model maker
Scott Bonnenfant...assistant effects animator
Dave Bossert...snow animator
Jeff Brewer...model maker
Mike Cachuela...effects animator
Thomas Cardone...color timing and paint
Joel Fletcher...animator
Joel Friesch...model maker
Chris R. Green...effects animator

Michael Grivett...assistant moldmaker
Michael Hinton...additional optical effects
Rebecca House...assistant model maker
Erik Jensen...moldmaker
Mike Jobe...moldmaker
Pamela Kibbee...assistant model maker
Aaron Kohr...assistant model maker
Pete Kozachik...visual effects supervisor
Victoria Lewis...moldmaker
Paula Lucchesi...model maker
Tony Preciado...assistant moldmaker
Tom Proost...set foreman
Jerome Ranft...assistant model maker
John Reed...mold maker supervisor
Marc Ribaud...model maker
Mitchell Romanauski...model shop supervisor
Rob Ronning...moldmaker
Kirk Scott...production assistant
Tom St. Amand...armature supervisor
Nathan Stanton...assistant effects animator
Eric Swenson...camera operator
Ariel Velasco-Shaw...digital effects supervisor
Harry Walton...additional optical effects
Wim van Thillo...moldmaker

Ed Wood

Directed by Tim Burton

Writing credits
Rudolph Grey (book *Nightmare of Ecstasy*)

Scott Alexander (written by) & Larry Karaszewski (written by)

Main Cast
Johnny Depp...Ed Wood
Martin Landau...Bela Lugosi
Sarah Jessica Parker...Dolores Fuller
Patricia Arquette...Kathy O'Hara
Jeffrey Jones...Criswell
G.D. Spradlin...Reverend Lemon
Vincent D'Onofrio...Orson Welles
Bill Murray...Bunny Breckinridge
Mike Starr...Georgie Weiss
Max Casella...Paul Marco
Brent Hinkley...Conrad Brooks
Lisa Marie...Vampira
George 'The Animal' Steele...Tor Johnson
Juliet Landau...Loretta King
Clive Rosengren...Ed Reynolds
Norman Alden...Cameraman Bill
Leonard Termo...Makeup Man Harry
Ned Bellamy...Dr. Tom Mason
Danny Dayton...Soundman
John Ross...Camera Assistant
Bill Cusack...Tony McCoy
Aaron Nelms...Teenage Kid
Biff Yeager...Rude Boss
Joseph R. Gannascoli...Security Guard
Carmen Filpi...Old Crusty Man

Produced by
Tim Burton...producer
Denise Di Novi...producer

Michael Flynn...co-producer
Michael Lehmann...executive producer

Original Music by
Ray Anthony (song "Bunny Hop")
Jon Arkell (song "Seringa")
Leonard Auletti (song "Bunny Hop")
Alan Braden (songs "Spring Fashion" and "Sweet and Lovely")
Bruce Campbell (song "Desolate Village")
Trevor Duncan (song "Grip of the Law")
Korla Pandit (song "Nautch Dance")
Dámaso Pérez Prado (song "Kuba Mambo")
Howard Shore

Non-Original Music by
Ray Evans (song "Que Sera Sera")
Jay Livingston (song "Que Sera Sera")
Pyotr Ilyich Tchaikovsky (from ballet "Swan Lake")

Cinematography by Stefan Czapsky

Film Editing by Chris Lebenzon

Casting by Victoria Thomas

Production Design by Tom Duffield

Art Direction by Okowita

Set Decoration by Cricket Rowland

Costume Design by Colleen Atwood

Mars Attacks!

Directed by Tim Burton

Writing credits
Len Brown (trading card series)
Woody Gelman (trading card series)
Wally Wood (trading card series)
Bob Powell (trading card series)
Norman Saunders (trading card series)
Jonathan Gems (screen story)
Jonathan Gems (screenplay)

Main Cast
Jack Nicholson...President James Dale/Art Land
Glenn Close...First Lady Marsha Dale
Annette Bening...Barbara Land
Pierce Brosnan...Professor Donald Kessler
Danny DeVito...Rude Gambler
Martin Short...Press Secretary Jerry Ross
Sarah Jessica Parker...Nathalie Lake
Michael J. Fox...Jason Stone
Rod Steiger...General Decker
Tom Jones...Himself
Jim Brown...Byron Williams
Lukas Haas...Richie Norris
Natalie Portman...Taffy Dale
Pam Grier...Louise Williams
Lisa Marie...Martian Girl
Brian Haley...Mitch, Secret Service Agent
Sylvia Sidney...Grandma Florence Norris
Jack Black...Billy Glenn Norris

Ray J...Cedric Williams
Paul Winfield...General Casey
Brandon Hammond...Neville Williams
Jerzy Skolimowski...Dr. Zeigler

Produced by
Tim Burton...producer
Paul Deason...associate producer
Larry J. Franco...producer
Mark S. Miller...associate producer
Mary Ann Marino...associate producer (uncredited)
Laurie Parker...producer (uncredited)

Original Music by
Danny Elfman
Victor Herbert (song "Indian Love Call") (uncredited)

Non-Original Music by Les Reed (song "It's Not Unusual")

Cinematography by Peter Suschitzky

Film Editing by Chris Lebenzon

Casting by
Matthew Barry
Jeanne McCarthy
Victoria Thomas

Production Design by Wynn Thomas

Art Direction by John Dexter

Set Decoration by Nancy Haigh

Costume Design by Colleen Atwood

Special Effects by
Astrig Akseralian...lead painter: Mackinnon & Saunders
Noel Baker...design sculptor: Mackinnon & Saunders
Colin Batty...design sculptor: Mackinnon & Saunders
Geraldine Corrigan...costume supervisor: Mackinnon & Saunders
Donald Elliott...special effects foreman
Lucy Gell...prototype fabricator: Mackinnon & Saunders
Georgina Haynes...mechanics designer: Mackinnon & Saunders
Thomas R. Homsher...special effects technician
Barry Jones...production supervisor: Mackinnon & Saunders
Christine Keogh...prototype fabricator: Mackinnon & Saunders
Louie Lantieri...special effects
Michael Lantieri...special effects supervisor
Ian Mackinnon...design supervisor: Mackinnon & Saunders
Graham Maiden...shop coordinator: Mackinnon & Saunders
Darren Marshall...design sculptor: Mackinnon & Saunders
Dan Ossello...special effects
Tom Pahk...special effects
Peter Saunders...design supervisor: Mackinnon & Saunders
Bridget Smith...mold designer: Mackinnon & Saunders
Stuart Sutcliffe...mechanics designer: Mackinnon & Saunders
Mark Thompson...prototype fabricator: Mackinnon & Saunders
Brian Tipton...special effects
Tom Tokunaga...special effects
Christine Walker...production supervisor: Mackinnon & Saunders
Simon White...shop coordinator: Mackinnon & Saunders

Sleepy Hollow

Directed by Tim Burton

Writing credits
Washington Irving...story *The Legend of Sleepy Hollow*
Kevin Yagher...screen story
Andrew Kevin Walker...screen story and screenplay

Main Cast
Johnny Depp...Constable Ichabod Crane
Christina Ricci...Katrina Anne Van Tassel
Miranda Richardson...Lady Mary Van Tassel/The Western Woods Crone
Michael Gambon...Baltus Van Tassel
Casper Van Dien...Brom Van Brunt
Jeffrey Jones...Reverend Steenwyck
Christopher Lee...Burgomaster
Richard Griffiths...Magistrate Samuel Philipse
Ian McDiarmid...Dr. Thomas Lancaster
Michael Gough...Notary James Hardenbrook
Marc Pickering...Young Masbath
Lisa Marie...Ichabod's Mother
Steven Waddington...Mr. Killian
Christopher Walken...The Hessian Horseman
Claire Skinner...Midwife Elizabeth 'Beth' Killian
Alun Armstrong...High Constable
Mark Spalding...Jonathan Masbath
Jessica Oyelowo...Sarah, The Servant Girl
Tony Maudsley...Van Ripper
Peter Guinness...Ichabod's Father

Produced by

Francis Ford Coppola...executive producer
Celia D. Costas...line producer: New York
Larry J. Franco...executive producer
Mark Roybal...associate producer
Scott Rudin...producer
Adam Schroeder...producer
Kevin Yagher...co-producer

Original Music by Danny Elfman

Cinematography by Emmanuel Lubezki

Film Editing by

Chris Lebenzon
Joel Negron

Casting by

Susie Figgis
Ilene Starger

Production Design by Rick Heinrichs

Art Direction by

Ken Court
John Dexter
Andy Nicholson

Set Decoration by Peter Young

Costume Design by Colleen Atwood

Planet of the Apes

Directed by Tim Burton

Writing credits
Pierre Boulle...novel *La Planète des Singes*
William Broyles Jr....screenplay
Lawrence Konner...screenplay
Mark Rosenthal...screenplay

Main Cast
Mark Wahlberg...Captain Leo Davidson
Tim Roth...General Thade
Helena Bonham Carter...Ari
Michael Clarke Duncan...Colonel Attar
Paul Giamatti...Limbo
Estella Warren...Daena
Cary-Hiroyuki Tagawa...Krull
David Warner...Senator Sandar
Kris Kristofferson...Karubi
Erick Avari...Tival
Lucas Elliott...Birn
Evan Parke...Gunnar
Glenn Shadix...Senator Nado
Freda Foh Shen...Bon
Chris Ellis...Lt. General Karl Vasich
Anne Ramsay...Lt. Col. Grace Alexander
Andrea Grano...Major Maria Cooper
Michael Jace...Major Frank Santos
Michael Wiseman...Specialist Hansen
Lisa Marie...Nova
Eileen Weisinger...Leeta

Deep Roy...Gorilla Kid/Thade's Niece
Rick Baker...Old Ape #2
Charlton Heston...Zaius, Thade's Father (uncredited)

Produced by
Ross Fanger...associate producer
Katterli Frauenfelder...associate producer
Iain Smith...line producer: London
Ralph Winter...executive producer
Richard D. Zanuck...producer

Original Music by
Danny Elfman
Paul Oakenfold (theme "Rule the Planet" remix)

Cinematography by Philippe Rousselot (director of photography)

Film Editing by
Chris Lebenzon
Joel Negron

Casting by Denise Chamian

Production Design by Rick Heinrichs

Art Direction by
Sean Haworth
Philip Toolin

Set Decoration by
Rosemary Brandenburg
Peter Young (UK)

Costume Design by
Colleen Atwood
Donna O'Neal

Big Fish

Directed by Tim Burton

Writing credits
Daniel Wallace...novel *Big Fish: A Novel of Mythic Proportions*
John August...screenplay

Main Cast
Ewan McGregor...Ed Bloom (Young)
Albert Finney...Ed Bloom (Senior)
Billy Crudup...Will Bloom
Jessica Lange...Sandra Bloom (Senior)
Helena Bonham Carter...Jenny (Young & Senior) & The Witch
Alison Lohman...Sandra Bloom (Young)
Robert Guillaume...Dr. Bennett (Senior)
Marion Cotillard...Josephine
Matthew McGrory...Karl the Giant
David Denman...Don Price (Age 18-22)
Missi Pyle...Mildred
Loudon Wainwright III...Beamen (as Loudon Wainwright)
Ada Tai...Ping
Arlene Tai...Jing
Steve Buscemi...Norther Winslow
Danny DeVito...Amos Calloway
Deep Roy...Mr. Soggybottom

Produced by

Bruce Cohen...producer
Katterli Frauenfelder...associate producer
Dan Jinks...producer
Arne Schmidt...executive producer
Richard D. Zanuck...producer

Original Music by

Danny Elfman
Buddy Holly (song "Everyday")
Eddie Vedder (song "Man of the Hour")

Non-Original Music by

Harry Akst (song "Dinah")
Dickey Betts (song "Ramblin' Man")
Otis Blackwell (song "All Shook Up")
Charles Hardin (song "Everyday")
Wilbert Harrison (song "Let's Work Together")
Norman Petty (song "Everyday")
Elvis Presley (song "All Shook Up")
Allen Reynolds (song "Five O' Clock World")

Cinematography by Philippe Rousselot

Film Editing by Chris Lebenzon

Charlie and the Chocolate Factory

Directed by Tim Burton

Writing credits
Roald Dahl...book
John August...screenplay

Main Cast
Johnny Depp...Willy Wonka
Freddie Highmore...Charlie Bucket
David Kelly...Grandpa Joe
Helena Bonham Carter...Mrs. Bucket
Noah Taylor...Mr. Bucket
Missi Pyle...Mrs. Beauregarde
James Fox...Mr. Salt
Deep Roy...Oompa Loompa
Christopher Lee...Dr. Wonka
Adam Godley...Mr. Teavee
Franziska Troegner...Mrs. Gloop
AnnaSophia Robb...Violet Beauregarde
Julia Winter...Veruca Salt
Jordan Fry...Mike Teavee
Philip Wiegratz...Augustus Gloop
Blair Dunlop...Little Willy Wonka
Liz Smith...Grandma Georgina
Eileen Essell...Grandma Josephine
David Morris...Grandpa George
Nitin Chandra Ganatra...Prince Pondicherry
Shelley Conn...Princess Pondicherry
Chris Cresswell...Prodnose
Philip Philmar...Slugworth

Tony Kirwood...Finckelgruber
Harry Taylor...Mr. Gloop
Francesca Hunt...Mrs. Salt
Geoffrey Holder...Narrator
Danny Elfman...Oompa Loompa Vocals (voice)

Produced by
Bruce Berman...executive producer
Graham Burke...executive producer
Felicity Dahl...executive producer
Katterli Frauenfelder...co-producer
Derek Frey...associate producer
Brad Grey...producer
Patrick McCormick...executive producer
Michael Siegel...executive producer
Richard D. Zanuck...producer

Original Music by Danny Elfman (also songs)

Non-Original Music by
Gardner DeAguiar (song "Mr. Quiet")
RaVani Flood (song "Mr. Quiet")
Manuel Ignacio (song "Mr. Quiet")
György Ligeti (from "Requiem")
Rafael Ruiz (song "Macarena")
Jesse Shaternick (song "Mr. Quiet")
Richard Strauss (from "Also sprach Zarathustra")

Cinematography by Philippe Rousselot

Film Editing by Chris Lebenzon

Casting by Susie Figgis

Production Design by Alex McDowell

Art Direction by
David Allday
François Audouy
Matthew Gray
Sean Haworth
James Lewis
Andy Nicholson
Kevin Phipps
Stuart Rose

Set Decoration by Peter Young

Costume Design by Gabriella Pescucci

Corpse Bride

Directed by
Tim Burton
Mike Johnson

Writing credits
John August...screenplay
Pamela Pettler...screenplay
Caroline Thompson...screenplay

Main Cast
Johnny Depp...Victor Van Dort

Helena Bonham Carter...Corpse Bride
Emily Watson...Victoria Everglot
Tracey Ullman...Nell Van Dort/Hildegarde
Paul Whitehouse...William Van Dort/Mayhew/Paul The Head Waiter
Joanna Lumley...Maudeline Everglot
Albert Finney...Finis Everglot
Richard E. Grant...Barkis Bittern
Christopher Lee...Pastor Galswells
Michael Gough...Elder Gutknecht
Jane Horrocks...Black Widow Spider/Mrs. Plum
Enn Reitel...Maggot/Town Crier
Deep Roy...General Bonesapart
Danny Elfman...Bonejangles

Produced by
Allison Abbate...producer
Jeffrey Auerbach...executive producer
Tim Burton...producer
Derek Frey...associate producer
Joe Ranft...executive producer
Tracy Shaw...line producer

Original Music by Danny Elfman

Cinematography by Pete Kozachik

Film Editing by Jonathan Lucas

Casting by Michelle Guish

Production Design by Alex McDowell

Art Direction by Nelson Lowry

Set Decoration by Colin Batty

Production Management
Harry Linden...production manager
Second Unit Director or Assistant Director
Joe Barlow...third assistant director
Mike Colley...second assistant director
Ezra Sumner...first assistant director

Art Department
Christopher Butler...storyboard artist
Padraig Collins...storyboard artist
Mark Cordory...props
Priscilla Elliott...art department researcher
Charles Fletcher...set constructor
Alex Hill...storyboard artist
Brendan Houghton...storyboard artist
Emma Lo Gatto...art department assistant
Emma Lo Gatto...art intern
Emma Lo Gatto...intern
Sean Mathiesen...previsualisation artist
Hannah Moseley...draughtsman
Rachel Myers...art department runner
Conor O'Gorman...art assist
Sam Page...digital set designer
Dean Roberts...storyboard artist
Neil Ross...conceptual artist
Sharon Smith...storyboard artist
David Stoten...storyboard artist
Tim Watts...storyboard artist

Andreas von Andrian...storyboard artist

Special Effects by
Kat Alioshin...project supervisor: Mackinnon and Saunders
Noel Baker...lead sculptor: Mackinnon and Saunders
Gary Faulkner...model rigger
Andy Gent...lead model rigger
Georgina Haynes...armature lead: Mackinnon and Saunders
Bethan Jones...foam lead: Mackinnon and Saunders
Christine Keogh...fabrication lead: Mackinnon and Saunders
Ian Mackinnon...puppets: Mackinnon and Saunders
Graham Maiden...puppet fabrication supervisor
Dan Pascall...puppet wrangler
Trevor Poulsum...junior puppet wrangler
Nick Roberson...lead painter: Mackinnon and Saunders
Denis Russo...model rigger
Peter Saunders...puppets: Mackinnon and Saunders
Michelle Scattergood...costumes lead: Mackinnon and Saunders
Bridget Smith...lead mould maker: Mackinnon and Saunders
Mark Thompson...silicone lead: Mackinnon and Saunders
Libby Watson...puppet coordinator

Appendix Three: List of Illustrations

Beetlejuice

Warner Bros

1. The Maitlands entering the beaurocratic afterworld where dark humour abounds
2. When Betelgeuse appears at the film's finale he has bat ears, hinting at future films
3. The use of stop-motion animation: the sandworms which bear a resemblance to creatures in *The Nightmare Before Christmas*
4. The terrible duo of Delia Deetz and Otho

Batman

Warner Bros

1. Batman is played by Michael Keaton and displays two traits common to Burton characters; alienation and a dual persona
2. We see Michael Keaton in one of three lead roles and the use of stripes, which can often be seen in Burton's early films
3. The impressive Gotham City which displays both gothic and expressionist influences, like many other locations in Burton's films
4. Jack Nicholson as the Joker is prominent due to his extroverted nature, while Batman hides in the shadows

Batman Returns

Warner Bros

1. The Bat Signal introduced at the end of the first movie is put to good use in *Batman Returns*

2. Michelle Pfeiffer as Catwoman, who displays an overt sexuality, something not seen in many other Burton films

3. Danny DeVito as the Penguin, in one of Burton's trademark graveyard scenes

Mars Attacks!

Warner Bros

1. Two Burton trademarks in *Mars Attacks!*: a dog and a severed human head

2. The alien ambassador prepares to address congress – and then to laser it to oblivion

3. Burton's once partner, Lisa Marie, makes a an appearance as a freaky alien in female disguise

4. The severed heads of Pierce Brosnan and Sarah Jessica Parker kissing in *Mars Attacks!*, showing dark humour and an unusual sexual attraction

Sleepy Hollow

Paramount/Mandalay Pictures/LLC

1. Ichabod Crane is alienated in the superstitious community and his companions are young, reflecting Burton's use of young people in pivotal roles

2. The lopping of heads in *Sleepy Hollow* was cathartic for Burton after spending a year on a *Superman* film which then fell through

3. The Hessian finally reclaims his head and becomes autonomous

4. The windmill in *Sleepy Hollow* was a homage to his earlier short

entitled *Frankenweenie*, and was also part of the gothic setting of the film

Big Fish
Columbia Tristar
1. Danny DeVito plays circus owner Calloway who also happens to be a misunderstood monster – a werewolf
2. The Hand-i-matic which Ed Bloom sells is reminiscent of Edward Scissorhands' hands
3. *Big Fish* contains a strong fairy tale element, something which creates a link with a number of other Burton movies, such as *Edward Scissorhands*
4. Burton's long-term partner Helena Bonham Carter as the witch in whose eye people can see their demise

Charlie & the Chocolate Factory
Warner Bros
1. Willy Wonka, played by Johnny Depp
2. The Buckets' run-down and slanted house, reflecting the same expressionist style used in *Beetlejuice*, the *Batman* films, *Sleepy Hollow*, and *Big Fish*
3. Willy Wonka's chocolate factory where things are not as sweet as they may at first seem
4. The all-singing, all-dancing Oompa-Loompas in the Nut Sorting Room

Corpse Bride
Warner Bros
1. Bonejangles putting his all into a good old knees-up in the underworld
2. The 'head' waiter in *The Corpse Bride*
3. The maggot living inside the Corpse Bride's head is a clear use